The Policing of Flows

Rectifying the fact that little criminological attention has been paid to the notion that the security of flows increasingly embodies concerns at the heart of contemporary policing practices, this book makes a significant contribution to knowledge about the policing and security governance of flows.

The book focuses on how the growing centrality of flows affects both contemporary 'risks' and the policing organisations in charge of managing them. The contributors analyse flows such as event security; border controls and migration; the movement of animal parts; security-related intelligence; and organisational flows. The emerging criminology of these, as well as flows of money, information and numerous commodities, from pharmaceuticals to minerals or malicious software, is leading to critical advances in the understanding of the changing harm landscapes and the practices that have developed to manage them.

Taken as a whole, the book opens up the conversation, and encourages the invention of new conceptual, theoretical and methodological tools to help criminology tackle and better understand the mobile world in which we live.

This book was originally published as a special issue of *Global Crime*.

Anthony Amicelle is Associate Professor in Criminology at the Université de Montréal, Canada. His research examines practices of policing, surveillance and intelligence at the interface of finance and security, especially with respect to counter-terrorism and financial crime such as money laundering.

Karine Côté-Boucher is an Associate Professor at the School of Criminology at the Université de Montréal, Canada. Her research focuses on border control – with a current focus on the relations between customs, logistics and the transportation industry.

Benoît Dupont is Professor of Criminology at the Université de Montréal, Canada, where he also holds the Canada Research Chair in Cybersecurity and the Research Chair in the Prevention of Cybercrime. He is the Scientific Director of the Smart Cybersecurity Network (SERENE-RISC), one of Canada's Networks of Centres of Excellence. His research interests include the co-evolution of technology and crime, as well as the polycentric governance of security.

Massimiliano Mulone is Associate Professor in Criminology at the Université de Montréal, Canada. His research interests include the privatisation of security, with a specific focus on the relations between the police and private security companies, as well as police deviance and its management.

Clifford Shearing is a Professor in the School of Criminology and Criminal Justice at Griffith University, Australia. He leads the Global Risk Governance Programme in the Law Faculty at the University of Cape Town, South Africa, and co-leads the New Securities Programme at the Griffith Institute of Criminology. A focus of his academic work has been on broadening boundaries of criminology, with a primary focus on 'security governance'.

Samuel Tanner is an Associate Professor in the School of Criminology at the Université de Montréal, Canada. His current research interests mainly focus on media, communication and security, especially on the role, policies, practices and impact of information and communications technologies for security purposes. He also works on violent extremism, focusing on Canada's far right.

The Policing of Flows
Challenging Contemporary Criminology

Edited by
**Anthony Amicelle, Karine Côté-Boucher,
Benoît Dupont, Massimiliano Mulone,
Clifford Shearing and Samuel Tanner**

LONDON AND NEW YORK

First published 2020
by Routledge
2 Park Square, Milton Park, Abingdon, Oxon, OX14 4RN

and by Routledge
52 Vanderbilt Avenue, New York, NY 10017

Routledge is an imprint of the Taylor & Francis Group, an informa business

© 2020 Taylor & Francis

All rights reserved. No part of this book may be reprinted or reproduced or utilised in any form or by any electronic, mechanical, or other means, now known or hereafter invented, including photocopying and recording, or in any information storage or retrieval system, without permission in writing from the publishers.

Trademark notice: Product or corporate names may be trademarks or registered trademarks, and are used only for identification and explanation without intent to infringe.

British Library Cataloguing in Publication Data
A catalogue record for this book is available from the British Library

ISBN 13: 978-0-367-28009-3

Typeset in Myriad Pro
by RefineCatch Limited, Bungay, Suffolk

Publisher's Note
The publisher accepts responsibility for any inconsistencies that may have arisen during the conversion of this book from journal articles to book chapters, namely the inclusion of journal terminology.

Disclaimer
Every effort has been made to contact copyright holders for their permission to reprint material in this book. The publishers would be grateful to hear from any copyright holder who is not here acknowledged and will undertake to rectify any errors or omissions in future editions of this book.

Contents

Citation Information	vii
Notes on Contributors	ix

Introduction – Criminology in the face of flows: reflections on contemporary policing and security 1
Anthony Amicelle, Karine Côté-Boucher, Benoît Dupont, Massimiliano Mulone, Clifford Shearing and Samuel Tanner

1. Managing flows during mega-events: taking account of internal and external flows in public order policing operations 12
Chad Whelan and Adam Molnar

2. Fluid interfaces between flows of rhino horn 34
Annette Hübschle

3. Regulation of cross-border law enforcement: 'locks' and 'dams' to regional and international flows of policing 54
Saskia Hufnagel

4. Crime analysis and cognitive effects: the practice of policing *through* flows of data 73
Carrie Sanders and Camie Condon

5. European border policing: EUROSUR, knowledge, calculation 92
Julien Jeandesboz

6. Liquid modernity and the police *métier*; thinking about information flows in police organisation 122
James Sheptycki

7. International flows, political order and social change: (in)security, by-product of the will of order over change 139
Didier Bigo

Index 159

Citation Information

The chapters in this book were originally published in *Global Crime*, volume 18, issue 3 (August 2017). When citing this material, please use the original page numbering for each article, as follows:

Introduction
Criminology in the face of flows: reflections on contemporary policing and security
Anthony Amicelle, Karine Côté-Boucher, Benoît Dupont, Massimiliano Mulone, Clifford Shearing and Samuel Tanner
Global Crime, volume 18, issue 3 (August 2017), pp. 165–175

Chapter 1
Managing flows during mega-events: taking account of internal and external flows in public order policing operations
Chad Whelan and Adam Molnar
Global Crime, volume 18, issue 3 (August 2017), pp. 176–197

Chapter 2
Fluid interfaces between flows of rhino horn
Annette Hübschle
Global Crime, volume 18, issue 3 (August 2017), pp. 198–217

Chapter 3
Regulation of cross-border law enforcement: 'locks' and 'dams' to regional and international flows of policing
Saskia Hufnagel
Global Crime, volume 18, issue 3 (August 2017), pp. 218–236

Chapter 4
Crime analysis and cognitive effects: the practice of policing through *flows of data*
Carrie Sanders and Camie Condon
Global Crime, volume 18, issue 3 (August 2017), pp. 237–255

Chapter 5
European border policing: EUROSUR, knowledge, calculation
Julien Jeandesboz
Global Crime, volume 18, issue 3 (August 2017), pp. 256–285

Chapter 6

Liquid modernity and the police métier; *thinking about information flows in police organisation*
James Sheptycki
Global Crime, volume 18, issue 3 (August 2017), pp. 286–302

Chapter 7

International flows, political order and social change: (in)security, by-product of the will of order over change
Didier Bigo
Global Crime, volume 18, issue 3 (August 2017), pp. 303–321

For any permission-related enquiries please visit:
http://www.tandfonline.com/page/help/permissions

Notes on Contributors

Anthony Amicelle is Associate Professor in Criminology at the Université de Montréal, Canada. His research examines practices of policing, surveillance and intelligence at the interface of finance and security, especially with respect to counter-terrorism and financial crime such as money laundering.

Didier Bigo is Professor of International Relations in the Department of War Studies at King's College London, UK, and MCU Research Professor at Sciences-Po Paris, France. He is also the Director of the Center for Study of Conflicts, Liberty and Security (CCLS), and Editor of the quarterly journal in French *Cultures et Conflits*.

Camie Condon is a contract academic staff member at Wilfrid Laurier University, Canada, and Academic Program Coordinator at Seneca College, Canada. She also works as a crime analyst for an Ontario regional police service. She conducts research on police use of force, crime and Intelligence analysis, and social media and violent extremist recruiting.

Karine Côté-Boucher is an Associate Professor at the School of Criminology at the Université de Montréal, Canada. Her research focuses on border control – with a current focus on the relations between customs, logistics and the transportation industry.

Benoît Dupont is Professor of Criminology at the Université de Montréal, Canada, where he also holds the Canada Research Chair in Cybersecurity and the Research Chair in the Prevention of Cybercrime. He is the Scientific Director of the Smart Cybersecurity Network (SERENE-RISC), one of Canada's Networks of Centres of Excellence. His research interests include the co-evolution of technology and crime, as well as the polycentric governance of security.

Annette Hübschle is a Senior Researcher and Postdoctoral Fellow with the Institute for Safety Governance and Criminology at the University of Cape Town (UCT), South Africa. Her research focuses on the governance of safety and security, with a specific focus on illegal wildlife economies and environmental futures, as well as the interface between licit and illicit economies, and environmental and social justice. She also acts as a Senior Research Advisor to the Global Initiative against Transnational Organized Crime.

Saskia Hufnagel is Senior Lecturer in Criminal Law at Queen Mary University of London, UK. Her main research areas encompass law enforcement cooperation in Asia, North America, the EU, and Australasia; comparative constitutional and human rights law with a focus on terrorism legislation; and the policing of art crime. She has published widely on national and international police cooperation, security, comparative constitutional law, and art crime. She is a qualified German legal professional and accredited specialist in criminal law.

Julien Jeandesboz is a Professor in the Department of Political Science and is a member of REPI and the Institute of European Studies at the Université Libre de Bruxelles, Belgium. His areas of interest are international political sociology, critical approaches to security, political sociology of European construction; European Union external relations, home affairs and internal security, border and migration control; and security and technology, and surveillance and liberties.

Adam Molnar is a Lecturer in the Department of Criminology and a member of the Alfred Deakin Institute for Citizenship and Globalisation at Deakin University, Australia. His research focuses on surveillance and technology in practices of policing and national security, and considers the impacts for privacy and social control.

Massimiliano Mulone is Associate Professor in Criminology at the Université de Montréal, Canada. His research interests include the privatisation of security, with a specific focus on the relations between the police and private security companies, as well as police deviance and its management.

Carrie Sanders is an Associate Professor and Graduate Coordinator of Criminology at Wilfrid Laurier University, Canada. She is a qualitative researcher who publishes in the areas of policing, intelligence and data analytics, and the social construction of technology. Her research has received funding from the Social Sciences and Humanities Research Councils of Canada.

Clifford Shearing is a Professor in the School of Criminology and Criminal Justice at Griffith University, Australia. He leads the Global Risk Governance Programme in the Law Faculty at the University of Cape Town, South Africa, and co-leads the New Securities Programme at the Griffith Institute of Criminology. A focus of his academic work has been on broadening boundaries of criminology, with a primary focus on 'security governance'.

James Sheptycki is Professor of Criminology at York University, Canada. His research is mainly in the area of transnational crime and policing, socio-legal theory and police organisation. He has written on a variety of substantive criminological topics including domestic violence, serial killers, money laundering, drugs, public order policing, organised crime, police accountability, intelligence-led policing, witness protection, and risk and insecurity.

Samuel Tanner is an Associate Professor in the School of Criminology at the Université de Montréal, Canada. His current research interests mainly focus on media, communication and security, especially on the role, policies, practices and impact of information and communications technologies for security purposes. He also works on violent extremism, focusing on Canada's far right.

Chad Whelan is an Associate Professor in the Department of Criminology and a member of the Alfred Deakin Institute for Citizenship and Globalisation at Deakin University, Australia. His research currently focuses on organised crime, terrorism and cyber-crime, and the use of technology in law enforcement and national security. He is the author of various publications addressing the structural and relational properties of security networks.

Criminology in the face of flows: reflections on contemporary policing and security

Anthony Amicelle, Karine Côté-Boucher, Benoît Dupont, Massimiliano Mulone, Clifford Shearing and Samuel Tanner

ABSTRACT

Much has been written about the governance of crime – indeed, this is the thread that has unified criminology. Yet, property crimes and attacks against individuals – traditionally at the core of the discipline – are plummeting in many societies. Meanwhile, harms and harm management emerge outside the narrowness of criminal justice definitions. Despite this, little criminological attention has been paid to the fact that the security of flows increasingly embodies concerns that are at the heart of contemporary policing practices. This introduction to this special issue takes stock of these changes and argues that to stay current and relevant, criminology must pay closer attention to these changing landscapes of harms and policing.

Our institutions of security governance have been profoundly shaped by eighteenth- and nineteenth-century European political developments that gave rise to the institutions of criminal justice.[1] Central to these developments has been the emergence of policing arrangements[2] that governments have developed to 'shape the flow of events'.[3] For the most part, those arrangements relate to the interpersonal 'hitting and taking' harms that criminal codes, and popular sensibilities, categorise as 'crime'.

One institutional development that has fundamentally shaped contemporary policing, particularly within the Anglosphere, was the emergence of the Marine Police Force in 1798, a private policing organisation. Established by the magistrates and security governance reformers Patrick Colquhoun and John Harriot, it was created to maintain security within the London's dockyards. This preventatively focused security organisation foreshadowed and provided inspiration for the establishment of the publically funded London Metropolitan Police three decades later. Both these developments arose in response to concerns, particularly by business interests, about the state of the 'institutions of privacy'.[4] At the centre of these concerns, both in the dockyards and in the City of London more broadly, was the secure flows of people and goods.

Much has been written about the governance of crime – indeed, this is the thread that has unified criminology. Yet, property crimes and attacks against individuals – traditionally at the core of the discipline – are plummeting in many societies. Meanwhile, harms and harm management emerge outside the narrowness of criminal justice definitions while 'securing circulation' of flows is still presented as the dominant liberal problematic of security.[5] Despite this, little criminological attention has been paid to the fact that the security of flows increasingly embodies concerns that are at the heart of contemporary policing practices.[6] Indeed, the focus within contemporary security governance of fortifying urban spaces, through gated communities and other spaces and securing the conduits that connect them,[7] only became a sustained focus of criminological attention during the last two decades of the twentieth century.[8] This logic of fortification has now spread beyond a concern for crime and into the management of mobile populations. The 'fortified enclaves'[9] that shape so much of contemporary life, at a variety of scales, and particularly the governance of flows that maintain these spaces – from gated communities to 'fortified continents'[10] and migrant imprisonment[11] – still receive little attention within criminology. This gap has created a failure to locate the security of the flows that define, and are maintained within, our fortified worlds.

Becoming a central feature of security governance at the centre of the criminological stage, such logics of fortification are also intersecting with a concern for filtering flows. From barriers to smart borders, mechanisms to govern global flows depend on 'socio-technical devices'[12] that aim to both intercept and facilitate the flows of people and things, while gathering information on those flows.[13] There is no better symbol than the airport to make clear the twin and apparently contradictory claims of our time: to maximise but to regulate flows.[14] The policing of crime has also begun to change significantly as the harm landscapes associated with terrorism – and more recently digital and environmental harms – have emerged as a defining feature of the twenty-first century. This has been evident notwithstanding scholarship on flows associated with the work of Manuel Castells. He identified the crucial role played by 'flows of capital, flows of information, flows of technologies, flows of organisational interaction [and] flows of images, sounds and symbols'[15] within our increasingly digital societies. In this context, the cyberspace and artificial intelligence have since become ubiquitous features of the global flows that characterise our 'world[s] in motion'.[16]

Taking stock of those changes, some policing and security research in the past two decades has started examining new types of harms in the form of flows and the regulation efforts that accompany these harms. Accordingly, criminological scholarship has developed its analysis of how flows of people, information and things have changed policing and how conversely policing intervenes and shapes those flows. The initial path-breaking forays into these novel conditions include interest for merging forms of transnational policing,[17] international drug-trafficking control,[18] the regulation of financial flows and 'dirty money'[19] and the role of information technologies in police work.[20] While continuing to receive interest, these contemporary trends in policing have been joined by investigations making sense of new complex phenomena related to the policing of/through flows. Recent advances have been made in areas as diverse as the policing of migration,[21] border security,[22] financial security,[23] criminal networks,[24] surveillance of transportation hubs, ports and supply chains,[25] cross-border environmental crime,[26] cybercrime and online radicalisation,[27] as well as online surveillance,[28] by private interests and governments. We argue that we are now dealing with a transition where we are less concerned with harm management narrowly conceived and more with the relation between harm management and the management of flows. This introduction sets the stage to ask: what kind of knowledge do we need to build to tackle this relation in order to set the course for a new vision of criminology for the twenty-first century?

In this perspective, we first refer to a conception of security that is both de-essentialised and disembodied from a classic and exclusive state-organised social control. Security remains an 'essentially contested concept'[29] used to capture very different sets of activities and issues inside the disciplines of anthropology, criminology, history, international relations, political science and sociology.[30] A nominative view is probably most common within these major social science disciplines, where security is treated as a public good, value or right, and it is given substance in the form of a human need. Here, security is thought as a set of measures and procedures that come to be seen as a normal part of our lives or are thought to be necessary to attain this normalcy. This 'normalisation' of security (as a necessary part of our lives, a sentiment of being secure) has the advantage of taking security away from statist reflexes that equate security with exception and the survival of the nation state. It opens up possibilities to reclaim the idea of security as emancipation from physical and human constraints for people.[31] Therefore, security here coincides with the possibility to improve one's sense of security. Yet, if security is, first and foremost, a sentiment[32] or an instrumental value,[33] our grasp of it becomes more elusive and more difficult to measure. When is there 'enough' security for 'whom' and from 'what'? Such questions open up the black box of security and leave aside an illusory search for its core meaning to privilege inquiries into 'what people do in its name' and 'the practices of governance'[34] that stem from this black box. Indeed, security is 'not only an analytical category, but also a category of practice, a way of framing and responding to social problems'.[35] In other words, 'when security policy and institutions enact a situation, they change the framing and legitimate repertoires of action by reiterating the existence of insecurities and by seeking to govern political and social relations as potentially inimical, dangerous or risky. In that sense, security practice always securitises; it necessarily inscribes insecurities in the world'.[36] While security as a practice with a political content is about securing against insecurities, it becomes more interesting to analyse what the securing process does rather than what security means.[37] Empirically, speaking of the relation between security, policing, harms and flows thus also requires investigating anew the contours of contemporary harms, who names, frames and manages them (or fails to do so) and is accountable for these harms. The emerging criminology of these and similar developments is leading to significant advances in understandings of the changing landscapes of harms and policing.

Presentation of the special issue

Held at the University of Montreal in November 2015, the workshop that inspired this special issue brought together scholars who recognized this elephant and explored its contours. The distinction that this workshop has incorporated in its title – namely policing *of*, and *through*, flows – emerged as a central thread and constitutes an integrating theme of the papers that make up this volume. The focus is therefore on how the growing centrality of flows affects both the nature of these contemporary 'risks' and the policing organisations in charge of managing them.

Together these papers make a significant contribution to the security governance of flows focus that inspired this workshop. These include, migration and animal parts considered in these essays, as well as flows of many other commodities, from pharmaceuticals to minerals or malicious software. The emerging criminology of these and similar developments portrayed in these papers is leading to significant advances in understandings of the changing harm landscapes and the practices that have developed to manage them.

In developing this *of* and *through flows* theme, Molnar and Whelan, in their essay, have looked to Michel Foucault and his ideas on 'circulation' for inspiration. With this concept in mind, they have turned their attention to what might be learned about the policing of and through flows from the arrangements, and associated practices, that were put in place to secure the G20 summit held in Brisbane, Australia, in September 2014. In their essay, they explore how the security of major events not only requires channeling the circulation of people but also depends on the work done by the police to manage their own internal flows of information with command and control structures. Through their analysis, they demonstrate how the 'policing of flows is … predicated on complex underlying systems of policing *through* flows'. They conclude by arguing that 'Policing is … heavily contingent on managing both the policing of flows … and the policing through flows'.

Hübschle, with a very different empirical focus, moves from the policing of the flows surrounding a single location, namely a mega event, to the complex task of policing that seeks to disrupt the global flows that characterise illicit economies. In doing so, she takes the reader away from the highly controlled spaces, like the Brisbane G20, to the complex terrains and pathways through which rhino horn is taken from the body of these endangered animals to the markets of East Asia, where, for a variety of reasons, their horns are regarded as having potent medicinal and status value. Hübschle traces how policing agencies have been, with disastrous results for wildlife conservation, unsuccessful in effectively disrupting flows of rhino horn.

Using the waterways metaphor of 'locks' and 'dams', Hufnagel's essay explores the governance of border security within the context of the European Union. The effective governance of external borders that have played such a vital role in enabling the opening up of internal borders has recently been fundamentally challenged by the massive flows of undocumented migrants fleeing the conflicts and poverty that today characterise some North African nations. Hufnagel compares this analysis of European border controls with an analysis of the governance of flows within Greater China. In developing her analysis, Hufnagel points to the importance of trust and legitimacy in shaping the organisational flows that enable the policing of flows. Trust and legitimacy, she argues, shape both the formal and informal forms of cooperation within and between organisations with regard, in particular, to the sharing of intelligence, upon which the policing *of* flows depends. Hufnagel concludes that legitimacy shapes trust and, hence, enhances levels of cooperation between police agencies.

Two papers within the special issue that focus attention very directly on flows of information (intelligence) within security governance organisations are Sanders and Jeandesboz. Both authors focus their fine-grained attention on the way in which information flows within and between security and policing agencies. For Sanders, a crucial feature of these intra- and inter-organisational flows is 'crime analysis and the practice of policing *through* flows of data have changed the *symbolic nature* of policing'. Sanders develops this line of thought in her conclusion, where she recognises the 'way in which the technological frames of crime analysts run counter to traditional action-oriented practices of policing'. In a complementary essay, Jeandesboz takes the reader into the very heart of border security practices within the European Union by exploring the central role given to technological developments in information processing and information exchange. Attention is drawn particularly to the 'centres of calculation' through which these policing flows are formed, transformed and directed.

In another essay focusing on organisational flows, Shepticky takes the reader inside the 'machine' to explore 'information flows in the police organisation'. He provides a trenchant analysis of the dilemmas and challenges facing twenty-first century police organisations as they are dealing with the competing logics of the cybernetic model of policing, those of the police métier, performance requirements and a reorientation towards "high-level social control". Ultimately in facing these challenges, Shepticky concludes that police organisations have little choice but to base their strategies on the democratic participation in intelligence production and governance.

Finally, Bigo takes a step back and proposes an in-depth reflection on the current state of scholarship about flows in the social sciences. He unravels the premise of contemporary security where flows are equated with chaos. The policing of flows responds to the international doxa where flows are seen as dangerous and in need of ordering and where the figure of the state continues to 'structure our relation to flows'. Yet, building on Bauman's 'liquid modernity', Bigo shows that flows responds to logics of distinction and social differentiation that go beyond the state. Alternatively, if, as Bigo suggests, we accept to view flows as 'the logic of the social', we may be able to resist their (in)securisation.

Why policing of/through flows in criminology?

Thinking of security in terms of flows, as the papers in this volume do, has scholarly precedents outside of criminology's established boundaries. For instance, Michel Foucault, in 'Sécurité, territoire et population', tackled the issue of flows and their management in his explorations of disease management strategies within seventeenth-, eighteenth- and nineteenth-century European cities.[38] What Foucault provided was an account of three political models of spatial control of flows of people and other mobile elements (carts, miasmas and so on) in relation to the management of leprosy, plague and smallpox. On the one hand, the first two models were based on a logic of enclosure with walls and related practices of territorial demarcation. While the management of leprosy relied on the *extra muros* exclusion of a certain segment of the population, the management of plague made quarantine compulsory with the *quadrillage* of city space to implement a strict regulation of movements *intra muros*. Both diseases thus refer to a problem of delimitation, whether the issue is about fixing an inside and an outside to block and exclude undesirable flows or it is about structuring territory to put and contain those flows in specific spaces. On the other hand, the management of smallpox through vaccination illustrated a third mode of spatial control with the 'emergence of a completely different problem that is no longer that of fixing and demarcating the territory, but of allowing circulations to take place, of controlling them, sifting the good and the bad, ensuring that things are always in movement, constantly moving around, continually going from one place to another, but in such a way that the inherent dangers of this circulation are cancelled out'.[39] In other words, the main problem becomes first and foremost the mobility as such rather than the delimitation of space to the extent that the issue is about monitoring an entire mobile population all over the territory.

In light of the special issue, the value of Michel Foucault's work is twofold. First, this concern with the spread of disease through flows of 'an indefinite series of mobile elements'[40] is at least as important today as it was in the nineteenth century – consider the recent outbreaks of Ebola and Zika. Second, and most importantly, Foucault also provides in this way three ideal types of flows management (e.g. through exclusion; containment; and traceability) to interrogate current policing configurations – whether they might predominantly relate to either one model or a specific articulation of various models or even the emergence of new modes of control.

For instance, today, the traceability and 'securitisation'[41] of flows is presented as central to the governance of security of population and the spaces they inhabit.[42] Indeed, the set of traceability techniques is designed and promoted to allow at any time the differentiation and relocation of flows without infringing upon the general principle of their circulation.[43] According to Hermitte, 'surveillance, this ancient reality, only becomes modern traceability when it is performed within an organised system, whose extension suggests that it is a genuine societal project, pursued by private powers as much as public powers'.[44] These developments extend the pluralisation of security governance – the securing of flows is 'nodal'[45] with heterogeneous networks that could be not only transnational but also hybrids between public and private actors.[46]

As a result, a significant aspect of this policing of flows is the multiplication of the governance practices that trace, filter, scan and survey flows. How these secure an ordered circulation – this constitutive aim of liberal regimes – also conveys questions about how we globally reformulate inclusion and exclusion, as well as 'social and political hierarchies, practices of rule and identities'.[47]

Therefore, thinking in terms of flows is conceptually promising, we argue, yet not new if one considers how this term is generalised when it comes to the study of security, but also when we account for the wide array of flows that is currently managed in different social spaces or sites of security. But what are flows, and how might this concept be useful in epistemological terms? What are the constitutive properties of flows that require a new conceptual model? How does this language of flows enable criminologists to explore new empirical terrains that were formerly ignored by traditional criminology?

In developing a criminology that pays attention to flows scholars need, through their research, to consider what is flowing, through what spaces, the strategies and practices that have been, and are being, developed to manage these flows and who engages in them. These are empirical questions that are likely to be answered differently in different contexts. This means highlighting the dynamic and adaptive nature of flows, such as being able to always find a path of least resistance (like water) to reach their goals, by contrast with a more static understanding of harms as located (or embedded) in physical spaces whose structural features represent powerful constraints. For instance, new technologies of communication and the Internet, mostly via social media platforms have now massively expanded the capacity of hate speeches to harm people in a way that is not just located in specific physical spaces, such as right-wing extremist demonstrations online. It is these questions that the papers included in this volume, through empirical explorations, have sought to address.

Thinking in terms of flows calls for the identification and discussion of the spaces/sites that permit or impede certain kinds of mobilities – urban, cross-border, financial, digital and so on. The papers in this volume explore the way in which people, information and goods, within very different domains, circulate between nodes or hubs where they are managed, shaped, directed and regulated. Through these processes of circulation, flows move from one space to another where they also shape processes, decisions and technologies. Those powerful social actors directing flows may also choose alternative pathways to avoid some regulations in favour of others (via different strategies such as 'forum shopping').[48]

Focusing attention on flows also necessitates a recalibration of established understandings of regulatory actors to include a wide range of 'actants'.[49] Who and what are involved in managing flows? What mentalities, technologies and practices do they employ? What outcomes are they seeking to realise? What vested interests are at stake? What resources are mobilised? In short, how and by whom are different sets of flows policed within different contexts? For example, how is the idea of flows impacting when we consider security actors whose core business is to provide security (law enforcement actors, private policing) versus those whose business is not to provide security/policing services per se (bankers, truckers, Internet companies)? One should identify them, assessing and studying their mentalities, the technologies they are mobilising, as much as their knowledge, resources and capacities.

The normative and legal frameworks (that are being produced and utilisedto manage flows should also become a focus of enquiry. How are classic questions of accountability, oversight and human rights renewed by the policing of and through flows? In light of the growing role of automated technologies in contemporary policing, we should investigate how and by whom these devices are produced, how and by whom they are domesticated, and how their publics and targets react. Indeed, machines and algorithms are increasingly mobilised to support the bureaucratic and technical management of flows, with a growing level of autonomy conferred to them by advances in artificial intelligence research. In that context, it is necessary to inquire into what these developments imply for the entanglements of humans and non-humans.

All these questions open new theoretical perspectives for criminologists, but will also spur methodological innovation. Being able to observe how flows move and are being controlled at multiple junctures of their stream will require ambitious research protocols that can capture a diversity of governance practices and rationalities being deployed at a global scale and over time. Understanding and explaining how their articulation forms a more or less coherent whole and how human–machine interactions influence their outcomes will require empirical creativity. What we hope to achieve with this special issue on *Criminology in the Face of Flows* is open the conversation for inventing new conceptual, theoretical and methodological tools to help criminology tackle and better understand the (im) mobile world we live in.

Disclosure statement

No potential conflict of interest was reported by the authors.

Notes

1. Brodeur, *The Policing Web.*
2. See for example, Radzinowicz, *A History of English*; and Beattie, *Policing and Punishment in London; The First English Detectives.*
3. Parker et al., 'Introduction in Regulation Law'.
4. Stinchcombe, 'Institutions of Privacy in the Detrmination'.
5. Boy, *Report on the Theory of Risk*; Dillon, *Politics of Security*; Langley, 'Toxic Assets, Turbulence'; and Lobo-Guerrero, "'Pirates', Stewards, and the Securitization'.
6. But see McCulloch and Pickering, *Borders and Crime.*
7. Shearing, 'Remarks on Zero Tolerance'.
8. For a review, see Bayley and Shearing, 'The Future of Policing'.
9. Caldeira, 'Fortified Enclaves'; and Brown, *Walled States, Waning Sovereignty.*
10. Aas, 'Analysing a World in Motion.'
11. Bosworth, *Inside Immigration Detention.*
12. Amicelle et al., 'Questioning Security Devices'.
13. Pallister-Wilkins, 'How Walls Do Work'.
14. Lyon, *Surveillance Studies: An Overview.*
15. Castells, *The Rise of the Network.*
16. See note 10 above.
17. Bowling and Sheptycki, *Global Policing.*
18. Nadelmann, *Cops Across Borders.*
19. Levi and Reuter, 'Money Laundering'.
20. Ericson and Haggerty, *Policing the Risk Society.*
21. Aliverti, *Crimes of Mobility.*
22. Côté-Boucher, 'The Paradox of Discretion'; and Loftus, 'Border Regimes and the Sociology'.
23. Amicelle and Jacobsen, 'The Cross-Colonization of Finance'; and De Goede, *Speculative Security.*
24. Morselli, *Inside Criminal Networks.*
25. Brewer, *Policing the Waterfront.*
26. White, *Transnational Environmental Crime.*
27. Dupont, 'Bots, cops, and corporations'.
28. Trottier, *Social Media as Surveillance.*
29. Buzan, *People, States & Fear.*
30. Bigo, 'Security, IR and Anthropology'.
31. Booth, 'Security and Emancipation'.
32. Delumeau, *Rassurer et protéger.*
33. Booth, *Theory of World Security.*
34. Valverde, 'Questions of Security,' 5.
35. Zedner, 'The Concept of Security,' 158.
36. Huysmans, *Security Unbound*, 4.
37. Balzacq et al., 'Security Practices'.
38. Foucault, *Security, Territory, Population.*

39. Ibid., 65.
40. Ibid., 20.
41. Schuilenburg, *The Securitization of Society*.
42. Gros, le *Principe sécurité*.
43. Torny, 'La traçabilité comme technique'.
44. Hermitte, 'La traçabilité des personnes', 3.
45. Shearing and Wood, 'Nodal Governance, Democracy'.
46. Bauman et al., 'After Snowden: Rethinking'.
47. Kotef, *Movement and the Ordering of Freedom*, 3.
48. Braithwaite and Drahos, *Global Business Regulation*.
49. See for example, Latour, *Reassembling the Social*.

Bibliography

Aas, K. F. 'Analysing a World in Motion. Global Flows Meet "Criminology of the Other".' *Theoretical Criminology* 11, no. 2 (2007): 283–303. doi:10.1177/1362480607075852.

Aliverti, A. *Crimes of Mobility. Criminal Law and the Regulation of Immigration*. London: Routledge, 2013.

Amicelle, A., C. Aradau, and J. Jeandesboz. 'Questioning Security Devices: Performativity, Resistance, Politics.' *Security Dialogue* 46, no. 4 (2015): 293–306. doi:10.1177/0967010615586964.

Amicelle, A., and E. K. U. Jacobsen. 'The Cross-Colonization of Finance and Security through Lists: Banking Policing in the UK and India.' *Environment and Planning D: Society and Space* 34, no. 1 (2016): 89–106. doi:10.1177/0263775815623276.

Balzacq, T., T. Basaran, D. Bigo, E.-P. Guittet, and C. Olsson. 'Security Practices.' In *International Studies Encyclopedia Online*, edited by R. A. Denemark, 1–30. Blackwell, 2010.

Bauman, Z. *Liquid Modernity*. Cambridge: Polity Press, 2000.

Bauman, Z., D. Bigo, P. Esteves, E. Guild, V. Jabri, D. Lyon, and R. B. J. Walker. 'After Snowden: Rethinking the Impact of Surveillance.' *International Political Sociology* 8, no. 2 (2014): 121–144. doi:10.1111/ips.12048.

Bayley, D., and C. Shearing. 'The Future of Policing.' *Law & Society Review* 30, no. 3 (1996): 585–606. doi:10.2307/3054129.

Beattie, J. M. *Policing and Punishment in London 1660–1720: Urban Crime and the Limits of Terror*. Oxford: Oxford University Press, 2002.

Beattie, J. M. *The First English Detectives: The Bow Street Runners and the Policing of London, 1750–1840*. Oxford: Oxford University Press, 2012.

Bigo, D. 'Security, IR and Anthropology: Encounters, Misunderstanding and Possible Collaborations.' In *The Anthropology of Security: Perspectives from the Frontline of Policing, Counter-Terrorism and Border Control*, edited by M. Maguire, C. Fruits, and N. Zurawski, 189–205. London: Pluto, 2014.

Booth, K. 'Security and Emancipation.' *Review of International Relations* 17, no. 4 (1991): 313–326.

Booth, K. *Theory of World Security*. Cambridge: Cambridge University Press, 2007.

Bosworth, M. *Inside Immigration Detention*. Oxford: Oxford University Press, 2014.

Bowling, B., and J. Sheptycki. *Global Policing*. London: Sage, 2012.

Boy, N. *Report on the Theory of Risk as a Societal Security Instrument*. Oslo: Societal Security Network, 2015. Accessed May 12, 2017. http://www.societalsecurity.net/sites/default/files/D5.1%20Report%20on%20the%20theory%20of%20risk%20as%20a%20societal%20security%20instrument_version2.pdf.

Braithwaite, J., and P. Drahos. *Global Business Regulation*. Cambridge: Cambridge University Press, 2000.

Brewer, R. *Policing the Waterfront. Networks, Partnerships, and the Governance of Port Security*. Oxford: Oxford University Press, 2014.

Brodeur, J.-P. *The Policing Web*. Oxford: Oxford University Press, 2010.

Brown, W. *Walled States, Waning Sovereignty*. Cambridge, MA: Zone Books, 2010.

Buzan, B. *People, States & Fear: An Agenda for International Security Studies in the post-Cold War Era*. London: Harvester Wheatsheaf, 1991.

Caldeira, T. 'Fortified Enclaves: The New Urban Segregation.' *Public Culture* 8, no. 2 (1996): 303–328. doi:10.1215/08992363-8-2-303.

Castells, M. *The Rise of the Network Society*. Oxford: Blackwell Publishers, 2000.

Côté-Boucher, K. 'The Paradox of Discretion: Customs and the Changing Occupational Identity of Canadian Border Officers.' *British Journal of Criminology* 56, no. 1 (2016): 49–67. doi:10.1093/bjc/azv023.

De Goede, M. *Speculative Security: The Politics of Pursuing Terrorist Monies*. Minneapolis: University of Minnesota Press, 2012.

Delumeau, J. *Rassurer Et Protéger. Le Sentiment De Sécurité Dans l'Occident D'autrefois*. Paris: Fayard, 1989.

Dillon, M. *Politics of Security: Towards a Political Philosophy of Continental Thought*. London: Routledge, 1996.

Ericson, R. V., and K. D. Haggerty. *Policing the Risk Society*. Toronto: University of Toronto Press, 1997.

Foucault, M. *Security, Territory, Population: Lectures at the Collège de France 1977–1978*. London: Picador, 2009.

Garland, D. 'The Limits of the Sovereign State: Strategies of Crime Control in Contemporary Society.' *The British Journal of Criminology* 36, no. 4 (1996): 445–471. doi:10.1093/oxfordjournals.bjc.a014105.

Gros, F. *Le Principe sécurité*. Paris: Gallimard, 1992.

Hermitte, M.-A. 'La traçabilité des personnes et des choses. Précaution, pouvoirs et maitrise.' In *Traçabilité et responsabilité*, edited by P. Pedrot, 1–44. Paris: Economica, 2003.

Huysmans, J. *Security Unbound: Enacting Democratic Limits*. London: Routledge, 2014.

Kotef, H. *Movement and the Ordering of Freedom*. Durham: Duke University Press, 2015.

Langley, P. 'Toxic Assets, Turbulence and Biopolitical Security: Governing the Crisis of Global Financial Circulation.' *Security Dialogue* 44, no. 2 (2013): 111–126. doi:10.1177/0967010613479425.

Latour, B. *Reassembling the Social: An Introduction to Actor-Network-Theory*. Oxford: Oxford University Press, 2005.

Levi, M., and P. Reuter. 'Money Laundering.' In *Crime and Justice: A Review of Research*, edited by M. Tonry, 289–375. Chicago: Chicago University Press, 2006.

Lobo-Guerrero, L. ''Pirates', Stewards, and the Securitization of Global Circulation.' *International Political Sociology* 2, no. 3 (2008): 219–235. doi:10.1111/j.1749-5687.2008.00046.x.

Loftus, B. 'Border Regimes and the Sociology of Policing.' *Policing and Society: An International Journal of Research and Policy* 25, no. 1 (2015): 115–125. doi:10.1080/10439463.2013.802788.

Lyon, D. *Surveillance Studies: An Overview*. Cambridge: Polity Press, 2007.

McCulloch, J., and S. Pickering. *Borders and Crime. Pre-Crime, Mobility and Serious Harm in an Age of Globalization*. London: Palgrave Macmillan, 2012.

Morselli, C. *Inside Criminal Networks*. New York: Springer, 2009.

Nadelmann, E. A. *Cops across Borders. The Internationalization of U.S. Criminal Enforcement*. University Park: Pennsylvania State University Press, 1993.

O'Malley, P. 'Risk and Responsibility.' In *Foucault and Political Reason: Liberalism, Neo-Liberalism and Rationalities of Government*, edited by A. Barry, T. Osbrone, and N. Rose, 189–208. Chicago: University of Chicago Press, 1996.

O'Reilly, C. 'The Transnational Security Consultancy Industry: A Case of State-Corporate Symbiosis.' *Theoretical Criminology* 14, no. 2 (2010): 183–210. doi:10.1177/1362480609355702.

O'Reilly, C., and G. Ellison. ''Eye Spy Private High': Re-Conceptualizing High Policing Theory.' *British Journal of Criminology* 46, no. 4 (2006): 641–660. doi:10.1093/bjc/azi090.

Pallister-Wilkins, P. 'How Walls Do Work: Security Barriers as Devices of Interruption and Data Capture.' *Security Dialogue* 47 (2016): 151–164. doi:10.1177/0967010615615729.

Parker, C., C. Scott, N. Lacey, and J. Braithwaite. 'Introduction in Regulation Law.' In *Regulating Law*, edited by C. Parker, C. Scott, N. Lacey, and J. Braithwaite Parker, 1–12. Oxford: Oxford University Press, 2004.

Radzinowicz, L. *A History of English Criminal Law and It's Administration from 1750: The Movement for Reform*. Vol. 1. London: Stevens & Sons, 1948.

Schuilenburg, M. *The Securitization of Society*. New York: New York University Press, 2015.

Shearing, C. 'Remarks on Zero Tolerance.' *Criminal Law Bulletin* 35, no. 4 (1999): 378–383.

Shearing, C., and J. Wood. 'Nodal Governance, Democracy, and the New 'Denizens'.' *Journal of Law and Society* 30, no. 3 (2003): 400–419. doi:10.1111/1467-6478.00263.

Stinchcombe, A. 'Institutions of Privacy in the Determination of Police Administrative Practice.' *American Journal of Sociology* 69, no. 2 (1963): 150–160. doi:10.1086/223544.

Torny, D. 'La traçabilité comme technique de gouvernement des hommes et des choses.' *Politix* 11, no. 44 (1998): 51–75. doi:10.3406/polix.1998.1761.

Valverde, M. 'Questions of Security: A Framework for Research.' *Theoretical Criminology* 15, no. 1 (2011): 3–22. doi:10.1177/1362480610382569.

Zedner, L. 'The Concept of Security: An Agenda for Comparative Analysis.' *Legal Studies* 23, no. 1 (2003): 153–176. doi:10.1111/j.1748-121X.2003.tb00209.x.

Managing flows during mega-events: taking account of internal and external flows in public order policing operations

Chad Whelan and Adam Molnar

ABSTRACT

The article examines the configurations and organisational dynamics of policing mega-events through the metaphor of 'flows'. Using the Brisbane 2014 Group of 20 Summit (G20) as an explorative case study, we suggest that the metaphor of flows may not only hold value with regard to understanding how objects of policing are rendered visible and manageable, but also how it might enable us to take stock of internal flows of data, information and intelligence within public order policing operations. We examine how police pursued their goal of containing and controlling protest flows as well as managing rapid intra- and inter-organisational flows. In particular, we examine how police and security actors designed what we call 'flow-based' architectures and the underlying organisational and situational contingencies shaping how these structures and systems form and function. The article concludes by calling for greater attention on internal dynamics of policing operations which, we argue, can potentially be advanced by drawing on the metaphor of flows.

Introduction

Foucault's lectures at the Collège de France on *Security, Territory, Population* focus on the relationship between security and circulation as an emerging expression of the liberal art of government. A new era of 'security' emerged within eighteenth-century liberalism that broke from a rights-based conception of security, which extends to sovereign territorial limits, and instead ushered in a model of security premised on the control and regulation of people, objects and events.[1] Foucault's insights invite nuance into conceptualisations of security and policing, particularly as security relates to how governments imagine, intervene upon and modulate risk in urban and digital environments.[2] Others have noted how practices of surveillance are situated within the onset of increasingly 'fluid' features of globalised modernity.[3] This research has considered how accelerations and mobility of information, capital and people have led to the deterritorialisation of traditional social institutions and boundaries in ways that shape practices of security.[4] While reflecting broader shifts in the field of security governance, these perspectives particularly call attention to, on the one hand, the traceability of flows and their regulatory management and control and, on the other, the ways in which social institutions are reorienting through rapid spatio-temporal fluxes in information, technologies, capital, political and symbolic life.[5]

Compared with the Foucauldian approaches of critical security studies that consider the regulation of 'risky' flows by security and policing institutions,[6] and surveillance studies that consider the fluidity and proliferation of data and informational flows,[7] one particular area where the institutional qualities of flows has seen less attention is in the internal dynamics of policing operations, particularly in the context of mega-events and public order policing.[8] Police agencies routinely adopt technologies and adapt strategies and tactics in ways that bring about new or altered institutional configurations,[9] especially in the context of mega-events.[10] Research on public order policing has noted how 'uncontainable' and 'transgressive' protest flows during events such as the G20 protests in London and Toronto 'have each stimulated tactical innovation, diffusion, and shifts in [police] practice'.[11] This research suggests that these developments in public order policing emerge through a form of interactive social learning between unpredictable protest tactics and subsequent police adaptation to neutralise those tactics, and how these policy developments diffuse as 'best practices', often on a transnational scale.[12] These shifts in police strategies and tactics are particularly evident in the context of mega-events such as international political summits and Olympic Games.[13] Much of the literature on mega-events concentrates on transformations in the physical environment as police and security actors pursue 'total' security. This involves configuring public and private space into controlled 'secure', even 'militarised' zones[14] and 'pre-crime' surveillance and intelligence efforts against potential threats in ways that blur the boundaries between criminal and security intelligence.[15]

We argue that in much of the mega-events literature such flows of people, objects and things are largely viewed as external threats subject to governance.[16] The literature is yet to sufficiently address the organisational configurations and situational environments of those aiming to control such flows. Combining work that seeks to recover the broader empirical nuance of institutional reconfigurations during mega-events[17] with research on the organisational complexities data, information and intelligence flows within policing organisations and networks,[18] we examine the extent to which flows might also be analysed as an *internal* mediating feature in terms of informational exchanges within and between security actors. We examine the utility of 'flows' as a concept with which to understand how objects of policing are controlled through novel developments in spatial and population management[19] as well as the internal workings of police operations through taking stock of intra- and inter-organisational flows. We aim to address how attempts to police territories and populations at mega-events shape, and are shaped by, an underlying 'web'[20] of structures and systems to manage data, information and intelligence flows.

The article proceeds in five sections. The first section provides a very brief review of Foucault's work as it has conditioned scholars to locate flows as objects of policing and security subject to risk-based classifications and sorting so that they can be regulated and controlled. Drawing on examinations of flow architectures in financial markets[21] and 'smart cities',[22] we then consider how flows might be considered as an internal characteristic of public order policing, reflective of developments in policing practices at mega-events that are customised to address the uncertainty of protest flows. The second section outlines the methodology for our case study, involving the analysis of internal police documentation and detailed interviews with key members of the Queensland Police Service (QPS), the organisation responsible for policing the 2014 G20. The following three sections draw on our empirical data as it relates to existing understandings of flows, as external to police organisations, and subsequently as it relates to the internal flows within police operations. We examine how police reconfigured the urban environment to regulate flows of people and manage populations during the event. We then focus on the often hidden relationships between technical architectures and organisational contexts that coordinate data, information and intelligence flows. In particular, we examine the underlying structures and systems designed to manage such flows and the organisational and situational contingencies shaping how these systems operate. The paper concludes by reflecting further on the properties of such internal flows in large scale policing operations.

Theorising the objects of security: existing perspectives on the policing of flows

Foucault's objective for his lectures was to theorise the relationship between security, territory and population as an attempt to better grasp techniques of power specific to a liberal art of government. As a biopolitical configuration, apparatuses of security sought to make the subjects and objects of circulation increasingly transparent, visible and subject to normative classifications in such a way that a security dispositif intervenes within and reshapes flows of people, objects, activities and information in ways that 'permit, guarantee, ensure circulations: of people, of goods, of air'.[23] Scholars have drawn on Foucault's lectures to consider the governmental rationalities and techniques of power implicated in managing circulations and mobility as part of contemporary security practices.[24] Critical geographers of security, in particular, have drawn on Foucault to theorise and research expressions of liberal governance in urban environments.[25] The first, and most common, attribute they focus on is a 'splintering urbanism',[26] a term that explains how the urban environment is separated into a patchwork of enclaves where 'more or less purified insides [are] separated from more or less dangerous outsides'.[27] Sometimes relying on the physical configurations of the built environment itself, once spaces are separated and enclosed, they can be differentially regulated in accordance with the security objectives and surveillance capacities of the apparatus.[28] Flows, insofar as they are said to exist as a series of risky or dangerous possibilities 'out-there' in the world, are predominantly located as a referent object that is external to security organisations. For example, in Haggerty and Ericson's work on the Surveillant Assemblage,[29] strongly indebted to Deleuze,[30] flows are viewed as people, things, objects or traces that have an independent reality and are made visible through the surveillance capacities of the security dispositif. Flows are rendered transparent and subsequently 'tamed' through classifications and sorting so they can be regulated, managed, entitled or controlled in accordance with the desired functional unity of the assemblage.

While these accounts provide vital critical explanations of practices of social control, it remains to be more thoroughly understood how the core institutions of security governance assemblages might be reconfiguring in important ways in relation to the government of flows, particularly in the context of mega-events. According to Klauser,[31] many studies into mega-event security 'often ignore the broader urban, national or international networks within which the studied micro-spaces of surveillance are positioned and monitored'. The wider picture of security governance is also quite often lost as researchers have instead concentrated on organisations as conduits for conducting risk analysis bound by a logic of 'worst-case' scenario planning[32] or engaging in threat construction, discriminatory forms of surveillance, and information and intelligence sharing.[33] How police and security organisations internally make sense of, and act upon, such risks is not always clear from studying their practices alone. Furthermore, although we know that formal and informal 'knowledge networks'[34] exist in mega-event policing, the underlying internal properties of intra- and inter-organisational networks facilitating real-time data, information and intelligence flows *during* major event security initiatives have yet to be captured in much of this literature.[35]

Furthering Klauser's call for a deeper assessment of the networks within which the regulations of flows take place,[36] public order policing literature has been somewhat more sensitive to the dialectic between classifications of 'external' flows as targets of regulation and the internal adaptations and reordering of policing organisations in response to them.[37] Gillham and Noakes note how the use of disruptive tactics by protest movements, particularly following the 1999 Seattle World Trade Organization protests, to avoid containment and negotiated management was thought to be the start of a new genre of protest tactics.[38] As protester groups became to be perceived as 'leaderless' and 'unpredictable',[39] thus rendering negotiated management risky, police and security actors widely discussed the need for innovations in police strategies and tactics. This development prompted significant revisions in public order policing across the United States, which resulted in the increasing use of tactics that sought to anticipate and pre-empt perceived disruptive behaviour.[40] A more recent example of this dialectical relationship can be found in the wake of the London 2011 riots, through what the UK's Her Majesty's Inspectorate of Constabulary terms a 'new period' of public order policing: an era that insists 'the game has changed' and that policing must strive 'to be as adaptable as possible' to respond to the inherent uncertainty of flows.[41]

Strategies and tactics used to manage the uncertainty of protest flows at mega-events have evolved into a convergence of a crime–security nexus. Researchers have traced how such tactics blend police-determined permit processes to sanction demonstrations,[42] spatial containment strategies,[43] the selective application of pre-emptive arrest[44] and pre-event surveillance and intelligence operations.[45] Interestingly, the regulation of flows at mega-events through real-time surveillance during the event has held less sustained focus in the literature. Police rely extensively on surveillance and information management for 'situational awareness' through the collection of data and information that is fed into a central command centre. These command centres form the basis for the real-time monitoring of the qualities of urban flows *and* simultaneously coordinate intra- and inter-organisational flows of data, information and intelligence. Flows are subsequently categorised and separated within the command centre, which facilitates police decision - making about how to manage them. In relation to the policing of protests, 'good' flows - those that follow along sanctioned routes that have been previously agreed upon through negotiated management – will be filtered accordingly, while 'potentially unruly' flows that may have strayed into 'no-go' zones or display suspicious characteristics are subject to more forceful interventions.[46] Such an elaborate urban surveillance system collects and processes a significant volume of images, sounds and data, to facilitate decisions in an institutional fashion that could be considered as a 'flow'-based architecture.

While the mega-events and public order policing literature has highlighted the significance of intra- and inter-organisational flows within and between police and security actors, this literature is yet to adequately focus on the underlying architectures that facilitate real-time data, information and intelligence flows during major events. To this end, useful studies can be found in relation to financial markets[47] and smart cities.[48] Global financial markets embody a 'flow architecture' through an integration of human actors and digital information communication networks that work to visualise, mediate and order information about the market in real time.[49] So called 'smart cities' harvest information gathered from digital devices and sensors embedded within the urban infrastructure. Data collated from CCTV cameras, traffic sensors, emergency response vehicles, air pollution sensors, water levels, seismic activity and a range of other areas might be drawn into a central hub to facilitate the understanding of real-time functioning and management of the urban environment.[50] The projected information, mediated through displays of 'real-time analytics', is a conglomeration of fragments representing a reality in a state of flux. In a dialectical fashion, this flow-based architecture is itself used as a means to more clearly understand and intervene upon flows within urban environments.[51]

Importantly, both of these human–technology interfaces of financial markets and smart cities weave together fragments of events with human and non-human actors into a modality that crafts a reality that is contingent on, but entirely distinct from, the events themselves. This mediated reality in the control room of the smart city, or on the market floor, is presented as always being in a state of flux, and yet, it exists as part of a broader situational and organisational context conditioning decision-making. In the context of public order policing environments at mega-events, the use of command centres providing situational awareness of flows (and protest flows in particular) depends heavily on various situational and organisational contingencies of policing operations. While such a flow-based architecture is inseparable from constructions of risk that inform the interpretation and use of data, it also extends beyond practices of risk calculation to the interface between information flows and the substantive shape of police and security interventions. The architecture is itself underpinned by organisational contingencies, such as command and control structures, which need to be considered alongside risk-based and technical initiatives to manage flows. We suggest that any efforts to coordinate internal flows of data, information and intelligence can only be properly understood when we also consider how these attempts are conditioned through such broader structures and systems.

Brisbane G20: case study

Brisbane 2014 took place on 15–16 November in inner-city Brisbane in Queensland, Australia. The event was coordinated by the G20 Taskforce, which was established in the Department of the Prime Minister and Cabinet (DPM&C) and was responsible for coordinating the policy agenda, logistics and venue security. The police organisation within the designated host city jurisdiction – the state of Queensland – established a G20 Group within the QPS, which conducted the core planning and coordinating work for the G20 which conducted the core planning and coordinating work for the G20 security operation, in conjunction with the G20 Taskforce. From the time the event was first canvassed in November 2011 to the time it was held 3 years later, Australia had 3 different prime ministers, with each having a somewhat different view on how the event would 'look and feel'; this resulted in seemingly constant shifting expectations for both the G20 Taskforce and QPS.

The security operation involved approximately 6650 police, including 4500 from QPS, 1500 from other state and territory police organisations and New Zealand and 650 members of the Australian Federal Police (AFP). It also involved many other agencies, including the Australian Defence Force, the Australian Customs and Border Protection Service (ACBPS)[52] and the Australian Security Intelligence Organisation (ASIO) as well as private security services within the secure event zones. As is the case with complex security environments,[53] Brisbane 2014 involved multiple overlapping security networks. The G20 Taskforce itself was a network – drawing together multiple agencies in an attempt to coordinate the event – and the G20 Group also involved co-located liaison officers appointed from the agencies listed above and many more. The total cost of the security operation was $AU450 million.[54]

This research draws on a larger project following an exploratory case study design[55] covering various aspects of the Brisbane 2014 G20, particularly the organisational dynamics of planning and designing complex security operations that mostly sit behind the scenes. The project is based on detailed, qualitative interviews with key stakeholders involved in the G20 security operation across a number of agencies, including the G20 Group and G20 Taskforce, and the analysis of available security documentation. Working closely with the G20 Taskforce, the G20 Group was set up in late 2012 to plan and coordinate the security operation for Brisbane 2014. The G20 Group involved a hierarchical structure, with an Assistant Commissioner as the Program Executive, a Chief Superintendent as Program Director, and then three Superintendents responsible for the portfolios of Operational Planning, Program Control and Support Services. Project managers, who were normally at the level of Inspector, were appointed under the respective superintendents. Examples of project managers from the operational planning portfolio include: command and control; dignitary protection; intelligence; investigations and offender processing; public safety and specialist support; traffic; and venue security. The programme control and support services portfolios included a further 10 project managers. Our focus within these portfolios was limited to the areas of information technology integration, logistics, risk and quality assurance, and training. The QPS also travelled extensively in the lead up to Brisbane hosting the G20 meeting and had international peer-reviewers and observers come to Brisbane before and during the event.

The project involves 15 interviews with members of the QPS G20 Group, 10 interviews with members of the G20 Taskforce and 3 interviews with international stakeholders from Canada, New Zealand and the United Kingdom. Other interviewees include members of the AFP. In total, 30 interviews were conducted. Interviews were semi-structured, between 45 and 90 min long and were conducted in 2015–2016. In this article, we concentrate on interviews with senior members of the G20 Group and the analysis of operational manuals and other internal documents, made available by

QPS. Our primary focus is the internal workings of the security operation and as such we draw heavily on interview data. While we recognise the limits of relying on interview data, including the potential for there to be a significant difference between what respondents may say in an interview and how they *actually* think and act, in-depth qualitative interviews are the only feasible methodology for addressing the *internal* configurations and practices of policing operations as much of the finer details are not captured in documents such as post-event reviews. Even methods such as observational research, should access be permitted, are almost practically impossible as the planning process underpinning the policing operation lasted over 2 years. We do not attempt to assess the effectiveness of the policing operation, but rather examine how police pursued their goal of securing the event from external flows and made sense of, and attempted to manage, their extensive internal flows of data, information and intelligence during the event.

The interview schedule contained open-ended questions, inviting interviewees to share their experiences of being involved in Brisbane 2014. For example, interviewees were asked to tell us about their role, the challenges they faced in carrying out their role and the main lessons they learnt for securing mega-events in the future. Formal representations were made to QPS to interview members involved in securing the G20 meeting. The QPS responded positively to our request, and many of the core members involved in planning the security operation made themselves available to participate in this project. Interviews were transcribed, and interviewees were given an opportunity to review and amend the interview transcript, principally to ensure that no security-sensitive information was inadvertently released, as a condition of the research agreements. Interview data were coded and analysed using NVivo 10. Coding concentrated on classifying emerging themes from the interviews. Data were cross-referenced across interviewees from each organisation as well as against official documents (where possible). It should be noted that it is the personal views of interviewees that are quoted in this article and these views are not necessarily representative of the QPS.[56]

Managing external flows: visibility, channelling and predictability

The police operation for the G20 involved multiple, overlapping approaches to securing territories. Similar to other events,[57] these include dividing and controlling spaces as part of a broader spatial containment strategy to filter flows of people and objects and provide territorial boundaries, enclosures and separations used to authorise surveillance and control of the spaces themselves.[58] The emergence of separated border zones, often through extensive physical barriers, enabled QPS to further structure space[59] to discipline flows through a combined strategy of physical separation, increased visibility through surveillance[60] and legal powers to facilitate stop-and-search and impose exclusionary bans.[61]

The governance of flows through border and access control was recognised as expanding far beyond the city itself. Reminiscent of upstream migratory controls concerning immigration flows,[62] with reference to public order policing at Brisbane, one interviewee uses the metaphor of concentric theory to conceptualise the differentiation

THE POLICING OF FLOWS

of territories and the distinct tactical manifestations of the securitisation of spaces surrounding the event:

> So, if you can imagine a concentric theory, the outer-ring is our intelligence services, our border agencies; they are vetting people coming into the country and identifying who is already here and what they are capable of. Then the next ring is our uniform police at venues, our bomb searchers, our crowd management, our tactical groups; they are the next ring that are around those dignitaries. The final ring is the close protection team.

Brisbane 2014 employed a familiar legal architecture as previous international political summits.[63] The event triggered the *G20 (Safety and Security) Act* 2013 (the 'Act'), which created new offences and powers for authorised officers in designated security areas. The Act was accompanied by the *G20 (Safety and Security) Regulation* 2014, which established the designated security areas for each of the meeting venues and accommodation precincts. The legislative package established a three-tiered separation of 'inner' security areas, 'outer' security areas and 'motorcade' areas as a strategy to regulate the urban landscape. Inner-security areas were considered 'restricted areas', which included spaces and buildings like venues for meetings and delegate accommodation. Motorcade security areas were temporarily enacted to provide exclusive access of authorised persons to utilise transport ways within and between restricted areas. A subsequent security buffer zone, called a 'declared area', blanketed both the restricted and motorcade areas.[64]

The differentiation of spatial enclosures allowed subsequent anchoring of lawful powers and associated manifestations of distinct discretionary powers for police, which could be leveraged as a means to identify, target, trace, exclude, ban or otherwise regulate types of flows within these distinct areas.[65] These powers placed prohibition on over 50 physical items and created new offences specifically applicable to the G20 event. For instance, an offence was introduced for any failure to comply with the requirement to disclose personal details in a declared area. An exclusion notice could ban individuals from security areas if they fail to comply with requests to disclose personal details, refuse a search, possess a prohibited item or have 'demonstrated an intention or the potential to disrupt a G20 event' (40).[66] The legislation encouraged (but did not lawfully compel) those intending to organise an assembly or protest to consult with a QPS 'liaison officer' to discuss the location, time and date (among other details) of the proposed assembly. In sum, the Act introduced a total of 18 additional powers and provisions that were leveraged to regulate access and control, including new legal definitions that regulated the lawfulness of protest assembly.[67] Official data indicate that 14 people were arrested for G20-specific offences, 4 were declared 'prohibited persons' and 27 were issued exclusion notices.[68] The legislation was criticised by various bodies following a post-event review, particularly by some of the more prominent protest groups, which expressed their perception that the legislation unnecessarily impacted on civil liberties and restricted democratic rights to freedom of protest.[69]

Physical security barriers and fencing were also deployed as a way to splinter, enclose and regulate the urban environment. As others have noted,[70] this strategy of government allows greater capability to modulate, surveil, track and provide relative access to different zones and populations as a form of 'passage point urbanism'.[71] While fencing and physical barriers can enclose and protect a certain territory, they also interfere with the visibility of circulations. One interviewee spoke to the benefits of developing physical barriers that could separate and enclose populations while simultaneously providing an optimal vantage point to monitor and respond to protest crowds:

> We had looked at fencing around the world. There are a lot of really effective security fences, but they are quite unpleasant to look at, they are quite difficult to install and remove. ... We did some research ... and we found a fence that was essentially designed to sort of keep people out ... and marshal people thru turn styles in a safe manner, but that couldn't be generally pushed over. ... We then approached the manufacturer about some modifications that we thought would be relevant for us to be able to use their fence. ... around our most at-risk venues. ... We asked them to investigate designing and installing some sort of polycarbonate for the ... fence that was clear, both so any officers we had behind the fence could look out and see any approaching danger, but it also softened the general look of the fence. It allowed the community standing at the fence line to look thru and see Obama or Putin – or whoever they wanted to see – clearly, safely and without feeling like they were looking inside or thru a jail or a security fence.

There was a concerted effort to combine the utility of 'fences that couldn't be pushed over', but that could also, according to the interviewee, ensure the fence was transparent and aesthetically pleasing. As a result, there are two distinct features that emerge in the spatial control of flows in the context of the Brisbane G20. First, with regard to the 'look and feel', control over flows at the Brisbane G20 accorded significantly with normative aesthetics: that is, the control of flows was designed to follow a more subtle and naturalised course.[72] The QPS engaged in 'reflexive dramatisation'[73] whereby police strategies and tactics are carefully 'stage managed', as a means to 'soften' the look and feel of the security operation.[74] However, the mobilisation of physical architectures to regulate people also preserves a capacity for continued visibility and traceability of flows.[75] The material structures of the fencing, for the policing of flows, afforded a tripartite capability – to separate and control flows within enclosed territories, while simultaneously providing an ability to continually trace and monitor the internal segments of risky populations.[76]

Regulating flows at mega-events also involves a range of additional operations directed toward policing the 'transgressive' qualities of population flows.[77] An 'issue-motivated group' (IMG) 'threat matrix' was established which assessed each known group based on their *intent* and *capability* to disrupt the event.[78] The QPS created an External Engagement Plan that set out detailed processes for engaging with IMGs, where the level and type of police engagement was commensurate with the perceived level of risk. According to our interviewees and QPS documentation, the emphasis placed on engagement was in many respects a result of learning – or their 'assessment'[79] – from other mega-events, particularly Toronto 2010. As stated in the QPS G20 Group *Policy and Procedures Manual*: '[a]n analysis of the lessons learnt from previous G20 events and other large scale diplomatic meetings has revealed that IMG engagement is an essential task associated with the planning and conduct of such events'.[80] The manual goes on to state: '[s]uccessful and timely IMG engagement may prevent unlawful and violent protest and provide IMGs an opportunity to voice their message effectively and without the need for conflict with police or the community'.[81]

Our interviewees suggest that the QPS placed considerable emphasis on engagement, as a form of 'relationship-building',[82] with protest groups very early in the planning process. As one senior QPS member states, 'We made a decision very, very early in the piece that we were going to support protests. In fact, we were going to facilitate them and we were going to have that dialogue of conversation early with them'. While engaging with protest flows was a set policy, the interviewee explains that implementing this policy would require that 'the entire organisation, all jurisdictions and all 6600 police had to have the same philosophy, the same narrative, the same brief'. As such, in a similar way to those who have studied the internal workings of police operations, the interviewee reminds us that the regulation of external flows is subject to variations in the organisational pathologies[83] or occupational subcultures[84] of policing organisations.

Relationship-building is also explained as an effective system of intelligent control.[85] For example, one officer discusses the effectiveness of protest engagement by comparing it to the more historically heavy-handed responses of 'escalated force',[86] when asked whether engagement was a 'soft' policing response:

> They are not really soft measures. … Over time, and particularly over my period of time, a lot of work was done particularly in the crowd management and public safety arenas to bring about a relationship-building process. So, it is not a them-and-us. And we worked hard to stop the them-and-us. It doesn't matter what your protest is; I don't care. There is no true them-and-us. We trained years ago to have what we called the Janus face, which is no emotion. You would just stand there and they would talk to you and it would be like a thousand-yard stare. I find that the most insulting thing in the world. … Our research showed that if I engage you and I can talk to you, I can have a totally opposing view as long as I respectfully argue that view with you, you and I will form a relationship regardless of what it is. … That holds true. It is not fake; it is real. … That's part of stopping that transition to a mob. … We can avoid that through relationship-building. The first thing I will do at a protest is go and shake your hand and you are disarmed from that time on.

All of these examples indicate the extent to which the policing of flows involves the continual adaptation and blending of multifaceted police strategies and tactics that span the crime–security nexus, through a tethering of overt – with subtler – forms of coercion, control and legitimation.[87] Making flows more visible and malleable is performed through crafted practices of sovereignty such as banning and exception,[88] physical partitions[89] and relationship-building,[90,91] while simultaneously upholding, and perhaps even extending, capacities for traceability and control. Notably, the particular blend of 'intelligent control'[92] present at the Brisbane G20 assumed its form based on local and historically specific characteristics.[93] The policing of flows, however, is further predicated on a more substantive understanding of the complex technologies and architectures underpinning policing operations.[94]

Managing internal flows: designing architectures for real-time situational awareness

The Brisbane G20 police operation was overlaid with an immensely complex, multi-layered command and control structure. This structure had to manage the input and output of flows, including information collected through surveillance, intelligence information and operational communications across over 6500 police. Given scope constraints, however, our focus is on the heart of the police operation, which is the

Police Operations Centre (POC), based in QPS headquarters. The POC was an integrated command and control infrastructure that made it possible to gather, organise and communicate data and information as a means to deliver security at the event. The POC was newly constructed for the QPS on the basis that existing capabilities were deemed insufficient to coordinate emergency management and public order operations to the scale and scope required for the Brisbane G20. The rationale was to provide a strategically designed flow-based architecture[95] in order to synthesise data and spatially visualise information as a means to 'tame' the risky contingencies of external flows. Data and information flows came from a number of sources, including CCTV and aerial surveillance, information gathered through extensive intelligence operations[96] and from front-line police during the event. For example, field intelligence officers were deployed with body-worn cameras to 'provide a discreet source of human intelligence collection with the ability to capture and relay timely information including photos, video and audio'.[97]

The collation of data streams – as representations of disparate events and pieces of data/information – interfaced with human analysts and decision makers across 30-plus agencies (and their associated information technology specialists), and were broken down into a series of distinct 'pods'. Each pod reflected the key functional areas within the security operation – including crowd management, dignitary protection, venue security and traffic management – and, instead of being passive receptors of information coming into the POC, each area was able to customise the data and information displayed in their pod. The ability to interpret and reflexively contribute to real-time intelligence streams provided the POC with a substantial flow-based architecture over the duration of the operation. For instance, in one description of the platform, an interviewee describes how the QPS moved away from the traditional design of command centres, such as with having a large so-called 'video wall', to provide flexibility for each of the pods to customise their own experience:

> We still had one big room, centre table for the commander, breakout areas to go and have quiet discussion, but around that room we created a video wall for each of the capabilities so that, for example, crowd management could put up the cameras that were focused on crowd; they could put up URL [uniform resource locator] tracking of their team leaders. ... So, we will give you the situational awareness, you cherry-pick what you need and put it up. ... When you ask other people, they say 'nobody ever looks at the wall'. Why? Because they don't have much say in what goes up there or they are sitting too far back to read it.

In addition to the technical configurations of the pods, the key functional areas were also able to coordinate on an interpersonal level when interpreting information flows and making decisions. In the centre of the POC was an Operational Coordination Group (OCG), comprised of at least one representative from each stakeholder agency involved in the operation and responsible for coordinating all internal information flows. In Brisbane 2014, the OCG was frequently referred to as the 'single point of truth', reflecting the fact that in large, complex policing environments it is very hard to manage the volume and validity of information flows.[98] According to one senior member of the QPS, the OCG was employed because:

The event was too big; there was so much happening we couldn't control the dispersal of information. There was no way in the world we could identify pieces of information that had to go to individual agencies and push it out, which is generally what we do.

Dividing streams of information coming into the POC and filtering it through the OCG established a further human circuit that was expected to improve the coordination and exchange of information. In the words of a project manager of one of these areas:

We would be side-by-side to make sure that we had everybody on the same sheet of music and we are all heading in the right direction, or if there was a protest occurring, because they were right there and that information was coming into us right there. We knew that if we did have to change some motorcades to go via a different route, it took a matter of seconds to actually then relay that information down to the team and get them to make that change.

While we are unable to assess whether this goal of being on the 'same sheet of music' was actually achieved, our focus is not to examine how these structures and systems worked at the event but rather explore their complex relational properties. In this context, we argue that to properly understand mechanisms such as the POC as a flow-based architecture requires considering how the gathering, processing, dissemination and actions based upon information are contingent on a wider set of situational[99] and organisational contingencies[100] shaping the governance of protest flows.

Organisational and situational dimensions of internal flows: reflexive systems of command and control

Designing the POC was only part of the picture when coordinating internal data and informational flows. Decision-making can be considered as a kinetic aspect of flows, particularly in relation to how flows of information scale into action-oriented public order responses. Information flows coming through the POC, and related police management of external flows, were mediated by a highly structured command and control system. The command structure involved three distinct levels: strategic, operational and tactical.[101] Both the strategic and operations commanders were based in the POC. Tactical commanders were located at meeting venues, accommodation venues and other locations.[102]

One of the most notable aspects of the policing response is that it involved a high level of centralised information management within the POC, but at the same time was overlaid with a decentralised system of command and control. Ordinarily, most key decisions would be made by commanders situated in the POC, including the respective capability coordinators.[103] Our interviewees suggest that they deliberately worked to devolve decision-making for crowd management operations, noting that QPS 'philosophy was that decisions should be made at the lowest level; in fact, [they] should be made down on the ground'. Nonetheless, our interviewees suggest that in most cases there is a tendency for those in command centres such as a POC to want to coordinate all decision-making centrally. As the same interviewee states: 'having been a commander in the field, you know that if all the technology is funnelling up to someone above you, they are going to think they know more than you ... and try to make decisions about what you are doing down on the ground'. QPS documentation suggests that they deliberately attempted to avoid this perception, stating: '[t]here is a strong expectation that decisions will be made locally and that unnecessary interference or escalation will be avoided', further noting that 'capability coordinators are authorised to make decisions on behalf of the Operations Commander'.[104] According to many of our interviewees, the revision in the organisational context of the command structure introduced greater flux and granularity in the public order response to regulating flows. For example, another officer mentioned how this strategy of decentralised command was purposely 'built in' to the operation as a 'mobility programme'.

According to our interviewees, the rationale behind the decision to tether a decentralised command and control structure with the POC stemmed from previous lessons learned in the wake of the Toronto G20. One senior member of the QPS states:

> What we learned out of Toronto; some of those key decisions, tactical decisions were waiting for support from the POC, where they had very little awareness and very little feel as to what was happening on the ground. So, we made a decision that there would be a tactical decision-maker. ... The next decision-making level was obviously the POC. ... Decisions in the past that were made in the POC were now pushed down to the Superintendents on the ground. And a lot of those decisions were made about how to interact with protesters; all of those decisions. I didn't have the situational awareness, even though I had vision, we had vision everywhere, I still couldn't sense the mood of the crowd sitting up there so that is why that decision had to come from them. ... I know in Toronto there were decisions about releasing protesters out of certain areas; it took hours and there were people on the ground saying 'we need to let these people go'. Well, that was up to the people on the ground to make that decision.

Tactical command in the urban environment was able to respond and adapt to protest flows, largely based on their particular proximity to interpret the sentiment and activities of protest flows and their ability to immediately respond. However, again, this response was contingent on organisational contexts. First, there was no guarantee that the organisation would respond to this adaptation. Second, our interviewees suggest that just as there is a tendency for command centres to want to coordinate all decision-making centrally, there is a bias among front-line police to defer decision-making 'up' to command centres. As the same officer notes:

> I had to train them, give them the confidence that they were allowed to make that decision and that they would have our support in making that decision. And that directly came out of the research we did out of Toronto.

The interviewee highlights the ways in which the *in-situ* adoption[105] of policing of flows is contingent on the socialisations of police organisations. Front-line police were used to deferring decision-making up to the POC, thinking that the POC knew more than what any individual actor could on the ground, because of the volume of data, information and intelligence flows. While the POC provided increased aerial 'visibility' of flows and an ability for each pod to reflexively interact and customise their user interface, it was simultaneously recognised as having limitations with regard to the degree of situational awareness that could facilitate decision-making about managing protest flows in near real time. Data and information from the POC were designed to support and supplement decisions on the ground, but were no substitute for expertise at the front line.

The rationale for this approach, according to our interviewees, was to recognise the validity of decision-making on the ground. Some of our interviewees would also suggest that putting more responsibility on front-line police provided more capacity for them to tailor their response to the relationships they may have with protest groups, in their specific context. While there may be some merits (and risks) in both of these points, we would suggest that there is another more practical reason as to why the QPS actively promoted devolved decision-making; if every decision was to be processed by the POC, the entire system was at risk of becoming paralysed under the sheer weight of internal information flows. The drive for enhanced situational awareness *of* external flows therefore necessitates adaptive strategies in managing such flows.

Conclusion

This article has not attempted to make any claim concerning the effectiveness (or otherwise) of the tactics employed at Brisbane 2014. Instead, we have examined how police pursued their task of managing external and internal flows while attempting to secure the event. Drawing on a Foucauldian-inspired approach, previously utilised by Klauser and Fussey,[106] we have addressed some of the ways that channelling the uncertainty of flows relies on techniques that combine spatial control tactics that filter populations through exceptional legislative and physical means and enhanced levels of surveillance that emanate well 'upstream' prior to the event. In short, the governance of flows at mega-events is reflected through complexity and paradox insofar as it focuses a blend of strategies and tactics on how people and objects are channelled, rendered transparent, monitored and filtered across spatial thresholds. Making divisions between good and bad circulation, however, was significantly bound up with a common strategic logic that attempted to render flows persistently visible in manifold ways, even as far as the material infrastructure, such as clear fencing, could be designed to further facilitate this monitoring.[107] However, the physical barriers served additional, perhaps more important, purposes in the context of Brisbane 2014. It was important for event organisers that the governance of flows was also practised in a way that was aesthetically acceptable. In what de Lint and Hall have termed 'reflexive dramatisation',[108] officials attempted to soften the look and feel of control over flows in ways that simultaneously maintained, or even extended, possibilities for the persistent traceability of uncertain flows.[109] Moreover, police reliance on the subtle interpersonal dynamics of 'relationship-building' with protestors in the context of crowd management also drew upon a similar logic that blends 'soft' forms of control with a strategic goal for persistent visibility and traceability of flows.[110]

Our objective in this article was particularly to extend insights into governance *through* flows, or the internal flows within public order policing operations, with an examination of the complex and heterogeneous configurations of governance specific to the Brisbane 2014 G20. While the constitution of the POC reflected a flow-based architecture that existed over the course of the event, analysing its particular features calls attention to the tensions and practices that mediate the governance through flows. In particular, we have emphasised how the vast technologically mediated flow-based architecture of the POC intersects with the organisational and situational contingencies underpinned by command and control structures. For example, tactical command experienced flows on the front line, adapting to their 'good' or 'transgressive' qualities, in part based on sensory experiences of 'mood' and behaviours in a close-knit *in-situ* environment. By contrast, strategic and operations command within the POC could interact through a flow-based centre that interpreted information from an aerial vantage point as a means to delineate negative from positive flows with respect to movement and circulation around the city (and in accordance with the conditions of previous negotiations with police on protest routes). While still maintaining many of the core principles of centralised information management, our interviewees suggest that promoting decentralised decision-making made the police operation far more responsive, in terms of speed *and* mobility, which they perceived as allowing them to better anticipate, manage and adapt to the inherent uncertainties of flows.

Acknowledgements

The authors would like to acknowledge the essential contribution of all of our interviewees, who willingly made time for this project in their busy schedules and who shared their experiences so openly. We would like to especially extend thanks to the QPS for responding very positively to our requests to conduct interviews across the planning team, for providing various documents and for often brokering access to other interviewees. We would also like to thank the editors of this special issue and anonymous reviewers for their helpful comments on an earlier version of this article.

Disclosure statement

No potential conflict of interest was reported by the authors.

Notes

1. Foucault, *Security, Territory, Population*.
2. Aradau, Lobo-Guerrero, and Van Munster, "Security, Technologies of Risk"; Dillon and Neal, *Foucault on Politics, Security and War*; Coté-Boucher, "The Diffuse Border"; and Klauser, "Through Foucault to a Political."
3. Bauman, *Liquid Modernity*; Bauman and Lyon, *Liquid Surveillance*; and Zedner, "Security."
4. Bauman and Lyon *Liquid Surveillance*, 2–14.
5. Bauman, *Liquid Modernity*.
6. See note 2.
7. Bauman and Lyon, *Liquid Surveillance*.
8. Klauser, "Spatialities of Security and Surveillance"; and Fussey, "Command, Control and Contestation."
9. Giacomantonio, "A Typology of Police Organizational Boundaries"; Wood, "Crisis and Control"; and della Porta and Tarrow, "Interactive Diffusion."
10. Bennett and Haggerty, *Security Games*; and Molnar, "The Geo-Historical Legacies."
11. Wood, "Crisis and Control," 20; and della Porta and Tarrow, "Interactive Diffusion."
12. See also Gillham and Noakes, "More Than A March in a Circle"; and Gillham, "Securitizing America."
13. Bennett and Haggerty, *Security Games*; Boyle and Haggerty, "Spectacular Security"; Boyle, Clément, and Haggerty, "Iterations of Olympic Security"; Coaffee, Fussey, and Moore, "Laminated Security for London"; Fussey and Coaffee, *Security Games*; and Whelan, "Surveillance, Security and Sports.'

14. Graham and Marvin, *Splintering Urbanism*; and Klauser, "Spatialities of Security and Surveillance."
15. Bigo, "Globalized (In)Security"; Fussey, "Command, Control and Contestation"; Kitchin and Rygiel, "Privatizing Security, Securitising Policing"; and Monaghan and Walby, "Making Up 'Terror Identities'."
16. Aradau and Van Munster, "Governing Terrorism Through Risk"; Boyle and Haggerty, "Spectacular Security"; and Klauser, "Spatialities of Security and Surveillance."
17. Coaffee, Fussey, and Moore, "Laminated Security for London"; Fussey, "Command, Control and Contestation"; Klauser, "Interacting Forms of Expertise"; and Molnar, "The Geo-Historical Legacies"
18. Sanders, Weston, and Schott, "Police Innovations, 'Secret Squirrels'"; and Sheptycki, "Organizational Pathologies in Police."
19. Pallister-Wilkins, "How Walls Do Work"; and Aradau, "Security that Matters."
20. Brodeur, *The Policing Web*.
21. Cetina, "From Pipes to Scopes."
22. Kitchin, "The Real-Time City?"; and Dodge and Kitchin, "The Automatic Management."
23. Foucault, *Security, Territory, Population*, 51.
24. Aradau et al., *Security and Global Governmentality*; Bigo, "Globalized (In)Security"; Dillon and Lobo-Guerrero, "Biopolitics of Security"; and Côté-Boucher, "The Diffuse Border."
25. Elden, "Governmentality, Calculation, Territory"; and Klauser, "Through Foucault to a Political" and; "Spatiality of Security."
26. Graham and Marvin, *Splintering Urbanism*.
27. Franzen, "Urban Order," 207.
28. Klauser, *Through Foucault*.
29. Haggerty and Ericson, "The surveillant assemblage," 608.
30. Deleuze, "Postscript on the Societies."
31. Klauser, "Spatialities of Security and Surveillance," 290.
32. Boyle and Haggerty, "Spectacular Security."
33. Monaghan and Walby, "Making Up 'Terror Identities'"; and Fussey, "Command, Control and Contestation."
34. Boyle, "Knowledge Networks."
35. Samatas, "From Thought Control."
36. Klauser, "Spatialities of Security and Surveillance."
37. McAdam, "Tactical Innovation"; della Porta and Tarrow, "Interactive Diffusion," 2013; Gillham, "Securitizing America"; and Wood, "Crisis and Control."
38. Gillham and Noakes, "More Than a March in a Circle."
39. Fernandez, *Policing Dissent*.
40. Gillham, "Securitizing America"; and Fernandez, *Policing Dissent*.
41. Her Majesty's Inspectorate of Constabulary, *Policing Public Order*, 3.
42. Gorringe and Rosie, "We Will Facilitate Your Protest."
43. Kitchin and Rygiel, "Privatizing Security, Securitising Policing"; and Fussey, "Command, Control and Contestation."
44. Gillham, "Securitizing America"; and Gillham, Edwards, and Noakes, "Strategic Incapacitation."
45. de Lint and Hall, *Intelligent Control*; and Monaghan and Walby, "Making Up 'Terror Identities'."
46. Gillham, "Securitizing America"; Fernandez, *Policing Dissent*; and Gillham and Noakes, "More Than a March in a Circle."
47. Cetina and Preda, "The Temporalization of Financial"; and Cetina, "From Pipes to Scopes."
48. Dodge and Kitchin, "The Automatic Management," 2011; and Kitchin, "The Real-Time City?"
49. See note 47.
50. Kitchin, "The Real-Time City?"
51. Dodge and Kitchin, "The Automatic Management"; and Kitchin, "The Real-Time City?"
52. The ACBPS became the Australian Border Force on 1 July 2015.

53. Brewer, *Policing the Waterfront*; Dupont, "Security in the Age"; and *Whelan, Networks and National Security.*
54. Crime and Misconduct Commission, *Review of the G20 (Safety and Security) Act 2013.*
55. Flyvbjerg, "Five Misunderstandings"; and Yin, *Case Study Research.*
56. The QPS requires that the following disclaimer be stated: The views expressed in this material are those of the authors and are not those of QPS. Responsibility for any errors of omission or commission remains with the authors. The QPS expressly disclaims any liability for any damage resulting from the use of the material contained in this publication and will not be responsible for any loss, howsoever arising, from use of or reliance on this material.
57. Klauser, "Spatialities of Security and Surveillance."; Coaffee and Fussey, "Olympic Rings of Steel"; and Gillham and Noakes, "More Than A March in a Circle."
58. Foucault, *Security, Territory, Population*; and Graham and Marvin, *Splintering Urbanism.*
59. Zedner, "Security."
60. See note 36.
61. Fussey, "Command, Control and Contestation"; and Gillham, "Securitizing America."
62. Clochard and Dupeyron, "The Maritime Borders."
63. Beare, Des Rosiers, and Deshman, *Putting the State on Trial*; and Gillham, "Securitizing America."
64. Queensland Police Service, *Policy and Procedures Manual.*
65. Foucault, *Security, Territory, Population*; and Bonditti, "Violence Archaeology of Terrorism."
66. See note 64.
67. Queensland Police Service, *G20 General Duties*; and *Policy and Procedures Manual.*
68. Queensland Police Service, *Post Operation Report.*
69. Brisbane Community Action Network, *Submission to: Review.*
70. See note 26.
71. Graham, *Disrupted Cities*,145.
72. de Lint and Hall, *Intelligent Control.*
73. Ibid.
74. Whelan "Security Networks and Occupational Culture."
75. See note 19.
76. Vitale, "The Command and Control."
77. Gillham, "Securitizing America"; Monaghan and Walby, "Making Up 'Terror Identities'"; and Gorringe and Rosie, "The Polis of 'Global'."
78. Queensland Police Service, *Policy and Procedures Manual*, 123.
79. della Porta and Tarrow, "Interactive Diffusion."
80. Queensland Police Service, *Policy and Procedures Manual*, 122.
81. Ibid., 122
82. Gorringe and Rosie, "We Will Facilitate Your Protest."
83. Sheptycki, "Organizational Pathologies in Police."
84. Sanders, Weston, and Schott, "Police Innovations"; and Whelan, "Security Networks and Occupational Culture."
85. See note 72.
86. Gillham and Noakes, "More Than a March in a Circle."
87. King, *When Riot Cops are Not Enough*; and Gillham, "Securitizing America."
88. Bigo, "Globalized (In)Security."
89. Pallister-Wilkins, "How Walls Do Work."
90. Gorringe and Rosie, "Long Way to Auchterarder."
91. See note 72.
92. See note 72.
93. See note 74.
94. Bonditti, "Violence Archaeology of Terrorism."
95. See note 47.

96. In the lead up to the event, a Joint Intelligence Group (JIG) was created, which comprised members of QPS, AFP, other seconded police, ASIO, ADF, the Australian Crime Commission (ACC – now the Australian Criminal Intelligence Commission) and ACBPS. Its principal role was to coordinate the intelligence effort for the G20, including updating and disseminating details of prohibited persons and persons or groups of interest, viewed as those who may pose a threat to the event, community or police. The JIG was essential to managing extensive intelligence flows while a Joint Analysis Group, which comprised all agencies above apart from the ACC and ACBPS, was designed to pool information, identify and reconcile contradictions in intelligence production by forming an agreed, shared interpretation of information, before it was fed into to the POC.
97. Queensland Police Service, *Policy and Procedures Manual*, 90.
98. See note 83.
99. Sanders, Weston, and Schott, "Police Innovations."
100. See note 83.
101. Queensland Police Service, *Command and Control Policy*.
102. The decision to separate these functions was modelled heavily on the UK Gold, Silver and Bronze command and control structure (London Emergency Services Liaison Panel 2015), and it was the first time the strategic and operational functions were demarcated in Australia (Queensland Police Service 2016). The role of the Police Strategic Commander, a Deputy Commissioner of QPS, was essentially to guide, advise and support the Police Operations Commander, an Assistant Commissioner, who assumed overall responsibility for planning and coordinating the police operation.
103. See note 68.
104. Queensland Police Service, *Policy and Procedures Manual*, 61.
105. Sanders and Hannem, "Police 'Empires' and Information Technologies."
106. See note 8.
107. See note 19.
108. See note 72.
109. See note 1.
110. Gorringe and Rosie, "Long Way to Auchterarder"; "The Polis of 'Global'"; and Bonditti, "Violence Archaeology of Terrorism."

Bibliography

Aradau, C. "Security that Matters: Critical Infrastructure and Objects of Protection." *Security Dialogue* 41, no. 5 (2010): 491–514. doi:10.1177/0967010610382687.

Aradau, C., T. Blanke, M. De Larrinaga, and M. Doucet. *Security and Global Governmentality: Globalization, Governance and the State*. London: Routledge, 2010.

Aradau, C., L. Lobo-Guerrero, and R. Van Munster. "Security, Technologies of Risk, and the Political: Guest Editor's Introduction." *Security Dialogue* 39, no. 2–3 (2008): 147–154. doi:10.1177/0967010608089159.

Aradau, C., and R. Van Munster. "Governing Terrorism through Risk: Taking Precautions, (Un) Knowing the Future." *European Journal of International Relations* 13, no. 1 (2007): 89–115. doi:10.1177/1354066107074290.

Bauman, Z. *Liquid Modernity*. Cambridge: Polity Press, 2000

Bauman, Z., and D. Lyon. *Liquid Surveillance*. Cambridge: Polity Press, 2013.

Beare, M., N. Des Rosiers, and A. C. Deshman. *Putting the State on Trial: The Policing of Protest during the G20 Summit*. Vancouver: UBC Press, 2015.

Bennett, C., and K. Haggerty. *Security Games: Surveillance and Control at Mega-Events*. Hoboken: Routledge, 2011.

Bigo, D. "Globalized (In)Security: The Field and the Ban-Opticon." In *Terror, Insecurity and Liberty: Illiberal Practices of Liberal Regimes after 9/11*, edited by D. Bigo and A. Tsoukala, 10–48. New York: Routledge, 2011.

Bonditti, P. "Violence Archaeology of Terrorism." In *Foucault and the Modern International*, edited by P. Bonditti, D. Bigo, and F. Gros, 155–175. New York: Palgrave, 2017.

Boyle, P. "Knowledge Networks: Mega-Events and Security Expertise." In *Security Games: Surveillance and Control at Mega-Events*, edited by C. Bennett and K. Haggerty, 169–184. Hoboken: Routledge, 2011.

Boyle, P., D. Clément, and K. Haggerty. "Iterations of Olympic Security: Montreal and Vancouver." *Security Dialogue* 46, no. 2 (2015): 109–125. doi:10.1177/0967010614543582.

Boyle, P., and K. Haggerty. "Spectacular Security: Mega-Events and the Security Complex." *International Political Sociology* 3, no. 3 (2009): 257–274. doi:10.1111/ips.2009.3.issue-3.

Brewer, R. *Policing the Waterfront: Networks, Partnerships, and the Governance of Port Security*. Oxford: Oxford University Press, 2014.

Brisbane Community Action Network – G20. *Submission to: Review of the G20 (Safety and Security) Act 2013*. Crime and Misconduct Commission. Brisbane: Queensland Government, 2015.

Brodeur, J. P. *The Policing Web*. Oxford: Oxford University Press, 2010.

Cetina, K. K.. "From Pipes to Scopes: The Flow Architecture of Financial Markets." *Distinktion: Scandinavian Journal of Social Theory* 4, no. 2 (2003): 7–23. doi:10.1080/1600910X.2003.9672857.

Cetina, K. K., and A. Preda. "The Temporalization of Financial Markets: From Network to Flow." *Theory, Culture & Society* 24, no. 7–8 (2007): 116–138. doi:10.1177/0263276407084700.

Clochard, O., and B. Dupeyron. "The Maritime Borders of Europe: Upstream Migratory Controls." In *Borderlands: Comparing Border Security in North America and Europe*, edited by E. Brunet-Jailly, 19–40. Ottawa: University of Ottawa Press, 2007.

Coaffee, J., and P. Fussey. "Olympic Rings of Steel: Constructing Security for 2012 and Beyond." In *Security Games: Surveillance and Control at Mega-Events*, edited by C. Bennett and K. Haggerty, 36–54. Hoboken: Routledge, 2011.

Coaffee, J., P. Fussey, and C. Moore. "Laminated Security for London 2012: Enhancing Security Infrastructures to Defend Mega Sporting Events." *Urban Studies* 48, no. 15 (2011): 3311–3327. doi:10.1177/0042098011422398.

Coté-Boucher, K. "The Diffuse Border: Intelligence-Sharing, Control and Confinement along Canada's Smart Border." *Surveillance & Society* 5, no. 2 (2008): 142–165.

Crime and Misconduct Commission. *Review of the G20 (Safety and Security) Act 2013: Consultation Paper and Invitation for Public Submissions*. Brisbane: Queensland Government, 2015.

de Lint, W., and A. Hall. *Intelligent Control: Developments in Public Order Policing in Canada*. Toronto: University of Toronto Press, 2009.

Deleuze, G. "Postscript on the Societies of Control." *October* 59 (1992): 3–7.

della Porta, D., and S. Tarrow. "Interactive Diffusion: The Coevolution of Police and Protest Behaviour with an Application to Transnational Contention." *Comparative Political Studies* 45, no. 1 (2012): 119–152. doi:10.1177/0010414011425665.

Dillon, M., and L. Lobo-Guerrero. "Biopolitics of Security in the 21st Century: An Introduction." *Review of International Studies* 34, no. 2 (2008): 265–292. doi:10.1017/S0260210508008024.

Dillon, M., and A. Neal. eds. *Foucault on Politics, Security and War*. London: Palgrave Macmillan, 2008.

Dodge, M., and R. Kitchin. "The Automatic Management of Drivers and Driving Spaces." *Geoforum* 38 (2007a): 264–275. doi:10.1016/j.geoforum.2006.08.004.

Dodge, M., and R. Kitchin. "The Automatic Management of Drivers and Driving Spaces." *Geoforum* 38, no. 2 (2007b): 264–275. doi:10.1016/j.geoforum.2006.08.004.

Dupont, B. "Security in the Age of Networks." *Policing & Society* 14, no. 1 (2004): 76–91. doi:10.1080/1043946042000181575.

Elden, S. "Governmentality, Calculation, Territory." *Environment and Planning D: Society and Space* 25, no. 3 (2007): 562–580. doi:10.1068/d428t.

Fernandez, L. *Policing Dissent: Social Control and the Anti-Globalization Movement*. New Brunswick, NJ: Rutgers University Press, 2008.

Flyvbjerg, B. "Five Misunderstandings about Case-Study Research." *Qualitative Inquiry* 12, no. 2 (2006): 219–245. doi:10.1177/1077800405284363.

Foucault, M. *Security, Territory, Population*. Basingstoke: Palgrave, 2007.

Franzén, M. "Urban Order and the Preventive Restructuring of Space: The Operation of Border Controls in Micro Space." *The Sociological Review* 49, no. 2 (2001): 202–218. doi:10.1111/1467-954X.00252.

Fussey, P. "Command, Control and Contestation: Negotiating Security at the London 2012 Olympics." *The Geographical Journal* 181, no. 3 (2015): 212–223. doi:10.1111/geoj.2015.181.issue-3.

Fussey, P., and J. Coaffee. "Balancing Local and Global Security Leitmotifs: Counter-Terrorism and the Spectacle of Sporting Mega-Events." *International Review for the Sociology of Sport* 0, no. 0 (2012): 1–18.

Giacomantonio, C. "A Typology of Police Organizational Boundaries." *Policing & Society* 24, no. 5 (2014): 545–565. doi:10.1080/10439463.2013.784302.

Gillham, P. "Securitizing America: Strategic Incapacitation and the Policing of Protest since the 11 September 2001 Terrorist Attacks." *Sociology Compass* 5, no. 7 (2011): 636–652. doi:10.1111/soco.2011.5.issue-7.

Gillham, P., B. Edwards, and J. Noakes. "Strategic Incapacitation and the Policing of Occupy Wall Street Protests in New York City, 2011." *Policing & Society* 23, no. 1 (2013): 81–102. doi:10.1080/10439463.2012.727607.

Gillham, P., and J. Noakes. "'More than a March in A Circle:' Transgressive Protests and the Limits of Negotiated Management." *Mobilization: An International Quarterly* 12, no. 4 (2007): 341–357.

Gorringe, H., and M. Rosie. "The Polis of 'Global' Protest: Policing Protest at the G8 in Scotland." *Current Sociology* 56, no. 5 (2008a): 691–710. doi:10.1177/0011392108093831.

Gorringe, H., and M. Rosie. "It's a Long Way to Auchterarder! 'Negotiated Management' and Mismanagement in the Policing of G8 Protests." *The British Journal of Sociology* 59, no. 2 (2008b): 187–205. doi:10.1111/j.1468-4446.2008.00189.x.

Gorringe, H., and M. Rosie. "'We Will Facilitate Your Protest': Experiments with Liaison Policing." *Policing* 7, no. 2 (2013): 204–211. doi:10.1093/police/pat001.

Graham, S., ed. *Disrupted Cities: When Infrastructure Fails*. New York: Routledge, 2010.

Graham, S., and S. Marvin. *Splintering Urbanism: Networked Infrastructures, Technological Mobilities and the Urban Condition*. London: Routledge, 2001.

Haggerty, K., and R. Ericson. "The Surveillant Assemblage." *British Journal of Sociology* 51, no. 4 (2000): 605–622. doi:10.1080/00071310020015280.

Her Majesty's Inspectorate of Constabulary. *Policing Public Order: An Overview and Review of Progress against the Recommendations of Adapting to Protest and Nurturing the British Model of Policing*. London: HMIC, 2011.

King, M. *When Riot Cops Are Not Enough: The Policing and Repression of Occupy Oakland*. New Brunswick, NJ: Rutgers University Press, 2017.

Kitchen, V., and K. Rygiel. "Privatizing Security, Securitizing Policing: The Case of the G20 in Toronto, Canada." *International Political Sociology* 8 (2014): 201–217. doi:10.1111/ips.2014.8. issue-2.

Kitchin, R. "The Real-Time City? Big Data and Smart Urbanism." *GeoJournal* 79, no. 1 (2014): 1–14. doi:10.1007/s10708-013-9516-8.

Klauser, F. "Spatialities of Security and Surveillance: Managing Spaces, Separations and Circulations at Sport Mega Events." *Geoforum* 49 (2013a): 289–298. doi:10.1016/j.geoforum.2012.11.011.

Klauser, F. "Through Foucault to a Political Geography of Mediation in the Information Age." *Geographica Helvetica* 68 (2013b): 95–104. doi:10.5194/gh-68-95-2013.

Klauser, F. "Interacting Forms of Expertise and Authority in Mega-Event Security: The Example of the 2010 Vancouver Olympic Games." *The Geographical Journal* 181, no. 3 (2015): 224–234. doi:10.1111/geoj.2015.181.issue-3.

London Emergency Services Liaison Panel. *Major Incident Procedure Manual, Version 9.4.* London: LESLP, 2015.

McAdam, D. "Tactical Innovation and the Pace of Insurgency." *American Sociological Review* 48 (1983): 735–754. doi:10.2307/2095322.

Molnar, A. "The Geo-Historical Legacies of Urban Security Governance and the Vancouver 2010 Olympics." *The Geographical Journal* 181, no. 3 (2015): 235–241. doi:10.1111/geoj.2015.181. issue-3.

Monaghan, J., and K. Walby. "Making Up 'Terror Identities': Security Intelligence, Canada's Integrated Threat Assessment Centre and Social Movement Suppression." *Policing & Society* 22, no. 2 (2012): 133–151. doi:10.1080/10439463.2011.605131.

Pallister-Wilkins, P. "How Walls Do Work: Security Barriers as Devices of Interruption and Data Capture." *Security Dialogue* 47 (2016): 151–164. doi:10.1177/0967010615615729.

Queensland Police Service. *Command and Control Policy (Internal Memoire).* Brisbane: Queensland Police Service, 2014a.

Queensland Police Service. *G20 General Duties Aide Memoire.* Brisbane: Queensland Police Service, 2014b.

Queensland Police Service. *G20 Group: Operation Southern Cross - Policy and Procedures Manual.* Brisbane: Queensland Police Service, 2014c.

Queensland Police Service. *G20 – 2014 Operation Southern Cross: Post Operation Report.* Brisbane: Queensland Police Service, 2016.

Samatas, M. "From Thought Control to Traffic Control: CCTV Politics of Expansion and Resistance in Post-Olympics Greece." In *Surveillance and Governance: Crime Control and Beyond*, edited by Mathieu Deflem, Jeffrey T. Ylmer, 345–369. Emerald Group Publishing, 2008.

Sanders, C., and S. Henderson. "Police 'Empires' and Information Technologies: Uncovering Material and Organisational Barriers to Information Sharing in Canadian Police Services." *Policing and Society* 23, no. 2 (2013): 243–260. doi:10.1080/10439463.2012.703196.

Sanders, C. B., C. Weston, and N. Schott. "Police Innovations, 'Secret Squirrels' and Accountability: Empirically Studying Intelligence-Led Policing in Canada." *British Journal of Criminology* 55 (2015): 711–729. doi:10.1093/bjc/azv008.

Sheptycki, J. "Organizational Pathologies in Police Intelligence Systems: Some Contributions to the Lexicon of Intelligence-Led Policing." *European Journal of Criminology* 1, no. 3 (2004): 307–332. doi:10.1177/1477370804044005.

Vitale, A. "The Command and Control and Miami Models at the 2004 Republican National Convention: New Forms of Policing Protests." *Mobilization: An International Quarterly* 4, no. 12 (2007): 403–412.

Whelan, C. *Networks and National Security: Dynamics, Effectiveness and Organisation.* Aldershot, UK: Ashgate, 2012.

Whelan, C. "Surveillance, Security and Sports Mega Events: Toward a Research Agenda on the Organisation of Security Networks." *Surveillance & Society* 11, no. 4 (2014): 392–404.

Whelan, C. "Security Networks and Occupational Culture: Understanding Culture within and between Organisations." *Policing and Society* 27, no. 2 (2017): 113–135. doi:10.1080/10439463.2015.1020804.

Wood, L. J. *Crisis and Control: The Militarization of Protest Policing*. Between the Lines. London: Pluto press, 2014.

Yin, R. *Case Study Research: Design and Methods*. 5th ed. Thousand Oaks, CA: Sage Publications, 2014.

Zedner, L. "Liquid Security: Managing the Market for Crime Control." *Criminology & Criminal Justice* 6, no. 3 (2006): 267–288. doi:10.1177/1748895806065530.

Zedner, L. "Security." In *Key Concepts in Criminology*, edited by Tim Newburn. Oxon: Routledge, 2009.

Fluid interfaces between flows of rhino horn

Annette Hübschle (iD)

ABSTRACT
In spite of the regulation, financial assistance and securitisation of responses to rhino poaching, rhino deaths have escalated over the past decade. This article discusses why efforts to disrupt illegal flows of rhino horn have been unsuccessful by honing in on structural and functional aspects of the broader rhino horn economy. Existing scholarly literature tends to focus on the legal–illegal binary in markets. The focus of this article is on grey flows in wildlife markets through an examination of rhino horn laundering and illegal hunting in the wildlife industry. Fluid interfaces of legal, grey and illegal flows have led to the creation of hybrid and highly adaptable flows. It is also argued that the international regulatory framework is not geared towards effective transnational enforcement and lacks social legitimacy amongst key actors. The article draws on research findings from a multi-sited ethnography, during which the researcher followed rhino horn from the source to the market.

Introduction

Three rhinoceroses are shot dead in the South African bush each day; their horns are chopped off and sold to intermediaries operating in lucrative wildlife markets. South Africa is home to 79% of the world's remaining rhinoceros. Of the 20 306 South African rhinos, 18 413 are southern white rhinos and approximately 1 893 animals belong to the black species.[1] Roughly one-third of South Africa's white rhinos are on private land, local communities protect 0.5 % of the black rhino population through a custodianship programme, and national and provincial parks authorities look after the remainder.[2] Although the South African Minister of Environmental Affairs[3] announced that poaching had stabilised in 2015 with 40 animals less killed than the previous year, the International Union for Conservation of Nature (IUCN) Species Survival Commission's African Rhino Specialist Group (AfRSG)[4] warns of ' the deepening rhino poaching crisis in Africa' with poachers killing 1377 rhinos across the continent in 2015 (see Table 1).

At the core of the rhino crisis is the tenacious demand for rhino horn in consumer markets. Powdered rhino horn has been used in Traditional Asian Medicine (TAM) for more than four millennia. Carved into hilts for traditional daggers known as 'yambiyas', rhino horn was also in great demand in Yemen during the 1970s and 1980s.[5] Another

Table 1. Known rhino killings in South Africa (2000-2016).

Year	Kruger National Park	Rest of South Africa	Total
2000	0	7	7
2001	4	2	6
2002	20	5	25
2003	14	8	22
2004	7	3	10
2005	10	3	13
2006	17	7	24
2007	10	3	13
2008	36	47	83
2009	50	72	122
2010	146	187	333
2011	252	196	448
2012	425	253	668
2013	606	398	1004
2014	827	388	1215
2015	826	349	1175
2016	662	392	1054

Source: Source: Department of Environmental Affairs (2014) & Molewa (2016).

centuries-old tradition relates to the trophy hunting of rhinos. The resultant hunting trophies are exported to the hunter's home country where they are kept in private collections, galleries and museums. Whilst these 'traditional' uses endure to lesser degrees, rhino horn is increasingly employed as an investment tool and as criminal currency. It also serves as a status symbol, religious or cultural artefact and gift amongst the upper strata of Asian societies. The price of rhino horn is contingent on provenance, use and type, averaging at US $ 45 to 65 000/kg in consumer markets.

The research for this article emanates from a multi-sited ethnography, during which the author followed rhino horn from the southern African bush to southeastern Asian markets. More than 420 research informants were interviewed during 14 months of fieldwork in 2013 and 2014[6], and follow-up visits to the field were conducted in 2015 and 2016. The sample included, amongst others, convicted rhino poachers, wildlife traffickers, private rhino breeders and farmers, anti-poaching rangers and state security forces, as well as affected local communities and Asian consumers. The article starts with a conceptualisation of markets and flows. It continues with an analysis of flows of rhino horn by honing in on flows that escape or bypass regulations. The focus is on specific structural, institutional and functional aspects of flows, which render regulation and enforcement difficult. Empirical examples are provided to illustrate the argument. The article concludes with an assessment as to why the illegal market continues to thrive and provides ideas on how to improve the policing of flows.

Markets and flows

Scholarly contributions on the illegal trade in wildlife have largely focused on individual segments or stages of the supply chain,[7] specific actor constellations[8] and disruptive measures.[9] Much of the literature has focused on the supply side of the market, identifying poachers as the main suppliers of illicit wildlife contraband.[10] The recent escalation of poaching and wildlife trafficking has not only been attributed to rising demand in consumer markets but also to the entry of organised crime networks in what is seen as a 'low risk, high reward' criminal activity. Scholars have analysed the role of organised crime networks in ordering, transporting and distributing wildlife products.[11] Agency in illegal wildlife markets is not only theoretically significant but also bears policy consequences in the real world. Little is known about the flow or onward journey along the supply chain once the wild animals have been poached, harvested or caught[12] or the demand side (two recent articles deal with the demand for rhino horn in China[13] and Vietnam.[14] The focus on either actors or market segments conceals the dynamic and fluid structure and functioning of the broader wildlife economy.

In a bid to move beyond existing analyses, this article proposes that the global rhino horn trade be understood in terms of a transnational market where different flows impact its sustainability, resilience and profitability. Markets, in this instance, are defined as 'arenas of regular voluntary exchange of goods or services for money, goods or services of equitable value.[15] Markets are considered illegal if the product per se, its exchange or consumption violates legal stipulations. The state has the power to prosecute market actors[16]; it denies property rights in such markets and sets and enforces no quality standards.[17] Legal definitions contained within a country's national legislation thus delineate whether an economic exchange registers as legal or illegal in a jurisdiction. Such legal definitions may differ across geographies and time. An economic exchange may be declared illegal in one country whilst being legal and legitimate elsewhere. In other words, segments of supply chains of any type of good or service may hold a different legal status in supply, transit or demand countries. An important distinction relates to economic exchanges that occur at the interface between legality and illegality; these markets are neither legal nor illegal as they hover in an undetermined grey zone. Some market actors may exploit legal or enforcement loopholes in what is termed as 'grey' markets or flows in this article. Actors capitalise on ambiguities of the legal/illegality nexus by falsifying the provenance of a traded good as a formerly legal good (e.g. pre-CITES horn)[18] or convert an illegally acquired good to a 'legal' good (e.g. poached horn is converted into trophy hunted rhino horn). The contested illegality of a good or service may legitimise participation in grey or illegal markets. Cultural norms, traditions and cognitive frames influence the social legitimacy pertaining to the exchange or consumption of a good or service. Thus, whilst lawmakers might have outlawed its exchange or consumption, the womxn in the street might not accept or know about the changed legal status. In some instances, contested illegality serves as a legitimisation mechanism, facilitating the participation in illegal or grey markets.[19]

A further consideration relates to the transnational nature of the illegal market in rhino horn. Historically, market and place were closely intertwined. Whilst markets often involved the inclusion of long distance trade and foreign merchants, markets were connected to the social and economic lives of local communities, occurring at fixed intervals and in specific places – the local marketplace.[20] With the emergence of migrant labour and hut taxes during the colonial era in the southern African context,[21] market and place started to separate. Producers, traders and consumers no longer had to be at a fixed time and location to engage in economic exchange. In the current climate of instantaneous capital flows, global transactions and virtual marketplaces, economic transactions are fluid and difficult to police or locate. In recognition of the fluid and dynamic structure of the global economy and markets, the concept of flows (instead of commodity or supply chains) is employed here. Asymmetries in legislation, knowledge, economy and culture shape the flow of goods.[22] The concept is useful in showcasing the fluid connections and crossovers between legal, illegal and grey economic exchanges. Castells[23] introduced the concept of 'spaces of flow', suggesting that 'material arrangements allow for simultaneity of social practices without territorial contiguity'. In later publications, Castells[24] and others[25] use the concept of flows with specific reference to the 'network society',[26] which is characterised by increasing fragmentation of individuals and communities, necessitating interdependent relationships among individuals, public services, the police, information communication technology (ITC) and modes of transport. According to this view, people, money, goods and information are in circulation, travelling to and from different places, employing different infrastructures and thereby generating different 'flows' which connect, collide or meet in nodes.[27] The governance of flows and nodes provides a complex conundrum to regulators whilst offering immediacy, connectedness and new opportunities for economic actors.

The application of the concept of flows allows flexibility with regard to trajectories, influences and contingent relationships that may evolve, develop or disappear between actors, flows and institutions. Taken in a literal sense, the concept of 'flows' invokes different imaginaries, such as bifurcation (flows split because of a blockage, disruption or intervention), directionality and interdependence (what happens upstream may have an impact downstream), the confluence of tributaries (flows that merge), dead ends (flows that dry up or disappear), deltas (a flow splits into myriad offshoots) and dry riverbeds that flow again upon new rains (re-joining flows). The idea of different flows forming constitutive elements of the aggregate market in rhino horn presents a dynamic model that integrates market processes, actors, social networks and institutions whilst also covering spatial–temporal considerations. It will be argued that illegal, grey and legal flows of rhino horn cannot be studied in isolation because they merge, converge and diverge, impacted by one another and by institutions, networks and cognitive frames found in the market field. Unlike the rather static concept of a singular supply chain, the concept of 'flows' allows for dynamic and interdependent relationships.

The existence of legal, grey and illegal flows out of South Africa

The United Nations Convention on International Trade in Endangered Species of Wild Fauna and Flora (CITES) provides the international regulatory framework for international trade in endangered plant and animal species. All rhino species were placed in Appendix I in 1977, effectively banning international trade except under exceptional circumstances.[28] In recognition of South Africa's success with rhino conservation and management (see below), the populations of white rhino in South Africa were moved to Appendix II in 1994. An annotation confined permissible trade to live rhinos to 'acceptable and appropriate destinations and hunting trophies only'.[29] Whilst CITES deals with international trade and trade bans, member states have to transpose CITES stipulations to the local level and regulate the domestic trade of endangered species. The domestic trade of rhino horn remained unregulated in South Africa until 2009 and presented a regulatory loophole, which criminal actors were readily exploiting. As an example, rhino horn deriving from illegal hunts and unregistered stockpiles was laundered into illegal markets.

In 2009, the Minister of Environmental Affairs and Water imposed 'a national moratorium on the trade of individual rhinoceros horns and any derivatives or products of the horns within South Africa'.[30] Citing a lack of public consultation prior to its issuance, the North Gauteng Division of the High Court[31] lifted the domestic trade moratorium in 2015. This was in response to two private rhino breeders instituting a lawsuit against the Department of Environmental Affairs (DEA). The purpose of the lawsuit is unclear as there is no known domestic market for rhino horn in South Africa.[32] In May 2016, the Supreme Court of Appeal refused the Minister of Environmental Affairs leave to appeal, upholding the High Court's ruling. By appealing to the Constitutional Court, the DEA reinstated, only temporarily, the 2009 ban. In February 2017, the DEA then issued draft regulations for the domestic trade in rhinoceros horn or a part, product or derivative of rhinoceros horn.[33] According to public officials and conservationists (personal communication with author, 2017), the draft regulations are a pre-emptive strike aimed at providing a regulatory framework in case the Department were to lose the Constitutional Court appeal. In April 2017, the Constitutional Court indeed lifted the moratorium. Since then, the domestic trade in rhino horn has been legal on paper; however, the existing regulatory framework requires permits for buying, selling or possessing rhino horn. In their current iteration, the new draft regulations on domestic trade remain vague, allowing room for interpretation and clever manoeuvring.[34] The regulations are likely to be fine-tuned, incorporating written representations and objections made by the public after a 30-day notice period.

The annotation of permissible trades and the relatively short lifespan of the CITES prohibition (42 years at the time of writing) have allowed for legal flows to co-exist with grey and illegal flows (see Figure 1). It is legal for live animals and hunting

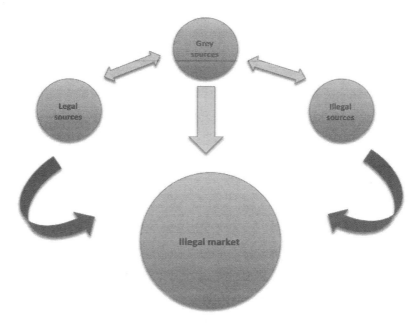

Figure 1: Flows of rhino horn entering the illegal market.

Legal sources: Hunting trophies, legal horn stockpiles, pre-Convention horn, live rhino exports, antique rhino artefacts. Grey sources: Horns emanating from sources where legal and regulatory loopholes were exploited.Illegal sources: Illegally killed rhinos, theft, fake horn.

trophies to be exported from rhino range countries to elsewhere in the world (certain safeguards apply). Once the live rhino or the hunting trophy leaves African shores, national regulatory agencies relinquish their responsibilities to authorities in receiving countries.

The existence of flows with differing legal status is not peculiar to the rhino horn economy. Many products do have associated illegal or grey flows and markets. The example of the rhino horn economy is used to show how shrewd market actors manipulate the interface between legality and illegality through clever schemes.

Context to private rhino ownership in South Africa

To understand why the private sector is well-situated to orchestrate both illegal and grey rhino horn traffic, a basic understanding of the private ownership of wildlife in South Africa is needed. South Africa constitutes a special case within the southern African region because private individuals are allowed to own wildlife including rhinos.[35] Wild animals are considered *res nullius* in South African common law, meaning that nobody owns them. Through successive changes in the law, game ranchers were granted ownership over wildlife and the right to derive income from consumptive utilisation, such as the killing of wild animals for profit.[36] The rhino plays an important role in the privatisation drive of wildlife in South Africa. The number of white rhinos in the Hluhluwe-Umfolozi Game Reserve[37] in KwaZulu-Natal had been reduced through unrestrained hunting to about 50 to 70 animals in the early twentieth century and had gone locally extinct elsewhere in South Africa. Through successful breeding and conservation programmes within the park, white rhino numbers had increased by the 1960s. Rhino numbers started exceeding the carrying capacity of the park and conservators feared that an outbreak of disease could revoke the recovery of the white rhino. It was at this point that the Natal Parks Board[38] commenced 'Operation Rhino', in which over the course of the 1960s and early 1970s saw more than 1200 white rhinos relocated from the Hluhluwe-Umfolozi Game Reserve to the Kruger Park, private game reserves, as well as zoos and safari parks abroad. Nowadays, the total size of South African private rhino reserves stretches over an area of about two million hectares incorporating about 330 separate properties. According to a survey conducted by the Private Rhinos Owner Association (PROA) in 2015, 33% of the national herd (about 6 200 animals) were kept on private land in South Africa (personal communication with Pelham Jones, Private Rhino Owners Association, 2016).[39] Until the end of the apartheid regime in 1994, black South Africans were excluded from private land and rhino ownership. Due to the slow pace of economic transformation in South Africa and other socio-economic factors, ownership patterns have changed little: black communities protect 0,5% of black rhinos through custodianship programmes. The vested interest of the wildlife industry in rhino conservation and management is clear from the above. Not only are rhino owners and wildlife industry professionals knowledgeable when it comes to rhino conservation, but they also know the tricks of the trade and the associated profitability of rhino horn.

Grey flows are largely linked to the harvesting of rhino horns on private land. The process may be consumptive (lethal) through the trophy hunting or illegal killing of a rhino, or non-consumptive by way of dehorning a rhino above the growth point. Unlike the tusks of elephants, rhino horns grow at a rate of 6 to 10 centimetres or 0,6 kg to 1 kg in female white rhinos and 0,8 kg to 1,5 kg in male white rhinos per annum. Horn growth is contingent on gender, sex, age, population type (i.e. free-range versus captive-bred) and species.[40] Rhino horn is thus a renewable resource, which is highly profitable on illegal markets. The dehorning of rhinos has been employed as an anti-poaching strategy.[41] The process is regulated through a permitting process, which includes the registering of rhino horn stockpiles with nature conservation officials. Currently, the international trade of rhino horn is banned through the Threatened or Protected Species (TOPS) regulations and the CITES prohibition while domestic trade is allowed if the seller and buyer stick to the new regulations (see section on regulatory framework).

Actors capitalise on the room to manoeuvre between legal and illegal forms of rhino horn trade. Bolstered by sentiments of contested illegality and legality,[42] criminal actors have no qualms to exploit or manipulate regulatory loopholes. Involved are wildlife industry professionals with intimate knowledge of the product (rhino horn) and of the institutional and legislative framework governing the international trade of rhino horn. Rhino owners, professional hunters, wildlife veterinarians, taxidermists, helicopter pilots, corrupt government officials and other categories of wildlife professionals are the principal actors. These actors belong to influential and transnational networks with links to political and economic elites in supply, transit and consumer countries. Actors from the formal wildlife sector did not only orchestrate illegal rhino hunts in private and public conservation areas and thefts from rhino horn stockpiles, but also they were involved in complex schemes that bypass existing conservation regulations, exploit regulatory loopholes and use legal trade channels to export illegally obtained rhino horn.

The pseudo-hunting phenomenon: appropriation and re-channelling of legal flows

A creative way of supplying Asian consumer markets with 'legally' attained rhino horn involved the recruitment of hunters originating from consumer countries that have no tradition and culture of sports hunting. In continuation of colonial big game hunting and safaris, the majority of 'traditional' rhino hunters herald from Europe and North America (data supplied by Professional Hunters Association of South Africa). As of the early 2000s, young Vietnamese nationals with no or a limited (sometimes falsified) track record of trophy hunting booked white rhino hunts with South African hunting outfitters. In terms of CITES stipulations and domestic laws in South Africa, hunters are allowed to shoot one white rhino per calendar year, whilst the annual quota for black rhinos is restricted to five animals. These hunting trophies may be exported as hunting memorabilia for non-commercial use. Vietnamese crime groups together with their local intermediaries recruited Vietnamese citizens as stand-in trophy hunters to bypass the rule of 'one white rhino, per person, per annum'. Their role was hence to pose as trophy hunters for the purposes of compliance with permit regulations, whilst a South African professional hunter would shoot the rhino on their behalf.

Vietnamese horn importers were using CITES export permits to import multiple rhino horns on the same single-use export permit to Vietnam until its expiration date was reached after six months.[43] Official records show that the export of 'legally' attained rhino trophies from South Africa to Vietnam was prevalent throughout the 2000s. Pseudo-hunting contributed 20% of all rhino horns leaving for Africa for illegal markets until the South African government closed down regulatory loopholes and instituted a national database that tracked actual trophy hunts taking place.[44] According to annual export and import data provided to CITES, the southeast Asian country acknowledged receipt of about 25% of the legally imported rhino horn trophies between 2003 and 2010. This suggests that approximately 487 of 657 'legal' rhino horns entered the illegal market in Vietnam.[45] Once South African authorities had identified the clever ploy, direct exports of rhino trophies from South Africa to Vietnam ceased. The manipulation of export permits and the failure of the relevant CITES management authorities to scrutinise trophy and rhino horn exports and imports allowed the laundering of horn that was ostensibly legally acquired, into illegal markets in Vietnam.

By the time, the legal loophole had been plugged and a temporary ban had been imposed on Vietnamese trophy hunters in 2012; a new type of 'non-traditional' hunters had slipped into the region. Czech trophy hunters were now posing as 'proxy' hunters for criminal networks. In this case, the export permits were forged and the horns redirected to Vietnam. The modus operandi changed again in response to law enforcement disruptions, and the horns were first flown to the hunters' home country before getting smuggled into Vietnam. Slovakian and Polish nationals were also implicated in the scheme (Interviews with law enforcement officials and conservators, 2013 and 2016). More recently, there have been suspicions that 'traditional' Big 5 hunters (notably American, Ukrainian and Russian nationals) were also hunting on behalf of Vietnamese groups (Interviews with organised crime investigators, 2015 and 2016). Discrepancies in the CITES trade data continue to provide cause for concern with South Africa's reported exports being far greater than the declared imports by receiving countries.[46]

What renders grey flows particularly efficient and safe is the early stage conversion of an essentially illegal good to legal status (the laundering of illegally harvested horn into legal trade flows), and contrariwise, the conversion of a legal product (hunting trophy) into an illegally traded good once it arrives in consumer markets. The early conversion curtails opportunity costs and risks further down the supply chain. From an illegal market actor's perspective, this mode of obtaining horn is not only the safest and most expedient method, but it also minimises the number of intermediaries required from the bush to the consumer market. It allows a largely unhindered passage of the horn through the minimal exposure to social control agents and measures aimed at disrupting the illegal market. Moreover, the horn stays in its original state, meaning that it is not processed into smaller pieces or powder form before reaching the consumer market. This is significant when it comes to quality control, valuation and pricing of the horn on the consumer market.

Case study: sex workers as rhino trophy hunters

The following case study provides an excellent example of the creativity of rhino traffickers and their ability to employ new strategies that bypass regulations and the law. Unlike the 'pseudo-hunters' who had to be flown in from their home country, a Laotian wildlife trafficking network using a front company called 'Xaysavang Trading Export-Import', employed an ingenious cost-saving measure. Chumlong Lemthongthai, the representative of the criminal network in South Africa, recruited Thai sex workers who were already based in South Africa to accompany him and his colleagues to private hunting reserves and farms to act as stand-ins for trophy hunters. The wildlife traffickers thus saved on financing travel costs from Southeast Asia to South Africa. The network's infamous pseudo-hunting scheme commenced in late 2010. Of significance was a clear separation of duties. The criminal network sought out South African wildlife industry professionals and conservation officials with a penchant for 'dodgy deals' that would facilitate their nefarious activities by availing their services and providing unhindered passage of rhino horn out of the country. To the wildlife network, cooperation with South African wildlife industry professionals involved little effort and operational risk. However, the 'legal' export of hunting trophies involved comparably more administrative and organisational footwork than a poaching excursion into a protected area would have (Interviews, 2013).

The local organiser of these pseudo-hunts was a South African game farmer and safari operator who employed the services of a professional hunter to shoot the rhinos on behalf of the Thai pseudo-hunters. The farmer also supplied rhinos, arranged rhino hunts, the removal and weighing of the rhino horns. The live rhinos were purchased at discounted prices at auctions as rhino farmers were starting to sell rhinos in the face of the escalating poaching crisis. He would also find farmers and outfitters who were willing to host the Thai pseudo-hunting party. Upon receiving the Thai nationals' passports, he would forward the necessary information as well as copies of passports to the outfitters or landowners who then applied on their behalf for the hunting permits.[47] The Thai sex workers would accompany the network members to game reserves and hunting farms to pose next to the dead rhinos in exchange for free food and drinks and R 5000 (475 €) for the 'job'.[48] A professional hunter killed the rhinos, and the farmer and his workers would dehorn the rhinos and take care of the carcasses. According to the hunting regulations, nature conservation officials ought to be present and monitor all rhino hunts. The Department of Environmental Affairs failed to provide proper supervision of these hunts [49] and Lemthongthai and other members of the network boasted later that 'everyone has a price in South Africa' (Interviews, 2013). Olivier's police statement[50] provides a list of contacts of the Xayasavang network within the North Western[51] nature conservation department, the customs and airports authority, as well as pliable taxidermists.[52]

Entry into illegal markets in Vietnam: regulatory and enforcement shortcomings

According to a report from the International Union for the Conservation of Nature Species Survival Commission African and Asian Rhino Specialist Groups and TRAFFIC to the CITES Secretariat ahead of the CITES CoP17, Vietnam[53] is one of four countries that is heavily involved in rhino horn trade transactions based on an analysis of global seizure data .[54] In January 2013, the Prime Minister of Vietnam issued Decision 11 on the prohibition of the export, import, selling and buying of specimens of some wild animal species listed in the

Appendices of CITES. This decision effectively bans all domestic sales of African rhino horn in Vietnam. An exception excludes 'imports for the purpose of diplomacy, scientific research, biodiversity conservation, display at zoos, exhibitions, non-profit circus performances, law enforcement and exchange of specimens amongst CITES management authorities of member countries are still allowed.'[55] The exceptions relating to the imports of rhino horn for the purposes of diplomacy and law enforcement are rather curious, as data collected for this project implicates both diplomats and law enforcement officials in the smuggling and distribution of rhino horn.[56] Despite these specified exemptions, Vietnam confirmed to the CITES rhinoceroses working group in July 2014 that no permit had been issued for ivory or rhino horn since the effective date of the decision on 24 January 2013.[57] Vietnam also banned 'non-commercial import of hunting trophies' unless cooperation agreements had been signed between the Vietnam CITES management authority and the CITES management authority in the exporting country.[58] At the time of writing, Vietnamese hunters were still banned from hunting in South Africa as the Vietnamese authorities had made no further progress in ensuring that the hunting trophies stayed with the original trophy hunter (Interview with government official, 2016, South Africa). This loophole relates to the lack of regulations and enforcement pertaining to what happens to hunting trophies once they have reached Vietnamese shores. Whilst rhino trophy hunters are not legally allowed to sell their trophies, there are no regulations preventing the owners from donating or gifting them. In fact, Vietnam's national civil law permits the trophy owner to decide how to use their trophies. Because hunting trophies are categorised as personal effects in the southeastern Asian nation, authorities said that they found it difficult to control and monitor them. In addition, there are no punitive measures or permit regulations[59] should the trophy owner decide to cut up the horn(s) or dispose of the trophy without prior authorisation.[60]

Vietnam was on the receiving end of a great deal of criticism at the CITES Conference of Parties (CoP) 16 in 2013 and CoP 17 in Johannesburg in 2016. Vietnamese government officials denied the role their country played in the illegal supply chain of rhino horn and pointed their fingers at their neighbour, suggesting that Vietnam served as a transit and processing hub for rhino horn en route to China (CITES Secretariat 2013, Interview with government official 6, Vietnam, 2013). At CoP 17, Vietnam claimed that rhino horn consumption had decreased and 21 rhino horn traffickers had been convicted. However, no supporting evidence was provided for both claims. Moreover, a revision to Vietnam's penal code has been postponed with no timelines for implementation provided. In its current form, the new code proposes monetary penalties of up to US $ 90 000 or a prison term of up to five years for minor offences and from 10–15 years for major offences. However, these penalties do not apply to individuals found 'illegally storing, transporting [or] trading' less than 50 grams of rhino horn (or 2 kg of ivory). Such infractions would be subject to lesser punitive measures in accordance with existing regulations.[61] Given the loopholes in the existing and proposed regulations and the lack of enforcement in Vietnam, illegally sourced rhino horns are likely to continue arriving via grey and illegal flows in Vietnam.

Transportation of rhino horn to the market

Due to the high incidence of fake horn, criminal actors, traders and consumers employ a number of measures to guarantee the authenticity of their acquisition. Criminal groups ensure that a trusted ally such as the rhino horn organiser or smuggling intermediary attends the hunt or receives the horn immediately after the hunt, without the precious good changing hands in the interim. By being present during the hunt and the subsequent dehorning of the animal, intermediaries safeguard the quality and the provenance of the horn. This mechanism is an important aspect of the valuation of rhino horn when it lands in Asia. Transport intermediaries who coordinate both grey and illegal flows of rhino horn ensure that the horn dispatched at the point of origin is the same as the one that arrives on the other side. The intermediaries stay connected by way instant or text messaging, or the horn is marked with concealed signs only known to the intermediaries. Of significance is the chosen route, mode of transportation, the length of the flow (how many segments or intermediaries are involved), and who receives the horn on the other side. The shorter and more direct the route (usually a legal flow), the lesser the risk of tampering with the expensive commodity. Should diplomats, law enforcement, customs, port or conservation officials be involved in the transportation or facilitation thereof; then, the risk of defection is reduced as the person's position or status holds sway and 'opens doors' (Interviews with rhino horn smugglers, South African correctional centres, 2013). Research elsewhere[62] and empirical data collected for this study at both ends of the supply chain[63] suggest that most rhino horn leaves the African continent by plane, and its onward journey from entrepôts depends on the connectedness of transport intermediaries. Rhino horn derived from legal or illegal trophy hunts and exported as hunting trophies is transported via an ostensibly 'legal' flow from the source to the supposed trophy hunter's home. Once the rhino horn reaches Asia, several pathways are possible including immediate distribution and trade, stockpiling or processing, distribution and trade.

Distribution and trade of rhino horn

Street- and shop-based Vietnamese wildlife traders are increasingly using social media platforms and instant messaging to sell wildlife contraband to their predominantly Chinese clientele. According to research undertaken by the Wildlife Justice Commission in 2015 and 2016, open trade of rhino horn, ivory and tiger bones is taking place in public view without law enforcement disruption in the village of Nhi Khe on the outskirts of Hanoi.[64] High-end dealers who sell to Vietnamese clientele prefer to enter into business arrangements with individuals whom they trust to pay the asking price for the right amount or quantity of horn. The preference is to sell whole horns or large quantities of horn as opposed to grams or pieces of horn (Interviews with intermediaries, 2013). The deal or exchange does not happen in a back alley or 'bad part of town' but at the buyer's, referent or dealer's residence or workplace (Interviews with consumers and intermediaries, 2013). The location of the deal serves the function of normalising the transaction as it happens in respectful surroundings such as the private or public sphere of the transacting parties. It also provides another layer of security[65] and legitimises the deal as a business transaction that can be safely and legitimately done from one's place of residence or work. This suggests that market participants are not concerned about law enforcement responses, stigma or social sanctions that might obtain from dealing or consuming rhino horn by their inner circle of family, friends or colleagues. In other words, these actions carry social and cultural legitimacy further cementing the legitimisation mechanism of contested illegality. These deals nevertheless form part of an informal underground economy in big urban centres and stand in direct contrast to the open trade of wildlife contraband in peripheral locations removed from the prying eyes of the international community and local law enforcement.

People in certain positions are assumed to be worthy of trust and respect by virtue of their status and role in society, as well as the access to horn supplies and influence the position confers upon them; consumers thus trust the provenance and authenticity of rhino horn if the supplier is either a 'trophy hunter', law enforcement, customs or conservation official, or a diplomat with legitimate connections to the source (Interviews with intermediaries, Johannesburg and Massingir, 2013; consumers, Hanoi and Ho Chi Minh City, 2013). Law enforcement and customs officers are believed to have easy access to confiscated rhino horn,[66] whilst government officials and diplomats who had been posted to South Africa in the past, or family members of diplomats on mission in South Africa were also perceived as credible suppliers of rhino horn with direct links to the source country (Interviews with consumers and suppliers, 2013). A forensic scientist in Hanoi supported this assumption, stating that horn confiscated at the airport and brought in for testing by the police, customs or CITES management authority was usually the 'real thing' (Interview, Hanoi, 2013). Some law enforcement officials are also known to abuse their position of power to seize illegal horn stocks that never enter the legal chain of custody but are laundered directly into illegal market flows (Interview with TCM trader and intermediary, 2013).

Regulation and grey flows

Grey flows originating in pseudo-trophy hunting, the dehorning of rhinos on private land and the laundering of horn from unregistered stockpiles or illegally hunted rhinos contributed their fair share to the illegal market in rhino horn until the late 2000s. Criminal actors pioneered the use of legal transport routes and flows, expanded the trade network and market reach and tested the legislative and regulatory frameworks for loopholes and enforcement weaknesses. Local South African intermediaries had access to wide-ranging social and professional networks that facilitated illegal and grey transnational trade with Asian trafficking and trade networks. The displacement of grey sources of rhino horn by the late 2000s is partially explained by the promulgation of tougher conservation regulations, including the moratorium on domestic trade in rhino horn in South Africa, as well as the private sector 'out-pricing' itself. Although pseudo-hunts carried the semblance of legality, operators had to shoulder punitive expenses, including the cost of the hunt, transport and security premiums (e.g. bribes to conservation, customs and law enforcement officials). Essentially, it became cheaper and more efficient to pay local hunters to poach rhinos in protected areas than to orchestrate pseudo-hunts or pay market-related prices for rhino horn deriving from private sources. Some poaching groups established their own organisational structures and trade connections, whilst criminal networks with experience in other illegal markets also became involved in wildlife trafficking. Criminal actors continue to rely on the transportation and distribution infrastructures and networks associated with these grey flows.

The attractiveness of grey markets and flows lies in the façade of legality through the use of legal operators, transport channels and trade networks. Whilst the private sector remained under-regulated, law-abiding rhino breeders saw no problem in selling rhino horn or hunts to fellow 'farmers' as they were not breaking the law. However, once the law became clear about what was legal and legitimate and what was not, the supply of sub-legal/grey rhino horn started to dry up. Given that the moratorium was lifted, the proposed regulations pertaining to the domestic trade in rhino horn in South Africa are pragmatic in light of the apparent need to control and regulate domestic trade. However, if not carefully worded, these regulations may open up new opportunities for circumvention and creative *flow-hopping*. As it stands now, South Africa lacks the conservation management and law enforcement systems to manage domestic trade without corruption playing a role or domestic and foreign illicit trade systems penetrating it (personal communication with security official, 2017).

Conclusion: how to disrupt the illegal rhino horn economy?

Central to disrupting the rhino horn economy is thus an understanding of the interface between legal, grey and illegal markets for rhino horn. The focus of this article was on grey flows and markets, whilst links to illegal and legal flows of rhino horn were shown. These flows were presented as distinct entities for the purposes of analytical clarity. However, they are interconnected and contribute to the structure and functioning of the overall rhino horn economy (refer back to figure 1). In essence, the broader rhino and rhino parts economy are constituted of complex hybrid flows that involve recurring actors who perform specialised functions. Bolstered by sentiments of contested illegality, criminal actors have no qualms to exploit regulatory loopholes or to diversify into unchartered territory. These actors belong to influential and transnational networks with links to political and economic elites in supply, transit and consumer countries. Scholars[67] and practitioners[68] point to the involvement of organised crime in transnational rhino horn flows. Organised crime has become a catchall concept with close to 200 definitions[69]; the focus is often on the 'underworld', whilst the role of the 'upperworld' is acknowledged but not sufficiently analysed. In the case of the rhino horn economy, the role of the wildlife and transport industries, and government officials and law enforcement agents (all arguably representatives of the 'upperworld'), is significant in explaining why the illegal market is resilient and difficult to disrupt. Insider knowledge, the ability to utilise and instrumentalise legal, grey and illegal flows and access to transport, distribution and trade networks gives criminal actors the edge over market disruptors and law enforcers. The international regulatory protection regime, meanwhile, is riddled with ambiguities such as allowing the trophy hunting of rhinos, which usually leads to a hunting trophy whilst not allowing other non-lethal forms of harvesting rhino horn and deriving financial benefit from it. Diffusion of the international trade ban to national jurisdictions is further complicated through the disconnection of legal rules from cultural norms and traditions in consumer markets.[70] Of importance is the recognition that the bifurcation of legal versus illegal forms of economic exchange is of limited use when a multilateral trade treaty is involved. Rhinos and their body parts enjoy differing legal status along the time-space continuum. Markets for hunting rights, for example, allow affluent trophy hunters to hunt rhinos and export trophies of the dead animal to their country of origin. Policing these hunting markets (and other linked markets and services) falls outside the purview of traditional law enforcement agencies that deal exclusively with policing issues (conservation agencies deal with hunting transgressions). Moreover, once the hunting trophy (or the live animal) leaves the country of origin, its onward journey and final destination move beyond the national jurisdiction and reach of national agencies. As is the case in many other illegal markets, international efforts have focused on disrupting the supply side of the illegal market.[71] With most rhino horn entering illegal markets nowadays originating from poached rhinos, southern African law enforcement and criminal responses have been directed at poachers. Despite the increasing militarisation, 100s of arrests and more than 200 confirmed deaths of poaching suspects in South Africa's Kruger National Park between 2010 and 2015,[72] rhino poaching statistics remain high, and the tipping point in rhino population growth is believed to have been reached with the number of rhino deaths outstripping births.[73] Whilst such measures may have achieved some measure of success in dealing with the piracy phenomenon along the East African coastline[74] and rhino poaching in India (Vira 2017)[75] and Nepal (Aryal et al. 2017),[76] they have contributed to further alienation of local communities from conservation and protected areas in South Africa.[77] Meanwhile, little attention has been paid to stopping actors and flows originating in the wildlife industry, transportation and conservation sectors. Corrupt practices within these sectors and in government entities facilitate the passage of horn through transport nodes and border points that are well policed. Professional associations and industry oversight groups should enforce professional standards and sanction bad apples in their peer groups. Regulating flows, plugging new loopholes and disrupting illegal flows will require multi-sectorial, multi-agency and transnational interventions that involve private–public and international partnerships.

Notes

1. Emslie et al., "African and Asian rhinoceroses," 1.
2. Ferreira, "Management and conservation of rhino populations," 2.
3. Molewa, "Minister Edna Molewa highlights progress."
4. IUCN, "IUCN reports deepening rhino poaching crisis."
5. Varisco, "Beyond rhino horn", 215–219.
6. The initial research project formed part of my doctorate at the Max Planck Institute for the Study of Societies. The chapter 'Researching illegal markets' provides an analysis of research, methodological and ethical challenges encountered in the field and how they were resolved or bypassed (compare with: Hübschle 2016a).
7. Lavorgna, "Wildlife trafficking," 1–12; Pires, "The heterogeneity of illicit parrot markets," 1–16.
8. Leberatto, "Understanding the illegal wildlife trade," 42–66; Wyatt, "The illegal trade of raptors," 103–123; van Uhm and Siegel, "The illegal trade in caviar," 67–87.
9. Elliot, "Fighting transnational environmental crime," 87–104; Di Minin et al., "Identification of policies," 1–11; Duffy, "Waging a war," 819–834.
10. Herbig and Warchol, "South African conservation crime," 1–16;
    Moreto, "Law enforcement monitoring in Uganda," 82–101.
11. Shelley, "Convergence," seminar presentation;
    Reuter and Bisshop, "Keeping the horn on the rhino,"149–185;
    Haas and Ferreira, "Combating rhino horn trafficking," 1–26.

12. For a comprehensive analysis of specific wildlife markets and flows, compare with Wong, "The organisation of the illegal tiger parts trade," 1–19;
Zabyelina, "The "fishy" business," 1–18;
van Uhm, *The illegal wildlife trade*.
13. Gao et al., "Rhino horn trade in China," 343–347.
14. Truong et al., "The marketplace management of illegal elixirs," 1–17.
15. Beckert and Aspers (2008) cited in Beckert and Wehinger, "In the shadow," 7.
16. The ability to prosecute actors within illegal markets is not restricted to illegal markets. The state may equally prosecute market actors in legal or grey markets.
17. Ibid.
18. The abbreviation CITES refers to the Convention on the International Trade in Endangered Species of Wild Fauna and Flora, which has been in place since 1975. Details are discussed below.
19. See Hübschle, "Contested illegality," 1–20.
20. Zukin, *Landscapes of power*, 6.
21. A similar pattern can be observed in Western Europe during Industrialisation.
22. Passas, "Cross-border crime," 19–37.
Bisshop and Valle, "Environmental victimisation," 34–54.
23. Castells, "Grassrooting the space of flows," 295.
24. Castells, *The rise of the network society*, 407.
25. van Sluis et al., "Nodal security in the ports," 73–96;
Côté-Boucher, "The paradox of discretion," 1–19;
van Sluis et al, "Nodal policing in the Netherlands," 365–371.
26. Castells, "Materials for an Exploratory," 5 suggests that the network society is a specific form of social structure emblematic of the Information Age.
27. van Sluis et al., "Nodal security," 73.
28. Milliken and Shaw, "The South Africa-Vietnam rhino horn trade nexus," 44.
29. CITES, "Resolution Conference 9.14: Conservation of and trade in rhinos."
30. Department of Environmental Affairs and Tourism, *Government notice on moratorium*.
31. North Gauteng High Court, "Kruger and another versus Minster of Water and Environmental Affairs."
32. Emslie et al., Ibid, 11.
33. Molewa, *Draft regulations for domestic trade in rhino horn*.
34. The draft regulations, for example, stipulate that a person 'may export a maximum of two rhinoceros horns, and then only for personal purposes' (Molewa 2017: 7). It is unclear whether a temporal limitation is in place, such as the regulation proposing an annual or once-off export rate of rhino horn for personal purposes. No definition of 'personal purposes' is provided.
35. Namibia also allows private ownership of wildlife.
36. Lindsey et al., "Economic and conservation significance of the trophy hunting industry," 463.
37. South Africa's oldest proclaimed nature reserve is now known as the Hluhluwe-iMfolozi Park.
38. The former province of Natal is known as KwaZulu-Natal since the end of apartheid, and its parks authority is known as Ezemvelo KZN Wildlife, the former Natal Parks Board.
39. PROA is lobbying for the lifting of the CITES trade ban.
40. See Pienaar et al., "Horn growth rates," 97–105.
41. See Lindsey and Taylor, *A study on the dehorning of African rhinoceroses*.
42. The notion of 'contested illegality' is conceptualised as a legitimisation mechanism employed by illegal market actors to justify their participation in grey or illegal flows.
43. Milliken and Shaw, Ibid, 58.
44. See note 32 above.
45. See note 43 above.
46. See note 32 above.

47. Navasa et al., "Lemthongthai versus the State," 9.
48. Kvinta, "The madness of modern-day poaching."
49. Navasa et al., Ibid, 12–13.
50. Johnny Olivier was a South African associate of the network, who was responsible for the 'administrative go-between activities'. He turned state witness during Lemthongthai's trial.
51. The North West Province is one of South Africa's nine provinces.
52. Olivier, "Police statement," 9.
53. See note 32 above.
54. The other three countries are China, Mozambique and South Africa.
55. Vietnam, "Illegal trade of rhinoceros horn in Vietnam."
56. The dubious role of Vietnamese embassy staff in South Africa came initially under the spotlight after South African journalists filmed the embassy's former first secretary receiving rhino horns from a known trafficker on the street outside the Vietnamese embassy in Pretoria in 2008 (50/50 2008). Since then, several Asian diplomats have been investigated for their involvement in rhino horn and ivory trafficking (compare with: Rademeyer 2016a). The smuggling of any contraband through diplomatic channels is the most secure (and "legal") flow because law enforcement bodies hold no jurisdiction to open and search diplomatic pouches (compare with: United Nations Conference on Diplomatic Intercourse and Immunities 1961: Article 27 of the Vienna Convention on Diplomatic Relations).
57. CITES Rhinoceros Working Group, "Species trade and conservation: Rhinoceroses," 5.
58. Vietnam, Ibid, 1.
59. CITES Secretariat, Species trade and conservation: Rhinoceroses," 7–8.
60. In its September 2012 report to the CITES Secretariat, Vietnam indicated that many hunters cut up their hunting trophies (the horns) and gifted pieces of rhino horn to friends and family. When the Management Authority in Vietnam undertook "random checks" of hunting trophies, only 7 out of 40 trophies were found in an unadulterated form whilst 11 hunters could not be contacted (CITES Secretariat 2013: 23).
61. See note 32 above.
62. Milliken, "Illegal trade in ivory and rhino horn," 20–21.
63. According to interdiction data of Vietnam's CITES Scientific Authority provided in 2013 (personal communication, 2013), all interdictions involving rhino horn had occurred at the two main international airports in Ho Chi Minh City and Hanoi, except for one interdiction along a major highway in 2004.
64. See for example Accountability Panel, "Decision on the Map of Facts."
65. Illegal business transactions (including drug deals) are commonly believed to take place at locations that appear to guarantee the anonymity of the market participants such as hotel rooms, restaurants, and busy or isolated public spaces. The corollary suggests that the dividing lines between public and private lives and work and leisure are blurred.
66. Amman, "The Rhino Horn Story" made a similar observation after talking to a horn dealer in the northern parts of North Vietnam who had his horn stocks confiscated by members of the drug enforcement unit claiming that they would pay the dealer later.
67. Ayling, "What sustains wildlife trade?" 57–80.
68. Milliken, Ibid.; Rademeyer, "Tipping point," 1–64.
69. Compare with Klaus von Lampe's database of 190 definitions of organised crime.
70. See Hübschle, "The social economy of rhino poaching," 427–447.
    Ayling, Ibid.
71. Several conservation NGOs are involved in demand reduction campaigns in consumer countries. Lack of objective measurement as to the size of the illegal market renders the impact of such campaigns an educated guess.
72. According to Joaquim Chissano, the former president of Mozambique, South African security forces had intercepted and shot dead close to 500 Mozambicans in the KNP over the same time period. SANParks officials confirmed that 134 alleged poachers had been killed between 2010 and August 2014. Recent media reports augment the figure to about 200 known deaths. The national parks authority no longer shares the death toll with the public.

73. See note 4 above.""
74. The use of armed guards on ships passing through the Gulf of Aden and the establishment of an international multi-agency Contact Group on Piracy off the Coast of Somalia are believed to have brought down pirate hijackings and demands for ransom. However, pirates appear to have diversified into new ventures, including the provision of protection to fishing trawlers involved in illegal fishing in the region.
75. Although the Kaziranga National Park in India has achieved rhino population growth, Vira, "India's Militant Rhino Protectors" argues that these conservation successes have come at a high cost affecting relationships with local people living near the park.
76. Aryal et al., "Global Lessons from Successful Rhinoceros" argue that beyond changes in policy and coordination of law enforcement, the role of local communities in protecting and profiting from wildlife was a crucial element of Nepal's success in reaching a zero-rhino poaching rate for four consecutive years.
77. Compare with Annecke and Masubelele, "A review of the impact of militarisation," 195–204; Hübschle, "The social economy of rhino poaching," 427–447.

Acknowledgements

A first draft of this article was presented at the 'Policing of/through flows: New perspectives' workshop organised by the Centre Internationale de Criminologie Comparée at the University of Montreal in Canada. The author would like to thank Karine Côté-Boucher and two reviewers for the insightful comments on an earlier version of the article. Many thanks also to the Max Planck Institute for the Study of Societies who provided the initial funding for the doctoral research project and the Global Initiative against Transnational Organised Crime who funded the postdoctoral fellowship at the University of Cape Town during which this article was finalised. Most importantly, many thanks to the research informants who were frank and generous with their time and information.

Disclosure statement

No potential conflict of interest was reported by the author.

Funding

Many thanks also to the Max Planck Institute for the Study of Societies who provided the initial funding for the doctoral research project and the Global Initiative against Transnational Organised Crime who funded the postdoctoral fellowship at the University of Cape Town during which this article was finalised.

ORCID

Annette Hübschle (iD) http://orcid.org/0000-0002-7566-7067

Bibliography

50/50. 2008. Vietnam embassy was caught red-handed in illegal rhino horn transaction.

Accountability Panel. *Accountability Panel Decision on the Map of Facts regarding Illegal Trade in Wildlife Products in Nhi Khe, Viet Nam*. Wildlife Justice Commission. The Hague, Netherlands, 2016.

AIM. 2015. "Mozambique: Chissano Says about 500 Poachers Killed in South Afrca." http://africa journalismtheworld.com/2015/09/23/mozambique-chissano-says-about-500-poachers-killed-in-south-africa/.

Amman, K. 2015. "The Rhino Horn Story at the Consumer End." *Karl Amman*. http://www.karlam mann.com/rhino-horn.php.

Annecke, W., and M. Masubelele. "A Review of the Impact of Militarisation: The Case of Rhino Poaching in Kruger National Park, South Africa." *Conservation and Society* 14, no. 3 (2016): 195–204. doi:10.4103/0972-4923.191158.

Aryal, A., K. P. Acharya, U. B. Shrestha, M. Dhakal, D. Raubenhiemer, and W. Wright. "Global Lessons from Successful Rhinoceros Conservation in Nepal." *Conservation Biology* (2017). doi:10.1111/cobi.12894.

Ayling, J. "What Sustains Wildlife Crime? Rhino Horn Trading and the Resilience of Criminal Networks." *Journal of International Wildlife Law & Policy* 16, no. 1 (2013): 57–80. doi:10.1080/13880292.2013.764776.

Beckert, J., and F. Wehinger. "In the Shadow: Illegal Markets and Economic Sociology." *Socio-Economic Review* 11, no. 1 (2013): 5–30. doi:10.1093/ser/mws020.

Bisschop, L., and G. V. Walle. "Environmental Victimisation and Conflict Resolution: A Case Study of e-Waste." In *Emerging Issues in Green Criminology: Exploring Power, Justice and Harm*, edited by R. Walters, D. S. Westerhuis, and T. Wyatt, 280. Basingstoke: Palgrave Macmillan, 2013.

Castells, M. "Grassrooting the Space of Flows." *Urban Geography* 20, no. 4 (1999): 294–302. doi:10.2747/0272-3638.20.4.294.

Castells, M. "Materials for an Exploratory Theory of the Network Society." *The British Journal of Sociology* 51, no. 1 (2000): 5–24. doi:10.1111/j.1468-4446.2000.00005.x.

Castells, M. *The Rise of the Network Society: The Information Age: Economy, Society, and Culture*. Chichester: Wiley, 2011.

CITES. 1994. Resolution Conference 9.14: Conservation of and trade in African and Asian rhinoceroses. edited by CITES.

CITES Rhinoceros Working Group. *Interpretation and Implementation of the Convention; Species Trade and Conservation: Rhinoceroses*. Geneva, Switzerland, 2014.

CITES Secretariat. 2013. Interpretation and implementation of the Convention, Species trade and conservation: Rhinoceroses.

Côté-Boucher, K. "The Paradox of Discretion: Customs and the Changing Occupational Identity of Canadian Border Officers." *British Journal of Criminology* (2015). doi:10.1093/bjc/azv023.

Department of Environmental Affairs and Tourism. 2009. Government notice on national moratorium on the trade in individual rhinoceros horns. In *No. 148*.

di Minin, E., J. Laitila, F. Montesino-Pouzols, R. O. B. Nigel Leader-Williams, P. S. Slotow, A. Goodman, J. Conway, and A. Moilanen. "Identification of Policies for a Sustainable Legal Trade in Rhinoceros Horn Based on Population Projection and Socioeconomic Models." *Conservation Biology* (2014). doi:10.1111/cobi.12412.

Duffy, R. "Waging a War to Save Biodiversity: The Rise of Militarized Conservation." *International Affairs* 90, no. 4 (2014): 819–834.

Elliott, L. "Fighting Transnational Environmental Crime." *Journal of International Affairs* 66, no. 1 (2012): 87–104.

Emslie, R. H., T. Milliken, B. Talukdar, S. Ellis, K. Adcock, and M. H. Knight. 2016. African and Asian rhinoceroses – Status, conservation and trade: A report from the IUCN Species Survival Commission (IUCN SSC) African and Asian Rhino Specialist Groups and TRAFFIC to the CITES Secretariat pursuant to Resolution Conf. 9.14 (Rev. CoP15). Geneva: CITES Secretariat.

Ferreira, Sam "Management and Conservation of Rhino Populations in the Face of Ongoing Poaching on State-Owned and Private Lands." In *Portfolio Committee on Environmental Affairs Colloquium on Anti-rhino Poaching*. Good Hope Chamber, Parliament of the Republic of South Africa, 2016.

Gao, Y., K. J. Stoner, A. T. L. Lee, and S. G. Clark. "Rhino Horn Trade in China: An Analysis of the Art and Antiques Market." *Biological Conservation* 201 (2016): 343–347. doi:10.1016/j.biocon.2016.08.001.

Haas, T. C., and S. M. Ferreira. "Combating Rhino Horn Trafficking: The Need to Disrupt Criminal Networks." *PLoS ONE* 11, no. 11 (2016): 1–26. doi:10.1371/journal.pone.0167040.

Herbig, F. J. W., and G. Warchol. "South African Conservation Crime and Routine Activities Theory: A Causal Nexus." *Acta Criminologica* 24 (2011): 2.

Hübschle, A. 2016a. "A Game of Horns: Transnational Flows of Rhino Horn." In. Cologne: International Max Planck Research School on the Social and Political Constitution of the Economy. http://pubman.mpdl.mpg.de/pubman/item/escidoc:2218357:10/component/escidoc:2262615/2016_IMPRSDiss_Huebschle.pdf.

Hübschle, A. "Contested Illegality: Processing the Trade Prohibition of Rhino Horn." In *The Architecture of Illegal Markets*, edited by J. Beckert and M. Dewey. Oxford: Oxford University Press, 2017.

Hübschle, A. M. "The Social Economy of Rhino Poaching: Of Economic Freedom Fighters, Professional Hunters and Marginalized Local People." *Current Sociology* 65, no. 3 (2016b): 427–447. doi:10.1177/0011392116673210.

IUCN. 2016. IUCN reports deepening rhino poaching crisis.

Kvinta, P. "The Madness of Modern-Day Poaching." *Outside Live Bravely* 16, no. March (2014): 2014.

Lavorgna, A. "Wildlife Trafficking in the Internet Age." *Crime Science* 3, no. 1 (2014): 1–12. doi:10.1186/s40163-014-0005-2.

Leberatto, A. "Understanding the Illegal Trade of Live Wildlife Species in Peru." *Trends in Organized Crime* 19, no. 1 (2016): 42–66. doi:10.1007/s12117-015-9262-z.

Lindsey, P. A., P. A. Roulet, and S. S. Romañach. "Economic and Conservation Significance of the Trophy Hunting Industry in sub-Saharan Africa." *Biological Conservation* 134, no. 4 (2007): 455–469. doi:10.1016/j.biocon.2006.09.005.

Lindsey, P. A., and A. Taylor. *A Study on the Dehorning of African Rhinoceroses as A Tool to Reduce the Risk of Poaching*. Pretoria: Department of Environmental Affairs and Endangered Wildlife Trust, 2011.

Milliken, T. 2014. Illegal trade in ivory and rhino horn: An assessment report to improve law enforcement under the Wildlife TRAPS Project USAID and TRAFFIC.

Milliken, T., and J. Shaw. *The South Africa–Viet Nam Rhino Horn Trade Nexus: A Deadly Combination of Institutional Lapses, Corrupt Wildlife Industry Professionals and Asian Crime Syndicates*. Johannesburg, South Africa: TRAFFIC, 2012.

Molewa, E. *Minister Edna Molewa Highlights Progress in the Fight against Rhino Poaching*. Pretoria: Department of Environmental Affairs, 2016.

Molewa, E. 2017. Draft regulations for the domestic trade in rhinoceros horn, or a part, product or derivative of rhinoceros horn. In *40601*, edited by Department of Environmental Affairs: Government Gazette.

Moreto, W. D., A. M. Lemieux, A. Rwetsiba, N. Guma, M. Dirciru, and H. K. Kirya. "Law Enforcement Monitoring in Uganda: The Utility of Official Data and Time/Distance-Based Ranger Efficiency Measures." In *Situational Prevention of Poaching*, edited by A. M. Lemieux, 82–101. Oxford: Routledge, 2014.

Navsa, A. D. P., J. J. A. Wallis, and J. J. A. Swain. 2014. Lemthongthai versus the State (849/2013) [2014] ZASCA 131 (25 September 2014). In *Case No. 849/2013*, edited by The Supreme Court of Appeal of South Africa.

North Gauteng High Court. *Kruger and Another V Minister of Water and Environmental Affairs and Others (57221/12) [2015] ZAGPPHC 1018; [2016] 1 All SA 565 (GP)*. Pretoria: SAFLII, 2015.

Olivier, J. 2011. *Police statement*. 13 May 2011.

Passas, N. "Cross-Border Crime and the Interface between Legal and Illegal Actors." *Security Journal* 16, no. 1 (2003): 19–37.

Pienaar, D. J., A. J. Hall–Martin, and P. M. Hitchens. "Horn Growth Rates of Free-Ranging White and Black Rhinoceros." *Koedoe* 34, no. 2 (1991): 97–105.

Pires, S. F. "The Heterogeneity of Illicit Parrot Markets: An Analysis of Seven Neo-Tropical Open-Air Markets." *European Journal on Criminal Policy and Research* (2014): 1–16. doi:10.1007/s10610-014-9246-6.

Rademeyer, J. *Beyond Borders: Crime, Conservation and Criminal Networks in the Illicit Rhino Horn Trade*. Geneva: Global Initiative against Transnational Organized Crime, 2016a.

Rademeyer, J. *Tipping Point: Transnational Organized Crime and the 'War' on Poaching*. Geneva: Global Initiative against Transnational Organized Crime, 2016b.

Reuter, E., and L. Bisschop. "Keeping the Horn on the Rhino: A Study of Balule Nature Reserve." In *The Geography of Environmental Crime: Conservation, Wildlife Crime and Environmental Activism*, edited by R. Gary Potter, A. Nurse, and M. Hall, 149–185. London: Palgrave Macmillan UK, 2016.

Shelley, L. 2016. "Convergence: What Kidneys, Cigarettes and Rhino Horn Have in Common." Seminar with Professor Louise Shelley on the convergence of rhino horn trafficking with other illicit activities, Environmental Security Observatory, University of Cape Town, 26 May 2016.

Truong, V. D., M. Willemsen, N. V. H. Dang, T. Nguyen, and C. Michael Hall. "The Marketplace Management of Illegal Elixirs: Illicit Consumption of Rhino Horn." *Consumption Markets & Culture* (2015): 1–17. doi:10.1080/10253866.2015.1108915.

United Nations Conference on Diplomatic Intercourse and Immunities. *Vienna Convention on Diplomatic Relations*. edited by United Nations. Neue Hofburg, Vienna: United Nations Treaty Series, 1961.

van Sluis, A., P. Marks, and V. Bekkers. "Nodal Policing in the Netherlands: Strategic and Normative Considerations on an Evolving Practice." *Policing* (2011): 365–371. doi:10.1093/police/par045.

van Sluis, A., P. Marks, F. Gilleir, and M. Easton. "Nodal Security in the Ports of Rotterdam and Ntwerp." In *Beyond Fragmentation and Interconnectivity: Public Governance and the Search for Connective Capacity*, edited by H. J. M. Fenger, M. Fenger, and V. J. J. M. Bekkers. Amsterdam: IOS Press, 2012.

van Uhm, D., and D. Siegel. "The Illegal Trade in Black Caviar." *Trends in Organized Crime* 19, no. 1 (2016): 67–87. doi:10.1007/s12117-016-9264-5.

Varisco, D. M. "Beyond Rhino Horn – Wildlife Conservation for North Yemen." *Oryx* 23, no. 4 (1989): 215–219.

Vietnam. 2013. Illegal trade of rhinoceros horn in Vietnam. edited by CITES.

Vira, B. 2017. "India's Militant Rhino Protectors are Challenging Traditional Views of How Conservation Works." https://theconversation.com/indias-militant-rhino-protectors-are-challenging-traditional-views-of-how-conservation-works-72828.

von Lampe, K. 2017. Definitions of organized crime.

Wyatt, T. "The Illegal Trade of Raptors in the Russian Federation." *Contemporary Justice Review* 14, no. 2 (2011): 103–123. doi:10.1080/10282580.2011.565969.

Zukin, S. *Landscapes of Power: From Detroit to Disney World*. Los Angeles: University of California Press, 1993.

Regulation of cross-border law enforcement: 'locks' and 'dams' to regional and international flows of policing

Saskia Hufnagel

ABSTRACT

Trans-jurisdictional policing can eventuate within a number of different environments: in federal states comprising different jurisdictions, in bilateral and multilateral settings and in regional contexts, for example, in the European Union (EU). Inter-jurisdictional flows of policing can be impeded by, for example, legal differences, lack of trust, lack of cooperative leadership, lack of knowledge about the other jurisdiction, etc. This article aims at exploring the facilitators of flows of policing by looking at two different systems and the obstacles within, as well as the interaction between them. The systems chosen are Greater China and the EU as they both comprise a number of different jurisdictions and are very distinct with regard to political, cultural and legal variables. It will be explored whether and how flows of policing are encouraged by legislation within and between the systems as well as what factors might determine the conclusion of a particular legal framework for cooperation.

1. Introduction

'Policing flows' can be understood in two ways, first as the 'policing of flows', for example, of illegal substances, weapons, migrants, or second as 'flows of policing', such as the exchange of information and intelligence between police and, at a later investigation stage, the transfer of evidence or suspects. Within one jurisdiction the flows of policing are rather contained and it can be expected that all police involved are privy to the same information, similar to water in a lake (although there is evidence that even within one jurisdiction – and even one organisation – information can be very unevenly distributed). One prominent example of insufficient information flow within one jurisdiction and its detrimental consequences is the Jean Charles de Menezes Case in the UK.[1] If multiple jurisdictions are involved the 'flows of policing' can be expected to be even more likely subject to obstacles or 'congestions' slowing down or even stopping the flows. 'Congestions' therefore have the potential to challenge the transfer of knowledge, evidence, people and anything else that is needed to detect, investigate and prosecute crimes between jurisdictions.

This article does not exclusively focus on the facilitation of flows of policing. Human rights are necessitating the building of 'locks', 'dams' or 'weirs'. This metaphor is used to imply that a 'free flow' of policing is not in anyone's interest. In democratic polities, the police are part of the executive branch of government, which is supposed to serve the people. Their services therefore have to be restricted by the rights of citizens. This could already explain why barriers to policing across jurisdictions should not just be broken down to enable flows, but the flows should be regulated to ensure controlled exchanges from one jurisdiction to the other.

Turning to the criminological research on flows, which is more often looking at the policing of flows rather than the flows of policing, we can see that trans-jurisdictional policing is predominantly aimed at the restriction of the individual.[2] Katja Franko argues in her article that there is a discrepancy between the high preservation of sovereignty of some nations as reflected in their border controls and 'the spirit of transnational flows of capital, goods and information'.[3] What 'locks', 'dams' or 'weirs' are supposed to achieve in the light of this discrepancy is a preservation of sovereignty and protection of national laws, while enabling the flows. One might also argue that like the policing of flows, flows of policing have to be regulated to achieve the protection and right to movement of the individual. Certain information, for example, should not be allowed to flow as it breaches individual rights, while other information protecting individuals should be facilitated. By not regulating flows – or completely obstructing them – flows might not be stopped, but only driven underground according to the metaphor that 'water finds its way'. This is true for crime as well as police information. Regulation might hence be a better way to tackle flows than erecting barriers. Another possible way to look at it would be the creation of weirs that can be overcome by water, while adjusting its flow – responding to the challenge of regulating the flows of policing without stopping them. If, for example, too many bureaucratic hurdles are built in, the water will not flow through the riverbed, but find a way around it.

More specifically with regard to the metaphors used, 'locks' can stop flows for specific purposes (letting a ship pass). 'Locks' can be seen as treaties or agreements with a specific condition attached to them (e.g. assurances in extradition cases). 'Dams' stop flows, but the possibility for letting through water in cases of emergency exists. Dams can therefore be compared to international cooperation with partners with very different human rights regimes where cooperation is not the rule, but the exception. Lastly, 'weirs' usually allow a constant flow while being able to restrict it when necessary. They are comparable to regions with existing broad regulation on cooperation that leaves the details to the discretion of the practitioners involved, but is still able to control the flow.

Using the three metaphors in the area of regulation of trans-jurisdictional policing means that some regulation, such as a unilateral legal assistance in criminal matters convention, might facilitate international legal assistance on a case-by-case basis ('dam'), while an international treaty or agreement between two or more states creates a general basis for all similar cases to be treated similarly ('lock' or 'weir'). When looking at the regulation of police cooperation across national and international jurisdictional boundaries it can be observed that it differs significantly and ranges from formal, legally binding international treaties and agreements, to informal custom applied between agencies. While these are the two most extreme cases of formality and informality, many types of regulation are situated somewhere on the continuum between these two points, such as Memoranda of Understanding (MoU) between agencies or Associations of Chiefs of Police. There are hence different 'states' of formalisation and enforceability of regulation. A customary good relationship between two police officers, two police stations or two agencies or departments can result in frequent exchange of information, mutual assistance and even joint investigations at a completely informal, unregulated level ('free flow'). In some instances, such informal cooperation has led to the establishment of more formalised initiatives, such as MoU between agencies, departments and nation states, or even to legally binding bilateral and multilateral treaties and agreements ('locks' or 'weirs'). Nation states have also established international regulation on police cooperation that was not based on developments in policing practice. This 'top-down' regulation can equally influence transnational policing. 'Locks' and 'weirs' are hence, somewhat counter-intuitively, not only introduced to limit policing powers across borders, but they seem to be a further stage in the evolution of well-working flows. If a flow is constant, but unregulated, 'locks' and 'weirs' are created. If a flow is not constant, policing seems more likely to be subject to 'dams'. This was one of the observations that could be made throughout the comparison.

With a view to the two systems, the European Union (EU) is assessed as a region that has formed its own human rights framework applying to a number of significantly different systems and has developed a number of 'locks' and 'weirs' through international (EU) treaties and agreements regulating police and justice cooperation. The four states forming Greater China, while not being sovereign nation states, have distinctly different histories, legal systems and police organisations, which presents obstacles for cross-border law enforcement. However, they did not regulate their policing flows through 'locks', but rather 'dams' or not at all.

The choice of systems was guided by the legal diversity within and between them. The EU was chosen as a system with a high diversity of jurisdictions at the criminal law and procedure level, but a high homogeneity of human rights requirements, while Greater China, [comprising Mainland China, Taiwan and the special administrative regions (SARs) Hong Kong and Macau], was chosen as a region with both diversity at the criminal law and procedure as well as the human rights level. While it is impossible to evaluate the quality or efficiency of flows within and between the systems, what can be assessed are points of congestion, facilitators and regulators of flows.

Points of congestion between the systems were addressed by taking stock of police practitioner perceptions in both the EU and China. First the author collected evidence of regulation and cross-border practices through desktop research. In a next step practitioner perceptions were gathered through both interviews and a review of the empirical literature to examine the actual practice with regard to the given regulation. To create a wider data sample considering limited fieldwork opportunities, the recent academic literature focusing on policing in the EU and China was evaluated. Apart from research by the author,[4] two other studies conducted by prominent EU and China policing scholars between 2006 and 2011 were examined in detail with a view to police perceptions on cooperation.[5] In the 2009 study by Sonny Lo,[6] Chinese police and criminal justice officials were interviewed on the formal and informal police cooperation between Hong Kong, Mainland China, Macau and Taiwan. Lo also interviewed representatives of the criminal justice system in other regions of Greater China. In the study by Hufnagel (2014),[7] interviews were mainly conducted with Hong Kong police and customs representatives to illustrate the importance of informal cooperation in Greater China. The study by Block[8] focused on the EU and interviews were conducted with 36 police officers and civil servants to find out about the actual implementation of EU Council instruments in EU policing. Similarly, the study by Hufnagel (2013)[9] based its findings on interviews with 40 police officers and prosecutors to investigate the implementation of cooperation instruments in cross-border cooperation practice in the EU and Australia. The author consulted 10 contacts for previous studies in the EU and Hong Kong again in 2016/17, to update the data on perceptions of cooperation barriers. The knowledge about informal cooperation and formalisation that has been gained through the above review of empirical studies on police cooperation in the EU and China and interviews conducted by the author for previous studies and to update the current study will be used here to highlight the interaction between regulation and policing practice.

A major difference between the systems assessed is that formal police cooperation frameworks have evolved at EU level in recent years, but police cooperation in Greater China still relies predominantly on informal police-to-police strategies in border regions.[10] The differences of formalisation levels could be related to the differences in legal diversity. There could furthermore exist a link between legal diversity, trust and human rights, which could explain why some systems build regulatory frameworks and others do not. What is even more interesting is the assessment of the two systems and their relationship towards each other. Between the EU and China, one single police cooperation framework exists, which is focused on the detection of precursor chemicals.[11] Precursor chemicals are shipped legally from China into EU member states where they are illegally distributed to drug manufacturers.[12] The criminal result of the flow therefore materialises in the EU, not in China. Such an agreement mainly benefits the EU. One might now state that rivers only flow in one direction, however, the idea of flows of policing is that they work both ways, which is where the metaphor comes to an end. Where the flow does not work in both directions, the interest of one party in cooperating might soon drain away. Unless, of course, there are political considerations not to stop it. This means that when looking at flows of policing, the assessment of existing 'congestions', 'locks', 'dams' or 'weirs' is not sufficient. One furthermore needs to address the directions of flows and the interests involved in maintaining reciprocity.

The present study will address directions of, barriers to and regulation of flows of policing in the EU and Greater China as well as between these two systems. With regard to barriers, trust will be examined as a potential major impact factor. Human rights are discussed more prominently with a view to regulating flows. Lastly, both concepts including political interests will be brought together when assessing the direction of flows. The systems discussed here have been chosen for their differences in the area of fundamental rights protection, which might impact on both trust between police and regulation of policing flows. There might be a relevance of shared fundamental rights, and in particular fair trial rights, between jurisdictions for the building of 'locks', 'dams' and 'weirs'. More broadly, the similarities and differences of human rights frameworks and the building of regulating barriers could be interconnected.

This article first addresses the concepts of trust and human rights as they apply to flows of policing. The two systems are then analysed separately with a view to 'congestions', 'locks', 'dams' and 'weirs' within them. Lastly, the article addresses directions of flows and the influence of national interests, taking policing flows between the EU and Greater China as a case study.

2. Human rights and the creation of 'locks', 'dams' and 'weirs'

Throughout the review of more or less 'legal' or 'formal' instruments regulating and facilitating flows of policing between jurisdictions, it could be observed that the existence of common human rights frameworks had a significant impact on the creation of 'locks', 'dams' and 'weirs'. The existence of human rights and their implementation therefore leads to the regulation of flows. With regard to the interconnection between human rights and international policing, much less literature has been produced than on human rights and domestic policing. Prominent exceptions include the work by Monica den Boer, Ben Bowling and James Sheptycki.[13]

This article uses the concept of human rights as being linked to the implementation of international human rights, as enshrined in the International Covenant on Civil and Political Rights (ICCPR) and the European Convention of Human Rights, within the systems addressed. National police agencies have to make sure they comply with their own state's human rights standards. This compliance could be endangered if the state they are cooperating with, for example, giving information to or getting information from, is not abiding by the same or at least similar standards.

Human rights are a crucial factor for police to determine which states they are cooperating with freely or warily. In cross-border police cooperation as in the relationship between a state and its subordinates, authority for certain actions is deferred upon the (another) state actor. This can be a rather specific act in the area of police cooperation, such as the carrying out of an arrest, search or seizure, or more oblique, like the transfer of information. As this act has to be carried out in a way that is accepted by the people, or the state in the case of police cooperation, there needs to be a similar benchmark as to what a 'good' act is. This, by contrast, can be perceived very differently in the 'people to state' relationship rather than the 'police to police' cooperation. In the former the act has to protect the rights given to the state's subjects, in the latter the act has to be fast, efficient and leading to the success of an investigation. However, it is impossible to assert that human rights are important in national, but not in international policing contexts. To the contrary, in international policing the human rights requirements of more than one state have to be observed as well as efficiency maintained. The more the human rights regimes to be obeyed differ, the more challenging this might become. In systems with very similar human rights regimes, 'weirs' might therefore be able to minimally correct the flow of policing as little attention needs to be paid to differences and the focus can be on efficiency. If the systems differ more significantly, but broadly adhere to the same standards, 'locks' can be used. They stifle the flow more, but aim at both maintaining or 'levelling' human rights as well as efficiency. Are the systems significantly different, human rights can completely hinder the flow of policing. There might, however, be great interests for cooperation, as in the case of terrorism where EU member states need the information from non-democratic states to maintain security in their jurisdictions. In these cases there are 'dams' that are opened in emergency situations, like a terrorist threat.

3. Trust and 'congestions'

In the various studies on trans-jurisdictional police cooperation that were conducted since the 1990s,[14] trust was mentioned by practitioners as a major positive impact factor on cooperation. Trust created a 'free flow' of information despite 'congestions', such as differences at the legal, cultural and political levels. Trust was furthermore often reported to circumvent 'locks' and 'dams' created to channel information from one jurisdiction to another in a controlled fashion. Trust therefore needs to be treated with extreme care. It can, on the one hand, be a very positive element facilitating flows of policing. On the other hand, it can contribute to the circumvention of legal regulation created to uphold the rights of all actors involved.

With regard to the link between trust and human rights, psychology research has shown that shared moral norms and values form a basis for trust. The more we perceive others as having a similar value system, the more we consider them to be trustworthy.[15] Applied to an organisation, such as the police, which is bound by legal frameworks, this should lead to the conclusion that the shared restriction by fundamental rights leads to common norms and values, which in turn lead to trust. Another factor that can lead to value commonalities is the need to produce results, to be efficient and to pursue a common goal. This might on many occasions complicate the maintenance of the legal values. However, it is important in the case of police to distinguish shared legal values and the shared goals. The distinction might explain why cooperation happens not only between agencies with similar human rights frameworks, but also with those that have very different legal restraints.

The adherence to international human rights might have a major impact on which police agencies are perceived as good cooperation partners. However, research in the area of inter-agency cooperation has shown that it often comes down to who is known in the other organisation personally.[16] It follows that there are three broad reasons for the establishment of a trust relationship between agencies: common norms, common goals and personal contacts.

By analysing 'congestions', 'locks', 'dams', 'weirs' and 'directions' of flows in the EU, Greater China and between them, the importance of trust can be established in different contexts. Lack of trust could create 'congestions', but when there is a dire need for information exchange, 'dams' might be created. Trust without regulation can create 'free flows', which can infringe individual rights. Long-established trust between systems perceiving each other as adhering to the same values could more often lead to the creation of 'locks' or 'weirs'. Lack of trust could impact on the direction of the flows of information, for example, if one party trusts, but the other does not, flows will only happen from the party that trusts to the one that does not. Political interests, however, could reverse this flow (e.g. in the case of terrorism).

4. Regulating flows of policing in the EU

A significant number of bilateral and multilateral police cooperation strategies exist between the member states of the EU.[17] They shall not be outlined here as there are more than 133 EU-level security provisions that highlight impressively the existence of 'locks' and 'weirs' for flows of policing in this region of the world. There were already 133

EU-level security provisions encompassing both substantive criminal law and procedural measures before the entry into force of the Lisbon Treaty in 2010. However, it should be noted that the bilateral and multilateral cooperation initiatives influenced EU-wide regulation. Some formalised cooperation initiatives between just two EU member states spread throughout the region, leading to a de facto harmonisation of 'locks' or 'weirs' created for a very select number of states at first. A strategy that developed in such a way are the 'Common Centres' [or Police and Customs Cooperation Centres (PCCCs)].[18] Other mechanisms started at a multilateral level (more than two states) and were then taken up at EU level, such as the Schengen Convention. With regard to the trust analysis, all mechanisms were based on a common goal: the fight against cross-border crime. However, despite the common goal, there were 'congestions' in the flow. In the case of the Common Centres, those congestions were mainly related to slow information flows and the bureaucratic hurdles involved.[19] The Centres brought police from different jurisdictions together in one building and thereby facilitated access to each other's databases and encouraged common border patrols and investigations.[20] The established strategy therefore seems to be less of a 'lock' and more a 'weir' or even the deepening of a channel. The same could be said in relation to the Schengen Convention. This mechanism facilitates cross-border incursions, surveillance and other measures, while not determining the legal limits of such cooperation. The application of legal limits is still left to the nation states. An EU 'lock' to cooperation was not created, but the Convention enabled trusting states to deepen their channels. This is different with regard to EU-level initiatives, such as Europol. Europol, discussed below, could be regarded a 'lock', while PCCCs and the Schengen Convention developed more organically as a 'weir' (regulating) or deepening of channels.

Seeing that many EU police cooperation initiatives started first between neighbouring countries, they were very likely also fostered by personal contacts. These were sometimes even the driving force and more crucial than the common goal, such as in the example of the Cross-Channel Intelligence Conference (CCIC) between the UK, France and Belgium.[21] While there was a clear need to cooperate in this region and hence a common goal, the personal and political animosities were too pronounced to lead to advanced cooperation. This changed when the head of the Kent police was replaced by a chief of police with a high level of diplomatic skills. The personal contacts thereby enabled the trust needed for a steady flow of policing. In this specific case, 'locks' were created, for example, the CCIC led to the establishment of the 'Sangatte Protocol' regulating the policing of the Channel region between France and the UK. This Protocol regulates in particular the mutual assistance within the Sangatte Fixed Link in the Channel region. The Protocol is supplemented by the 2005 Agreement on the carrying of Service Weapons by French Officers on the territory of the United Kingdom of Great Britain and Northern Ireland, which was necessary because French, unlike UK police officers, are required to carry service weapons other than batons. One could therefore conclude that 'locks' are created when there are significant differences between the cooperating legal systems that need regulation – also for the protection and legal security of the citizens policed.

EU regulation of policing across jurisdictions thereby consists of broadly two types. One is the deepening of channels and establishment of 'weirs' by creating international legislation that reduces bureaucratic hurdles. The other type of regulation is 'locks', which are more specific treaties and agreements between systems with significant legal differences. The 'locks' are necessary to overcome legal differences with practical implications and to create legal security for the 'policed'. Initial trust between the jurisdictions establishing the strategies first at a more contained bilateral and multilateral level was crucial to facilitate the process. Legislation was possible as EU member states abide by the same human rights standards. A third and more complex type of regulation does exist with regard to strategies that have not evolved from smaller initiatives, such as Europol.

The most prominent formalised cooperation mechanism so far is the 'Europol Convention' (signed by the then 15 EU member states on 26 July 1995), which came into effect on 1 July 1999 and has, since 2010, been replaced by a Council Decision, which has been transformed in 2016 into a Europol Regulation.[22] Europol can be divided into four different parts. It has a board of management consisting of representatives of the member states and a representative of the Commission (Art 37, Europol Decision). It therefore employs an intergovernmental structure of governance. The head of Europol is its director. Europol further consists of the actual database, a liaison officer network and the national units. Falling short of operational powers is the EU-wide network of liaison officers, who exchange information and intelligence on transnational crime.[23] Liaison officers from all EU member states are situated at Europol to enable easier access to information (Art 9, Europol Decision). In addition to liaison officers, there are national units of Europol established in each member state, which are the only competent liaison bodies between Europol and the member state authorities. Direct contacts between Europol and designated competent authorities in the member states, governed by national law, are allowed since 2004.[24] This indicates a growing ceding of sovereignty concerns by the member states in relation to Europol. This is not only advantageous in relation to efficiently providing information and accessing the database but also in relation to face-to-face contact and informal information exchange between the officers stationed at Europol. Europol's liaison officer network is of particular importance as the exchange of sensitive information requires a high level of trust, not only between the member states but also between the police practitioners on the ground.[25] The liaison officers of all member states, and even non-EU member states, are co-located in one building to encourage the establishment of close working relationships. The liaison officers are not supervised by Europol, which gives them greater freedom to cooperate informally.[26] Practitioners have accepted this network immediately and appreciate the opportunity to know their counterparts from other member states personally as it enhances trust and informal cooperation.[27] The possibility to cooperate both formally and informally within this network was stated to be an advantage.[28]

Within Europol, both types of regulation observed in the EU previously come together. First, Europol fosters completely informal cooperation by bringing police from different jurisdictions together enabling the 'free flow' or relatively unregulated flow under a broad legal framework ('weir'). Furthermore, it enables advanced multi-jurisdictional information exchange through the Europol database. This mechanism is highly regulated for reasons of data protection, but also national sovereignty and can therefore be called a 'lock'.

Another important EU-level strategy is the 2000 EU Convention on Mutual Assistance in Criminal Matters.[29] Apart from other aims, it established joint investigation teams

(JITs) in the EU. JITs were included in the Convention as a new mechanism to coordinate cross-border investigations, which aims at changing the established practice of parallel investigations. While initially a resisted mechanism by practitioners, they are today a commonly used strategy to investigate cross-border crime.[30] According to Article 13 of the Convention, a JIT is an 'operational investigative team consisting of representatives of law enforcement and other authorities from different member states and possibly from other organisations like Europol and Eurojust'. The purpose of a JIT is jointly to investigate a criminal case; the teams are bi- or multinational, likely operating from one location, possibly multidisciplinary and are set up for a single investigation within an agreed time frame. An important aspect of the introduction of JITs was their advantage compared to 'traditional' cross-border investigations, the so-called 'parallel investigations'. Parallel investigations focus on cooperation through exchange of international letters of request (ILOR) in cross-border investigations, commonly based on the 1959 Council of Europe Convention, but specified in bilateral and multilateral agreements (e.g. Arts 39 and 40 of the Schengen Convention). When a parallel investigation is set up between two or more member states, investigation teams can work on the same case within their respective jurisdiction simultaneously. Information exchange and the coordination of the investigation are conducted through ILOR exchanges between the participating countries.[31] In the best-case scenario, ILORs establish a legal basis for the direct and immediate exchange of intelligence and determine the preliminary measures necessary in the course of the investigation that can be taken. If particular investigative measures become necessary in one jurisdiction, such as communication interception, searches, interrogations or confiscation, additional ILORs can be issued.[32] This cumbersome back and forth of requests is not needed within JITs established under the 2000 Convention, which makes them a useful tool in cross-border cooperation. While practitioners were initially reluctant to use them, they have since their establishment in 2000 become a frequent tool in EU cooperation.[33] JITs are furthermore assisted by Eurojust, which is legally based on the Eurojust Decision.[34] Eurojust national members can, for example, assist in the setting up of JITs, provide resources and help determine under which rules of procedure evidence needs to be gathered to be applicable in the relevant trial jurisdiction. Eurojust also has further competences in the area of judicial cooperation.

Again, the 2000 Convention, in particular with a view to JITs, is combining both types of regulation discussed for the EU above. On the one hand it establishes a strict legal framework, a 'lock' for JITs regulating the setting up of the group and the exchange of knowledge within it. On the other hand, it enables the free or barely regulated flow ('weir') of information within the JIT and is aimed at breaking down bureaucratic hurdles thereby deepening channels.

Trust and legitimacy were important factors in establishing the above 'locks' and 'weirs'. In the case of Europol and Eurojust, the fact that they gather together practitioners from all (and more) member states is an important factor as they establish personal contacts, which in turn have proven to lead to greater trust. JITs could be said not to initiate personal contacts for further cooperation, but to enable personal interaction during an investigation that crosses borders. Another element of trust, common norms/values, is to a certain extent also fulfilled by all three mechanisms as they prescribe a certain way of engaging with each other (e.g. prescribing competences and data protection regimes). All agents participating in these instruments have to adhere to the same rules even though they might come from different systems, explaining the creation of 'locks' and 'weirs' rather than the mere deepening of channels. Lastly, the common goal defined for these instruments is cross-border law enforcement within the EU. While this broader goal will apply to all agents cooperating through EU mechanisms, the more specific goals could nevertheless be different. Consideration might have to be given to protecting the identity of a source or not endangering a further domestic investigation. This can lead to conflicting goals. The interesting observation on the three above mechanisms is, however, that they provide the forum to harmonise goals. For example the Netherlands and the UK overcame their major differences in disclosure regimes by resorting to the Europol channel. Under UK law, sensitive information about police operations, such as the identity of informants or operational technique, can be withheld from disclosure to the defence (the doctrine of public interest immunity),[35] while Dutch practitioners are bound to potentially disclose all information in criminal proceedings.[36] If information is therefore classified as sensitive, it cannot be disclosed to the JIT by the UK. Faced with this major impediment, the UK authorities used the Europol channel to provide the JIT with the Netherlands with sensitive information and the source of the information remained protected.[37] The shortcomings of the 2000 Convention can hence be overcome by innovative ad hoc practitioner cooperation efforts, using another EU cooperation mechanism. What proved to be important in carrying out the investigation was not the legal framework, but 'good personal contacts, the ability to bridge cultural differences, a shared interest and a good knowledge of the legal system of the cooperation partner'.[38] While these 'good relationships' or trust could have previously led to the circumvention of legal barriers, police could here use the 'lock' or 'weir' established by EU legislation to legally transfer information from one jurisdiction to the other. This shows again that in cases of specific legal differences regulation is important to manage flows. It can also be concluded from this example that trust has become less necessary in a system with 'locks' and 'weirs' as information can be given legally and securely.

Another initiative that is worth mentioning here is CEPOL, the European Police College, which was founded in order to create a network of police officials from all member states and harmonise European policing standards through training.[39] CEPOL promotes training and education through seminars, workshops and the exchange of police officers at senior levels; they can work for a limited period of time in other countries and learn about another system.[40] Cooperation mechanisms with a focus on training and more generally knowledge exchange can be found in both systems examined for this study. They are not only crucial in promoting trust between practitioners, but can also contribute to the harmonisation of practice and enhance cooperation. Practitioners participating in a number of seminars given by the author for CEPOL stressed that the major advantage of the events was that they got to know practitioners in other member states who they can then contact directly in cross-border investigations. CEPOL thereby fosters the 'free flow' of information, although this interpretation is too simplistic. Personal connections only give the officer a contact point willing to cooperate and make the process as un-bureaucratic as possible. This does not necessarily mean that legal regulation is circumvented. Personal contacts do rather lead to a 'deepening of channels'. Legal challenges will still have to be channelled through the specific 'locks' and 'weirs', but the process could be faster.

With a view to 'congestions' it can be concluded that the reason for the creation of cooperation initiatives was the overcoming of bureaucratic hurdles as well as legal differences. 'Locks' and 'weirs' in the EU context were therefore not prominently created to overcome a lack of trust. What needed to be facilitated was a freer flow of information through the deepening of channels (practitioner training) or the overcoming of specific legal issues through the establishment of 'locks' and 'weirs' (legal regulation).

5. Regulating flows of policing in greater China

While Greater China only includes four distinctly different jurisdictions, the differences between them are great and the challenges to police cooperation significant. Article 2 of the Basic Law of Hong Kong[41] provides the 'one country, two systems' political settlement. However, there are more than two systems at play in the region. The Mainland Chinese system draws heavily on foreign legal models.[42] The Chinese criminal code[43] and the code of criminal procedure[44] in particular borrow from both, the Soviet and German civil systems.[45] Hong Kong, as a former British colony is governed by the common law system, which continues even after recession to the PRC in 1997.[46] Macau, the other SAR in Greater China and until 1999 under Portuguese rule, has a 'potpourri' system similar to the mainland, based on Portuguese law, which in turn borrowed from German law.[47] Macau, like Hong Kong, does not apply the death penalty, which distinguishes the two administrative regions from the Mainland and has the potential to complicate police and justice cooperation between these jurisdictions.[48] Taiwan, like Mainland China and Macau, is a civil law (inquisitorial) system.[49] It contains a mixture of Imperial Chinese law, contemporary Chinese law, principles and concepts of civil law systems, such as Germany and Japan, as well as the US. These differences in systems and legal heritage also have an impact on the regulation and structure of policing within them.

Furthermore, the international and national human rights situation in Greater China is complicated. China is a signatory to the ICCPR, but has not ratified it. For this reason, Taiwan can equally not ratify it. Hong Kong and Macao have granted adherence to the ICCPR in their Basic Laws and therefore to some extent implemented it without being able to be a party to the Convention.[50] There is hence a far greater human rights discrepancy between the systems in China than in the EU.

Unsurprisingly, a common legal framework on police cooperation does in fact not exist in Greater China. However, a number of formal agreements were established bilaterally. An example for a bilateral cooperation framework is the 1988 Mutual Case Assistance Scheme (MCAS) between Mainland China and Hong Kong.[51] MCAS was established to investigate cross-border corruption cases. The agreement was first limited to Procurator Departments in Guangdong, but in 2000 was further extended through collaboration with the Supreme People's Procurator Department to other provinces.[52] This manifests a harmonising effect of this agreement on other regions within Mainland China. It also shows that a common goal seems to overcome the general rule that regulation is only established between systems that are based on a similar value system.

With regard to this specific crime (corruption), MCAS therefore provided a broadening of channels.

An example for trust between systems that have similarly limited international human rights standards is the 2009 *Cross-Strait Joint Crime-Fighting and Judicial Mutual Assistance Agreement*, which was concluded between Taiwan and Mainland China.[53] It is a formal agreement and to a higher degree binding than, for example, an MOU. This agreement is the most comparable to EU mechanisms and encompasses measures similar to those available through the Schengen Convention, such as cross-border incursions and mutual legal assistance. The closeness of Taiwan and Mainland China in the area of police cooperation is very surprising as Taiwan is not recognised by the PRC as a sovereign nation state. However, under the *Cross-Strait Agreement* both sides had established diplomatic organisations through which cooperation, for example, in criminal matters, could be conducted.[54] A possible explanation is that the PRC and Taiwan both apply the death penalty and have a similar approach to fair trial rights. Cooperation between them, despite political discrepancies, relies on jurisdictional similarities, considering that both systems rely more on Imperial and contemporary Chinese law than Macau and Hong Kong. This stresses that a common value system can lead to closer cooperation. However, human rights are here put to the test as both their existence, as well as their lack can lead to greater cooperation between organisations. Regulation is here brought in through a deepening of channels rather than through 'locks' or 'weirs' regulating the flow and overcoming legal differences.

The level of engagement between all four systems forming Greater China is more comparable to international cooperation than to the close and regulated EU cross-border law enforcement. The '1994 Agreement' was established between Mainland China and Hong Kong and confirmed the principle established between both systems previously on three different channels for mutual legal assistance. The first was Interpol, the second a direct link between the Hong Kong and the Guangdong province, and the third were liaison officers of the Ministry of Public Security stationed in Hong Kong.[55] Cooperation through Interpol had been long-established practice of operational police cooperation between the two parties during the 99-year British lease on Hong Kong. The 1984 Sino-British Joint Liaison Group decided in 1989 that cooperation through Interpol should persist even after the return of Hong Kong to Chinese Sovereignty in 1997.[56] The fact that the two systems chose international cooperation mechanisms (Interpol and liaison officers) rather than measures more tailored to a regional context shows that the assumption of differences is greater than in regions with more coherent value systems, such as the EU. International mechanisms like Interpol can be seen as 'dams' rather than 'locks' or 'weirs' as cooperation on their basis is not automatic, but follows a case-by-case assessment.

While several bilateral regulated mechanisms exist in Greater China, cross-border law enforcement is still predominantly based on informal cooperation mechanisms. However, between Taiwan and Mainland China a formalised framework can be observed. At the same time both of these entities have not ratified the ICCPR and still apply the death penalty. It appears that similarities in human rights foster formalisation of cooperation mechanisms. If the common goal is considered a priority in the systems, the differences in the value base do not hinder cooperation as the anti-corruption cooperation between Mainland China and Hong Kong shows. China therefore provides a very good case study. Between all four systems in Greater China, formalisation did not occur, but bilateral formal cooperation exists between systems with greater similarities or with common goals. It also needs to be mentioned that despite the differences between the four systems there are common education and training initiatives, for example, between Mainland China, Macao and Hong Kong. These initiatives were described by officers to generate trust and enhance cooperation. The concept of trust seems therefore independent of human rights similarities in the police cooperation context.[57]

While the establishment of 'dams' in China is more prominent than in the EU, the deepening of channels through training can be observed in both systems. 'Dams' are therefore more likely created when human rights frameworks differ. 'Locks' or 'weirs' could not at all be observed despite the differences in legal systems that needed to be overcome. They therefore seem to be established when there is dissimilarity of criminal law and procedure and similarity of human rights, as well as a long cooperation history between systems.

6. Policing flows between the EU and China

China has opened up to cooperation with EU member states since the 1990s and has a number of mutual legal assistance agreements with EU member states. While all EU member states seem to be dealing with China at the international level in criminal matters, the nature and wording of the agreements is mainly not binding. However, specific cooperation exists in areas such as drug crimes.

The ideas of 'congestions', 'locks', 'weirs', 'dams' and 'directions' of flows shall now briefly be tested on the example of the EU and China. Observations on practitioner perceptions in this area could be made in particular throughout a study conducted in 2013 on police cooperation in China and the EU.[58] The differences in human rights regimes were the major impediment according to EU practitioners for the lack of cooperation with China. Cooperation between EU member states and the SARs of China was reported to be well working and supported by bilateral treaties on mutual assistance in Criminal Matters.[59] However, many EU member states (such as France, Estonia, Greece, Poland, Cyprus, Romania, Portugal, Spain, Bulgaria and Latvia) also have bilateral treaties established with China itself, though cooperation in practice remains limited.

Human rights discrepancies seem to lead to a lack of trust between agencies and practitioners. The treaties, in this case 'dams', that have been created between some EU member states and China do not create a higher level of trust. If the trust is lacking, treaties will not be used by practitioners and not enable flows of policing. This is an interesting observation as here the practitioner seems to have more impact on the protection of suspects than the nation state. This is a consequence of the creation of 'dams' rather than 'locks' or 'weirs' as a 'dam' allows only for case-by-case assessment concerning transfer of information, suspects, evidence, etc., while 'locks' and 'weirs' provide a permanent legal basis. A 'dam' regulation is therefore likely only as good as the trust between agencies and practitioners in the different systems using it, as it is up to their discretion to cooperate.

When looking at the creation of instruments between the EU and China more generally, it can be stated that there is only one treaty between the two systems concerning the detection of precursor chemicals.[60] As mentioned above, this treaty was a reaction to a specific type of crime (precursor chemicals are shipped legally from China into EU member states where they are illegally distributed to drug manufacturers).[61] The direction of the crime flow is here exclusively from China to the EU. However, with a view to individual member states, it can be observed that the cooperation with regard to precursors has led to wider cooperation and training initiatives between China and these member states, for example, meetings, seminars and training initiatives on the tracing of precursor chemicals.[62] While this cooperation is geared towards the creation of trust rather than a deepening of information channels, it could be seen as a training that enables police to at some stage use their discretion in favour of cooperating with China more extensively. With regard to Germany and China the project seems to be even more perspicacious. While Germany does not have a mutual legal assistance treaty with China, it has an MoU on Exchange and Cooperation in the Legal Area.[63] This MoU is supplemented with a number of 3-year programmes between China and Germany, for example, including the education of judges in China.[64] More than trust building between practitioners, these programmes are aimed at bringing the Chinese Criminal Justice System to a level acceptable for cooperation with Germany.

Opportunities for cooperation with all EU member states seem to exist mainly in specialised areas with a defined 'need' for cooperation. At the EU level, cooperation with China appears so far to be a one-way street. Information is given from China to the EU, but there is so far little evidence the other way. However, the existence of agreements on mutual legal assistance in criminal matters with some EU member states shows a growing trend for more formalised two-way cooperation. The existence of liaison officer exchanges between China and EU member states (and Europol) furthermore gives rise to the expectation that information exchange is not exclusively a one-way street from China towards the EU. The same is true for the Interpol channel, which is used between EU member states and China. However, both the Interpol channel and liaison officers are 'dams' to flows of policing and individuals can bar the information flow on a case-by-case basis.

Many member states also have established exchange programmes for officers and other law enforcement training programmes with China.[65] Engagement through exchanges and training is therefore a common strategy between EU member states and China. This engagement seems to be mainly geared at overcoming differences in human rights regimes that inhibit cooperation. The criminal law of China still specifies the death penalty for a number of offences. Cooperation in the area of these crimes is hence not possible for EU member states. However, cases in which EU cooperation is sought are usually high-level cases with considerable publicity and international relations implications attached to them. It is therefore highly unlikely that China would abuse the trust put into it by a cooperating EU member. However, fears of practitioners in Europe, in particular with a view to data protections laws and similar technicalities, can prevent information flows to China. An important point in creating trust and fostering cooperation would be education with regard to the systems involved. Knowledge about China and in particular offences and penalties as well as the related judicial and law enforcement practices is crucial to start building trust between the systems. Mechanisms like the German 3-year cooperation initiatives might eventually lead to practitioners using their discretion in favour of cooperating with China.

7. Conclusion

It can be concluded that 'congestions' or blockages exist in all relationships assessed. While these are mainly bureaucratic and legal in the EU, lack of trust resulting from different human rights regimes inhibits cooperation in Greater China and in the EU–China relationship. Within the EU, cooperation based on regulation deepened existing channels or overcame specific legal differences. The lack of similar human rights regimes led to the creation of 'dam' legislation in Greater China and the EU–China cooperation. Personal trust became crucial in the latter contexts as the 'dam' would only be opened when practitioners trusted each other. Lack of trust hence creates 'congestions'. These can be overcome in situations of political or institutional interests (creating institutional rather than personal trust). If the type of crime is a political priority or has a serious impact on society, 'dams' are opened as the example of corruption cooperation in Greater China and of precursor chemicals in the EU–China context show. It follows that political and institutional interests can overcome political differences and lack of personal trust.

Personal trust without regulation can create 'free flows', which can be observed in China and the EU, but not between them. Free flows are also dangerous as they have the potential to infringe individual rights. Only long-established personal and institutional trust between systems leads to the creation of 'locks' and 'weirs' as observed in the EU. Lack of institutional trust prevents the creation of regulation and impacts on the direction of flows. While, for example, China extradites suspects and prisoners to Hong Kong, Hong Kong does not extradite to China. While China provides information on precursor chemical shipments to the EU, similar information is not given to China.

Generally, personal and institutional trust is established in all systems by common goals, common norms/values and personal contacts. This becomes particularly apparent through the fact that all systems foster personal contacts through education and training. However, the three trust indicators do not have to be present at the same time. A common goal/interest can be the driver of institutional trust and even ensuing regulation despite major differences of human rights regimes between the cooperating systems. It also becomes very clear that the personal trust established to promote cross-border law enforcement is not necessarily related to institutional trust between the systems or agencies in general.

Common goals/interests and personal contacts can create personal and institutional trust independently of human rights similarities (common values). This is likely to produce outcomes detrimental to the rights of the defendant. This is today particularly apparent in the area of intelligence and information exchange on terrorism. The systems that own valuable information are not necessarily trusted systems (neither personally nor institutionally). Nevertheless, without their information terrorism policing in Western democracies would be impossible. So, despite the value discrepancies, political and criminal justice priorities force police to cooperate.

What can be asserted is that human rights do influence personal and institutional trust. The common human rights frameworks in the EU have impacted on how police can cooperate. Where a common norm/value basis is present, formal cooperation mechanisms are more likely to occur. This was also confirmed in the Chinese case study as similar systems cooperated more likely with a formalised legal basis. The major problem remains the specific situation of a discrepancy at the value level, but a similarity at the goal level.

Notes

1. Gordon and Miller, "The Fatal Police Shooting of Jean Charles de Menezes."
2. Franko, "Analysing a World in Motion," 291.
3. Ibid., 292.
4. Hufnagel, *Police Cooperation Across Borders*; and Hufnagel, "Strategies of Police Cooperation."
5. Lo, *The Politics of Cross-Border Crime*; and Block, *From Politics to Policing*.
6. Lo, *The Politics of Cross-Border Crime*.
7. Hufnagel, "Strategies of Police Cooperation."
8. Block, *From Politics to Policing*.
9. Hufnagel, *Police Cooperation Across Borders*.
10. Hufnagel, "Strategies of Police Cooperation."
11. Agreement between the European Community and the Government of the People's Republic of China on drug precursors and substances frequently used in the illicit manufacture of narcotic drugs or psychotropic substances, 30 January 2009, OJ 2009, L56/8.
12. BKA, *Synthetische Drogen und Grundstoffüberwachung*.
13. See, for example, den Boer, Hillebrand and Nölke, "Legitimacy under Pressure"; and Bowling and Sheptycki, *Global Policing*.
14. See for an overview of the literature considered in this article Hufnagel, 'Cross-Border Cooperation in Criminal Matters'.
15. Breakwell, *The Psychology of Risk*, 160.
16. See, for example, Hufnagel, *Police Cooperation Across Borders*, 86–87.
17. Ibid., Chapter 2.
18. Felsen, "European Police Cooperation."
19. Ibid.
20. Ibid.
21. Gallagher, "Sheer Necessity," 111, 121.
22. Council Decision of 6 April 2009 Establishing the European Police Office (Europol), [2009] OJ L 121/37; also 'Europol Decision', previously Europol Convention: Council Act of 26 July 1995 Drawing up the Convention based on Art K.3 of the Treaty on European Union on the Establishment of a European Police Office (Europol Convention), [1995] OJ C316/2.
23. Loader, "Policing, Securitisation and Democratisation in Europe," 126, 128.
24. Protocol Drawn up on the Basis of Article 43(1) of the Convention on the Establishment of a European Police Office (Europol Convention), Amending that Convention (Danish Protocol), [2004] OJ C2/3.
25. Mitsilegas, *EU Criminal Law*, 165.
26. Ibid., 165–166.
27. Hufnagel, *Police Cooperation Across Borders*, 85.
28. Ibid.
29. EU Council Act of 29 May 2000 Establishing in Accordance with Article 34 of the Treaty on European Union the Convention on Mutual Assistance in Criminal Matters between the Member States of the European Union, [2005] OJ C 197/3 (entered into force 23 August 2005); also '2000 Mutual Legal Assistance Convention' or simply 'Mutual Legal Assistance Convention'.

30. Hufnagel, *Police Cooperation Across Borders*, 221.
31. Block, "Combating Organised Crime in Europe," 76.
32. Ibid.
33. Hufnagel, *Police Cooperation Across Borders*, 218–219.
34. Council Decision of 15 July 2009 on the strengthening of Eurojust and amending Council Decision 2002/187/JHA setting up Eurojust with a view to reinforcing the fight against serious crime, (2009) OJ L 138/14; (henceforth also 'Eurojust Decision').
35. Criminal Procedure and Investigations Act 1996 (UK) p1, ss 1–21; Criminal Justice Act 2003 (UK) ss 32–39.
36. Rijken, "Joint Investigation Teams," 113.
37. Ibid., 114.
38. Interview with UK-NL JIT member cited in Block, "Combating Organised Crime in Europe," 80.
39. European Police College, "About CEPOL."
40. Ibid.
41. The Basic Law of the Hong Kong Special Administrative Region of the People's Republic of China (April 1990) (Basic Law) adopted on 4 April 1990 by the Seventh National People's Congress of the People's Republic of China at its 3rd Session.
42. Potter, "The Chinese Legal System," 673–674.
43. The Chinese Criminal Code, adopted at the Second Session of the Fifth National People's Congress on 1 July 1979; revised at the Fifth Session of the Eighth National People's Congress on 14 March 1997 and promulgated by Order No.83 of the President of the People's Republic of China on 14 March 1997.
44. The Chinese Code of Criminal Procedure, adopted by the Second Session of the Fifth National People's Congress on 1 July 1979 amended pursuant to the Decision on Amending the Criminal Procedure Law of the People's Republic of China adopted by the Fourth Session of the Eighth National People's Congress on 17 March1996 and amended 14 March 2012.
45. Potter, "The Chinese Legal System," 674.
46. Ghai, "The Intersection of Chinese Law and Common Law in the Special Administrative Region of Hong Kong," 13–14.
47. Luke, "The Imminent Threat to China's Intervention in Macau's Autonomy," 731.
48. Ibid.
49. Chiu and Fa, "Taiwan's Legal System and Legal Profession."
50. Greenleaf, *Asian Data Privacy Laws – Trade and Human Rights Perspectives*, 474.
51. Choy and Fu, "Cross-Border Relations in Criminal Matters," 227.
52. Ibid.
53. Cross-Strait Joint Crime-Fighting and Judicial Mutual Assistance Agreement between the Taiwan Straits Exchange Foundation and the Association for Relations Across the Taiwan Straits, 25 July 2009.
54. Lo, *The Politics of Cross-Border Crime in Greater China*, 173.
55. Choy and Fu, "Cross-Border Relations in Criminal Matters," 228.
56. Lo, *The Politics of Cross-Border Crime in Greater China*, 177.
57. Hufnagel, "Strategies of Police Cooperation," 394–398.
58. Ibid.
59. See, for example, Agreement between the Government of the Federal Republic of Germany and the Government of the Hong Kong Special Administrative Region of the People's Republic of China concerning Mutual Legal Assistance in Criminal Matters (29 January 2009).
60. Agreement between the European Community and the Government of the People's Republic of China on drug precursors and substances frequently used in the illicit manufacture of narcotic drugs or psychotropic substances, 30 January 2009, OJ 2009, L56/8.
61. BKA, "Synthetische Drogen und Grundstoffüberwachung."
62. Ibid.

63. Deutsch-Chinesische Vereinbarung zu dem Austausch und der Zusammenarbeit im Rechtsbereich, 30 June 2000.
64. Dreijahresprogramm zur Durchfuehrung der Deutsch-Chinesischen Vereinbarung zu dem Austausch und der Zusammenarbeit im Rechtsbereich 2013–2015.
65. UNODC, "Mutual Legal Assistance."

Disclosure statement

No potential conflict of interest was reported by the authors.

Bibliography

BKA (Bundeskriminalamt). Synthetische Drogen und Grundstoffüberwachung: BKA intensiviert Zusammenarbeit mit der Volksrepublik China. Wiesbaden: Bundeskriminalamt. Accessed March 17, 2016. http://www.polizei.de/DE/Presse/Pressemitteilungen/Presse2012/121128__PMSymposium__China.html Accessed February 26, 2016.

Block, L. "Combating Organised Crime in Europe: Practicalities of Police Cooperation." *Policing* 2 (2008): 74–81. doi:10.1093/police/pan009.

Block, L. *From Politics to Policing – The Rationality Gap in EU Council Policy-Making*. The Hague: Eleven International, 2011.

Bowling, B., and J. Sheptycki. *Global Policing*. London: Sage, 2012.

Breakwell, G. M. *The Psychology of Risk*. Cambridge: Cambridge University Press, 2007.

Chiu, H., and J.-P. Fa. "Taiwan's Legal System and Legal Profession." In *Taiwan Trade and Investment Law*, edited by M. A. Silk, 21–42. Oxford: Oxford University Press, 1994.

Choy, D. W., and H. Fu. "Cross-Border Relations in Criminal Matters." In *Introduction to Crime, Law and Justice in Hong Kong*, edited by M. S. Gaylord, D. Gittings, and H. Traver, 223–242. Hong Kong: Hong Kong University Press, 2009.

den Boer, M., C. Hillebrand, and A. Nölke. "Legitimacy under Pressure: The European Web of Counter-Terrorism Networks." *Journal of Common Market Studies* 46 (2008): 101–124. doi:10.1111/j.1468-5965.2007.00769.x.

European Police College (CEPOL). About CEPOL. Budapest: CEPOL. Accessed March 18, 2016. https://www.cepol.europa.eu/who-we-are/european-police-college/about-us

Felsen, O. "European Police Cooperation: The Example of the German-French Centre for Police and Customs Cooperation Kehl (GZ Kehl)." In *Cross-Border Law Enforcement Regional Law Enforcement Cooperation - European, Australian and Asia-Pacific Perspectives*, edited by S. Hufnagel, S. Bronitt, and C. Harfield, 73–86. London: Routledge, 2012.

Fichera, M. Mutual Trust in European Criminal Law. *Working Paper Series* 10. Edinburgh: University of Edinburgh, 2009.

Franko-Aas, K. "Analysing a world in motion - Global flows meet 'criminology of the other." *Theoretical Criminology* 11, no. 2 (2007): 283–303. doi:10.1177/1362480607075852.

Gallagher, D. F. "Sheer Necessity: The Kent Experience of Regional Transfrontier Police Cooperation." *Regional and Federal Studies* 12 (2002): 111–134. doi:10.1080/714004776.

Ghai, Y. "The Intersection of Chinese Law and Common Law in the Special Administrative Region of Hong Kong: Question of Technique or Politics?" In *One Country, Two Systems, Three Legal Orders – Perspectives of Evolution*, edited by J. Oliveira and P. Cardinal, 13–50. Berlin: Springer, 2009.

Gordon, I., and S. Miller. "The Fatal Police Shooting of Jean Charles de Menezes: Is Anyone Responsible?" In *Shooting to Kill: Socio-legal Perspectives on the Use of Lethal Force*, edited by S. Bronitt, M. Gani, and S. Hufnagel, 215–238. London: Hart, 2012.

Greenleaf, G. *Asian Data Privacy Laws – Trade and Human Rights Perspectives*. Oxford: Oxford University Press, 2014.

Hufnagel, S. *Police Cooperation Across Borders – Comparative Perspectives on Law Enforcement within the EU and Australia*. Farnham: Ashgate, 2013.

Hufnagel, S. "Strategies of Police Cooperation along the Southern Chinese Seaboard: A Comparison with the EU." *Crime, Law and Social Change* 61, no. 4 (2014): 377–399. doi:10.1007/s10611-013-9494-2.

Hufnagel, S. "Cross-Border Cooperation in Criminal Matters." In *Oxford Bibliographies in International Law*, edited by T. Carty. Oxford: Oxford University Press, 2014.

Lo, S. S.-H. *The Politics of Cross-Border Crime in Greater China – Case Studies of Mainland China, Hong Kong, and Macao*. New York: M.E. Sharpe, 2009.

Loader, I. "Policing, Securitisation and Democratisation in Europe." *Criminal Justice* 2 (2002): 125–153. doi:10.1177/1466802502002002716.

Luke, F. M. "The Imminent Threat to China's Intervention in Macau's Autonomy: Using Hong Kong's Past to Secure Macau's Future." *American University International Law Review* 15 (2000): 731–757.

Mitsilegas, V. *EU Criminal Law*. London: Hart, 2009.

Potter, P. B. "The Chinese Legal System: Continuing Commitment to the Primacy of State Power." *The China Quarterly* 159 (1999): 673–683. doi:10.1017/S0305741000003428.

Rijken, C. "Joint Investigation Teams: Principles, Practice, and Problems. Lessons Learnt from the First Efforts to Establish a JIT." *Utrecht Law Review* 2 (2006): 99–118. doi:10.18352/ulr.28.

United Nations Office on Drugs and Crime (UNODC). Mutual Legal Assistance. Vienna: UNODC. Accessed March 18, 2016. https://www.unodc.org

Crime analysis and cognitive effects: the practice of policing *through* flows of data

Carrie Sanders and Camie Condon

ABSTRACT
Crime analysis is the systematic analysis of crime for identifying and predicting risks and efficiently directing police resources. Adopting a social construction of technology framework, we explore the work of crime analysts to understand how they police through flows of data and how their work informs policing practices on the ground. Specifically we look at: (1) the organisational and cultural integration of crime analysis in Canada, (2) the technological support of analytic practices, and (3) the incorporation of crime analysis for policing practices. From this analysis, we argue that organisational understandings of crime analysis combined with the analytic platforms utilised have forced crime analysts to work within traditional police performance initiatives that both respond to and reinforce reactive policing practice. Crime analysis and the practice of policing through flows of data have changed the symbolic nature of policing while reaffirming traditional ways of knowing and policing.

Introduction

The early identification and subsequent arrests of the attempted Via Rail bombers in Ontario and the Boston Marathon bombers in the United States have highlighted the role crime analytics plays in contemporary crime control.[1] Crime analysis is described as the systematic analysis of crime for the purposes of assisting in crime prevention and control, the identification and apprehension of criminals, and evaluation of policing strategies.[2] The movement towards 'pre-emptive policing' through the identification of targets, risks and threats has led to the development of a new profession of people, crime analysts, with specialised analytical skills in policing.[3] Crime analysts turn raw information into 'actionable intelligence' that is used for predicting and managing crime.[4]

The utilisation of data analytics in new policing strategies, such as intelligence-led and predictive policing, is part of a recognition among police professionals that policing has evolved from the traditional model of random, reactive, and response-based activities[5] to encompass the pre-emptive management of a wide set of problems concerning risks to security.[6] These new policing missions, therefore, are organised around the collection and analysis of flows of data. To date, there has been much research and theorising on the policing *of* flows, such as flows of people, money, and transportation.[7] However, much less is known about how we police *through*, or by means of, flows. Crime and intelligence analysis presents an ideal setting for empirically studying policing through flows of data.[8] Adopting a social construction of technology framework, we qualitatively study the sociotechnical work of crime analysts for understanding *how* the flow of data informs contemporary policing practices.

Research in the social construction of technology has identified the importance of attending to the way users' interpret and interact with technology for understanding how technological innovation shapes and is shaped by organisational structures.[9] It recognises that technologies and users are co-constituted and embedded within socio-structural networks that facilitate and impede users' choices and actions.[10] Objects are not static entities, but instead are shaped by the meaning users ascribe to them and their 'processes of production, translation, circulation, appropriation, experimentation and resistance'.[11] For example, research on security devices illustrates how technologies affect and/or reflect 'the logics, rationalities and modes of reasoning of security practices'.[12] Such research has demonstrated how technologies have 'cognitive effects' wherein the normative and political ideals of their designers facilitate and constrain particular modes of interpretation and action.[13] Thus, close attention to the sociotechnical relations of crime analysts and intelligence technologies provides much-needed empirical insight into the production of intelligence and the impact policing *through* flows of data has on contemporary crime control.

In what follows, we review the literature on crime and intelligence analysis. We then look empirically at crime analysts' perspectives of: (1) the organisational and cultural integration of crime analysis in Canada, (2) the technological support of analytic practices, and (3) the utilisation of crime analysis and its perceived impact on policing practices. From this investigation, we argue that crime analysis, and by extension crime analysts, occupy a tenuous position in contemporary policing that is shaped by, as well as reinforced through, the integration of database policing. We argue that the division of labour, organisational context, and cultures of policing are configured into police technologies and shape intelligence production. This social shaping of technology, we argue, has led crime analysis to be oriented towards, while also reinforcing, what Manning (2010) refers to as the 'police métier' – a set of habits and assumptions that 'envisions only the need to control, deter and punish the visible and known contestants'.[14] The police métier reproduces 'deeply held assumptions about people, society, crime and its causes' that 'sustains the validity' of police practices.[15] Thus, crime analysis and the policing *through* flows of data have changed the *symbolic nature* of policing without significantly altering police practices on the ground.

Intelligence technologies and database policing

The available research on crime analysis originates largely from the United States and the United Kingdom, where police training, practices, and policies differ from those in Canada.[16] While scholarship on the *actual* work and *culture* of crime analysts is sparse, the few studies that are available identify a lack of fit and integration between crime analysts and their organisations due to poor analytical thinking, a culture that doesn't support innovation, and fragmentation and occupational divides.[17] This scholarship has identified challenges for the integration of analytic knowledge in policing due to an occupational police culture that values and relies upon experiential knowledge.[18] Crime analysis, therefore, represents the 'antithesis of traditional action-oriented work, which police officers have long valued over more mundane paperwork tasks'.[19] Cope's qualitative analysis on crime analysts identifies the importance of negotiating the differences between the contextualised and experiential knowledge of police officers and the decontextualised and analytical knowledge of analysts for generating 'legitimacy and respect for the knowledge produced by analysts so they can be viewed as a new generation of crime experts'.[20] Her research has also shown the perception of analysts and analytical products to be influenced by the gendered nature and hierarchical structure of police organisations.[21]

A larger body of research exists that focuses on the methodological techniques (such as social network analysis, hotspots, kernel density mapping) and technologies involved in crime analysis and their effectiveness for crime reduction and control.[22] Such scholarship, we fear, has become trapped within the 'police métier' by 'reflect[ing] the conventional wisdom about why and how policing works'.[23] It focuses on what works and 'what the police can do' – placing the focus on fighting crime by using measures such as crime rates and number of arrests to evaluate success – rather than studying the means and practices by which the work is being conducted, and the implications these practices have on the citizens they police.[24] For example, much of the research available on crime analysis focus on the technological with little attention to the organisational and cultural contexts in which the work occurs and the interpretive work that shapes the analysis.[25] Yet, ethnographies of police information technologies have identified 'functional disconnects'[26] in the practical implementation of technology because of the organisational and operational (i.e. cultural) contexts of their use.[27] For example, Chan nicely illustrates how police culture can act as an impediment to police innovation, technological adoption and police reform, while Sanders et al. illustrate how the police occupational culture of secrecy and silos facilitates and constrains how police officers make sense of and utilise technologies and intelligence-led strategies.[28] Thus, understanding crime analysis requires a focus on the interpretive actions and understandings of analysts within the structural and cultural contexts and material realities that influence, shape, and guide them.[29]

Further, by researchers treating analytic technologies and crime analysts as distinct objects of analysis, the scholarship has ascribed objectivity to analytic products that ignore the 'subjective and interpretive practices … involved in their manufacture, and the contingencies and limitations of the products'.[30] However, as research in the social construction of technology has shown, the 'authority of a scientific fact is socially produced, rather than an inherent quality of the object being studied'.[31] Objectivity, they argue, is 'tied to a relentless search to replace individual volition and discretion in depiction by the invariable routines of mechanical reproduction'.[32] For example, sociological analyses of policing have shown how information stored on police records management systems (RMS) are not objective measures of crime and offending, but are instead the product of police practices and subjective decision-making on the ground.[33]

Police data, therefore, is dirty data – often containing inaccuracies that are 'routinely compensated for and often glossed over by crime analysts'.[34] Crime analysts spend their time doing 'database policing' (Ericson and Haggerty 1997); they find, collect, preprocess, and 'design and conduct analyses in response to ever-changing crime conditions, review and interpret the results of these analyses and exclude erroneous findings, analyse the integrated findings and make recommendations about how to act on them'.[35] A central part of crime analysis involves the analyst evaluating information for both its credibility and reliability.[36] In fact, the 'importance of evaluation in intelligence production cannot be underestimated as a failure to conduct it properly will undoubtedly result in a failure of intelligence'.[37] Joseph and Corkhill conducted a focused group interview with six intelligence analysts to interrogate this evaluation process and found that these analysts do not use formal evaluation processes, but instead rely predominately on informal processes that are self-taught on the job.[38] Yet, the interpretive and subjective decisions embedded within these evaluations, and the construction of crime data, become hidden by the use of non-transparent technologies and algorithms.[39] Interestingly, while crime and intelligence analysts are perceived to hold a central role within the production of policing intelligence,[40] there is little empirical research available on the work they do.[41] In fact, Innes et al. were the first scholars to open this line of inquiry by drawing upon the sociology of scientific knowledge framework to understand and make sense of the everyday work and practice of crime analysts.[42] Their groundbreaking research not only identified the subjective and interpretive work embedded within analytic products but also drew attention to the need for more grounded analyses on the sociotechnical work practices of analysts.

Methodology

In order to conduct a study of crime analysis that is critically attentive to the sociotechnical relations that make up analytic products, we employed ethnographic methods. By studying the *in situ* use of analytic technologies, we were able to uncover the way organisational users 'enact structures which shape their emergent and situated use of that technology'.[43] Ethnography provided analytic leverage for understanding how meanings ascribed to crime analysis become embedded within analytic technologies, which in turn facilitate and constrain use.[44]

We conducted 42 intensive interviews with crime analysts from eight different police services across Canada. While both crime and intelligence analysts participated in the study, for the purposes of this paper, we focus only on the perspectives and experiences of the 42 crime analysts (also referred to as district analysts or generalists). Unlike intelligence analysts who are often assigned to speciality units (such as gang crime units, drug units, homicide), crime analysts worked more closely with administration and front-line patrol officers. Whenever possible, we conducted interviews in the work settings so as to see the technologies and skills in action, while being attentive to the 'infostructure' and 'info-culture' that shape analytic work.[45] Interviews were supplemented with observation at crime analytic workshops and conferences. All data were stored and analysed in NVivo 10, a qualitative data analysis software program, using a constructivist-grounded theory approach.[46] Constructivist grounded theory prioritises the participants' understandings of their experiences, while incorporating a reflexive analysis that draws upon pre-existing theories and concepts (such as: technological frames, police métier, cognitive effects, and crime analysis) to guide the interpretation and focused coding. From this analysis, we provide empirical insight into the way analysts construct crime knowledge through flows of data. Not unlike previous ethnographic scholarship on the integration of information technologies and analytics in policing, we argue that the integration of analytics has not changed front-line practice, but instead has altered the *symbolic* nature of policing. Specifically, we argue that the sociotechnical work of analysts has been informed, and shaped, by the broader police métier and thus provides cognitive effects that reaffirm the world as it is known to police.

Defining and understanding crime analysis

Crime analysis is a relatively new and nascent profession in Canadian policing. It was not until 2000 that Ontario police services were mandated to have a crime analysis capacity to enhance intelligence gathering and reporting.[47] While a crime analysis capacity was mandated, there was little specificity provided regarding its implementation. As a result, there are significant variations among crime analysis units – with some units consisting of 1 crime analyst while others having 20 or more. There are also variations in operational models, with some services having only civilian crime analysts, and others having police officers, while still others include a mix of civilian and police analysts.

Civilian analysts are a heterogeneous group made up of internal transfers from other administrative positions 'where they are already embedded within the culture of policing' (I19) and external applicants. *Police analysts*, on the other hand, have been assigned to the unit. Many police analysts describe their placement in analysis as one of being 'parachuted' (I21) and 'dropped into the position' (I11, I13) or being sent to the 'penalty box' (I21).

> The biggest disadvantage for me was that *I was just put into this position* … it's not like I applied for it and it's not like I really did know exactly what it was about before I came to it, other than the fact that you know *they did some street checks and they sent out a report* … (I11, *emphasis added*).
> I'd *gotten myself into some trouble* … You get dropped in the *penalty box* – whether that's the central alternate response unit, where they take the reports over the phone … or the crime analyst's office where you have no public contact. *They get you off the street* … so typically your cadre of crime analysts are typically made up of your troubled coppers … or they're walking wounded, or they're retirees … that's pretty much what the penalty box consists of. And we're satisfied with that, because you *do no harm in an office, right*? (I21)

The experiences of the officers above shed important insight into the integration and organisational 'fit' of data-driven practices in policing. The first officer (I11) was placed into analysis after an injury. He was largely unaware of the position and had very little analytic training, skill, or knowledge. The second officer, who also had little analytic training and expertise, described his placement in crime analysis as a form of 'punishment'. His description of analysis as the 'penalty box' illustrates a division between what is perceived as 'real police work' and the work of 'crime analysts'. This perception of crime analysis as a 'penalty box' – a place for injured, ill or 'troubled coppers' (I21) – carries important cultural implications for crime analysis, as it devalues both the work that analysts do and who is doing the work. As the following analyst explains, 'the culture of policing has a "pecking order" and the culture dictates the order, and as an analyst you are down on that pecking order – you are an administrator' (field notes).

Analysts' education background (e.g. high school, college, undergraduate, and graduate school) and disciplinary training (e.g. policing, city planning, social work, geography, computer science, sociology, psychology, and criminology) also varied. Although there are no required training courses, analysts typically complete the Tactical and Strategic Intelligence Analyst courses delivered by the Canadian Police College. As one analyst explains,

> We really have no accreditation accepted or unified accreditation program north of the border in Canada. So what we typically do as analysts is either attach ourselves to the International Association of Law Enforcement Intelligence Analysis (IALEIA) and grab their Fiat course and their certification, or you know, you go to the International Association of Crime Analysts (IACA) and get their certification. Either way you are getting some type of training (I21).

For many analysts, and in line with previous research on crime analysis, training, 'experience and expertise were developed' (I06) through peer learning.[48] Services would send one person to a training course and that person would then become the 'resident expert and was expected to walk everybody through it' (I19). While there are limited training opportunities for crime analysts, there is even less provided to police officers.

The following field note excerpt highlights how the lack of organisational training provided on crime analysis both constrains and impedes data analytics and algorithmic practices.

> The real problem is that the officers are dictating the end product. *The officers are giving us the problem and asking us to verify it.* We don't have the chance to do analysis because the bar set within the police service is low, we are simply 'query clerks'. Even when an analyst is sent away on a workshop or training conference and learns these great analysis skills, *how do you develop skill sets when you are forced to continue doing what you were doing before? For analysis to be analysis, we need to stop having them give us the problem and instead let us tell them something.* For something to be an analysis product means it must have strategic and tactical utility. Strategic and tactic focus needs to be our goal, but we end up simply 'crime reporting'. Its not that analysts need autonomy within the organization, they need 'creative licence' to educate someone and to educate consumers as to what types of analysis can be done for various types of consumers (Fieldnotes, *emphasis added*).

The field note excerpt above illuminates how the lack of analytic knowledge provided to police officers both *constrains* analytic development and *impedes* the integration of analysis. As the analyst explains, the police officers that supervise analysts often dictate what the end product is to be, but without knowledge of what analysis is, or what it can do, analysts are often left to provide products that 'verify' and reaffirm problems already known to police. Crime analysis, as a result, has become oriented towards, while also reinforcing, the broader police métier; it is used to report and verify known and visible crimes. Further, while the integration of analytics is *impeded* by a lack of organisational knowledge of crime analysis, it is also *constrained* by this lack of knowledge because analysts are not provided opportunities to utilise and learn advanced analytic skills and techniques.

The lack of organisational investment in analytic training combined with the placement of civilians and 'troubled coppers' (I21) in analysis has rendered it a marginalised field within policing. As one analyst remembers:

I had this boss that didn't know, and he was kind of a little bit bullying at first, because he goes, '... how much do you get paid? *Like is it worth having someone like you, what are you, a data entry clerk?'*... And there is a joke that 'oh, you're the civilians, oh, you guys go for coffee and you guys sit pretty up in the office.' And there is that joke, but then they know that no, it's not easy, like we're not kicking up our shoes and watching Oprah all day. ... yeah we're doing *real work* (I36).

The analyst's experience above identifies the tenuous position crime analysts occupy within policing wherein they are faced with a cultural perception of their work as being administrative 'data entry' clerical work that is not *'real'* police work. The above quote highlights a lack of organisational understanding around what crime analysis *is*, and by extension, what crime analysts *do*. As another analyst explained, 'it's such an undefined position that anything that has to do with information, organisations will be like, "oh, let's just make a crime analyst do it"'(I30). One analyst went as far as to say that police administrators (those with decision-making powers) don't have a desire to understand analysis, but have 'done what the government mandated. They have crime analysts [who can] provide that statistical data, *which they see as intelligence* ...'(I18). Thus, how organisations perceive and define intelligence and analysis shapes how they integrate and utilise their crime analysts.

Crime analysts explained how much of what they do in a day is writing 'crime reports' and 'making pretty pictures' for police administrators and management. Such crime reports focus on,

telling [administration] 'here are your problem areas and your priorities,' *I don't tell them where their priorities are*, but here are your strengths and weaknesses and here's what's going on in the city, long term wise here is how it relates to what's been happening in the past' and from *that [they] can choose what [their] priorities and ... focuses are as a depart-ment* (I30).

Analysts, as described above, use flows of information to develop reports that identify past crime rates and trends. Interestingly, these crime reports do 'not tell them where their priorities are', but instead allow the administrators to 'choose what their priorities and focuses are'. In this way, the analyst has consolidated and synthesised the crime data for her manager, but the analysis – the turning the data into actionable intelli-gence – is left to the administrator. The use of crime analysts for crime reporting, and not for intelligence analysis is clearly evidenced in the following quote:

Crime analysis *is a necessity for managers to reach their goals*. So I mean crime analysis is *pretty robust* across the board because of that reason. If the manager needs the information, it's Comp Stat, or they need the information to show their bosses their accountability, you will always find a manager who has an analyst at hand to do that kind of work for them. *Intelligence is a frill* ... when you're talking about dollar and cents within departments. It is a luxury to have a good intelligence unit and it's a luxury to have intelligence analysis (I31, *emphasis added*)

The analyst above identifies how crime analysis has become 'robust' because of its perceived managerial and accountability value. He also identifies a clear hierarchical distinction between crime and intelligence ('frill') analysis.[49] Further, the analyst draws attention to the economic and organisational shaping of analysis by inferring that crime analysis (in this particular case, the reporting of crime) is less expensive than what 'good intelligence' costs police services.[50] The little education and training provided *coupled* with the lack of an agreed-upon definition and understanding of crime analysis has led analysts to spend their time synthesising information for the purposes of identifying and reporting on *past* crimes and crime trends, which, as one analyst explained, 'is crime reporting. There's no analysis there – [it] describes things that have happened'(I21).

Interestingly, the emphasis placed on 'report writing' and 'making pretty pictures' is in line with earlier research on crime analysis [51] and reinforces the argument that 'introducing crime analysis ... may not produce expected returns for new policing paradigms that incorporate these approaches ... unless officers see these alternative approaches as "real police work"'.[52] Further, our analysis signals that regardless of the growing discussions and enthusiasm for predictive policing and algorithmic analysis, the everyday practices of crime analysts do not appear to have significantly changed.[53]

Technological platforms and the shaping of analysis

While many analysts felt that their work was not well integrated or utilised by their organisation, they also believed they were not doing sophisticated analysis because they 'don't have the programs that are capable of pushing that analysis' (I10). Questions regarding the functionality of technology are essential for understanding or assessing its effectiveness.[54] Technical effectiveness is not only about its performance but also includes 'its management and implementation, for example, the adequacy of infrastructure, degree of integration with existing tools, and availability of high-quality training and support'.[55] Similar to previous ethnographic research on the integration of information technologies in policing, analysts identified numerous technological problems, such as a lack of interoperability with different databases and technological platforms, inadequate technological infrastructures, poor data quality, and poor analytic and technological training. For example, as described above, many analysts noted that they lacked training in important analytic skills and were required to learn through on-the-job training. The lack of high quality training provided to analysts draws attention to user capacity and capability constraints in regards to their analytic skill. Further, the technological challenges facing analysts, we argue, raise important questions about the organisational support and utilisation of analysis, and, more interestingly, the *type* of analyses being conducted.

Research in the social construction of technology has illustrated how the adoption and rejection of technology is shaped by the definition and meaning users ascribe to their interactions with it.[56] The perceptions and meanings crime analysts ascribe to their technologies are situated within their particular 'technological frames'.[57] As the following crime analyst explains:

> There is a challenge of us trying to get the information out ... because the operation of Niche and our needs [differ]. Just to give you a small idea, if I'm looking for a male, white, six feet with red hair, I need my query to meet all those criteria. And with Niche it checks each thing individually, so then I will get all the male, whites, and then I'll get all the six foot, and I'll get all the red hair. It won't give me all of them .... So our hands have ... been tied ... by the fact that our service has decided that everyone shall use Niche and that will be your only resource, which is difficult for the crime analyst because our use is a lot different from other people. It is hard to pull data out of there (I04).

THE POLICING OF FLOWS

The analyst above identifies the existence of differing 'technological frames' among crime analysts, police officers, and administrators that impact the effectiveness of police technologies for analysis. As another analyst explains, the police RMS has been designed for police services to comply with the Canadian Centre for Justice Statistics (CCJS) for the Uniform Crime Reporting (UCR). UCR codes are 'applied traditionally to a maximum of four violations or offences per incident. Every police service across Canada is mandated to submit their UCR data to Statistics Canada'.[58] Many analysts discussed the difficulty the RMS and UCR processes pose to crime analysis because 'the 5th and 6th offences, while not perceived as necessary for reporting, are very important for analysis' (I21).

Further, the standardised format for CCJS reporting has placed the *incident/occurrence* as the object of analysis. However, crime analysts are often interested in both the occurrence and the people. The different objects of analysis have introduced a 'fundamental flaw' (I02) in the technologies utilised for crime analysis (Regional crime analysis training workshop field notes, 2014). The following quote illuminates this 'fundamental flaw:'

> I can do an occurrence search in Niche, I can tell you how many thefts of autos we had between this date and this date ... [But] who did them? That's a problem because a person query is different ... there is no way to set up a query that'll say 'okay, it relates to charges of the person rather than to the occurrences, so they never meet.' It's like a magnet on the wrong end (I02).

The differing objects of analyses, therefore, have left analysts having to navigate 'orphaned databases' and 'flat files' and to spend the 'majority of their time working to access data and not doing analysis' (I21). Analysts being forced to work with technological platforms that focus on the incident undermines meaningful analyses by 'undercut[ting] systematic and generalisable modes of performance evaluation and analysis of long-term crime patterns'.[59] Using the incident as the object of analysis, we argue, orients crime analysis towards the police métier, while the intelligence product produced reinforces the police métier.

Presently, there are no standards or regulations regarding technological adoption in Canadian police services. The lack of regulation means that police services not only make individual decisions regarding IT adoption and enhancement[60] but also create agency-specific IT guidelines. Analysts frequently noted that when technology decisions and policies are made they are not being consulted, and by default, analytic needs and purposes are not incorporated. For example, police IT guidelines dictate what external databases, websites, platforms, and programs can be used and accessed on the police network. Many analysts noted that their services have limited, and in some cases denied, access to social media platforms (e.g. Facebook, Twitter). This is an important insight as our findings above demonstrate how different technological platforms (such as Niche, Versaterm, i2) construct different affordances. If police services are turning to algorithmic analysis for guiding contemporary policing strategies than it is important that analytic needs be incorporated in IT decisions. Further, the IT constraints experienced by crime analysts raise important questions about the size and variety of data sets analysts *actually* work with when conducting analysis. This is an important finding because it raises questions about the technological, organisational, and cultural capabilities of Canadian police services to undertake algorithmic and predictive analytics that are dependent on large quantities of data.[61]

The technological infrastructures crime analysts work with require them to do creative workarounds and 'invisible labour'[62] in order to find, gather, consolidate, and analyse data. For example, analysts have brought in stand-alone computers, not connected to the police network, to access different platforms, and designed their own databases, such as a 'tactical occurrence database' (I02), 'sex crime Modus Operandi template' (I30) or 'relational database' (I39), in order to overcome the challenges they face when doing database queries because of the 'flat files' (I30) stored in traditional RMS. As the following analyst explains,

> The only way you can do a [relational query] is if you pull the unstructured data (intelligence narratives) out of your records management system, compile it into a relational database, and reorganize it … and draw the table and link relationships so that you can then run these queries against it (I 39).

These technological challenges illuminate the existence of differing, and at times competing, 'technological frames' that impact the effectiveness of police technologies for crime analysis. The existence of differing technological frames and invisible labour reaffirms how analytic reasoning and automated methods appear to run counter to traditionally valued, experiential, action-oriented ways of using information in policing.[63] These organisational and technological challenges facing crime analysis, therefore, leave analysts having to 'pull the unstructured data out' in order to conduct analyses (I39). Interestingly, much intelligence data are generated in ways that are not necessarily digital or easily digitised and thus require the interpretive work of analysts. It is the 'translation of raw information into operationally viable intelligence that analysis plays its crucial role'.[64] It is to this invisible and interpretive labour that we turn to now in order to understand how policing through flows of data shapes policing practices.

Cognitive effects and the reappropriation of analysis

Crime analysts construct a variety of analytic products, such as crime maps, crime reports, and linkage charts. As noted earlier, much of what an analyst produces is dictated by his/her direct supervisor. Analysts noted that they spend much of their time creating weekly crime reports and bulletins to assist officers with routine patrols and investigation duties. The weekly report is a compilation and summary of index occurrences such as theft from auto, break, and enter and robbery. The formatting of this data typically covers a designated, previous week, date rage; however, other formats include the previous 30, 60, or 90 days. The weekly report serves to inform patrol of active crime areas and assist with directing patrols. A bulletin is designed to seek out and share information regarding ongoing investigations. Bulletins include information such as suspect photos, target locations, offender modus operandi and trends in date and time of offences. Depending on technological capabilities, including IT configurations and bandwidth capabilities, some services allow officers to access these reports through the patrol car mobile computer terminals. Many of the analysts noted how much of the data incorporated in their weekly reports and crime bulletins come from street checks. Street checks are notes provided by officers on occurrences or activities occurring in their zones that appear suspicious or seem noteworthy for others. As the following analyst explains:

THE POLICING OF FLOWS

> we put out a weekly crime report … based on all of the incidents the officers do, based on
> the street checks, so all of our officers have the ability to put in street checks. Which is just
> intel that they gather together when they're on the street … so we gather all this data and
> we do our analysis on all the reports and the incidents. We talk to other police services and
> we do our maps and our stats and everything and we put these reports together and it goes
> to the streets and they can access it from their Mobile Data Terminals (I10)

Not only did analysts provide a weekly crime report but they also create crime maps that highlight the major crimes of interest to the district officers (such as break and enters, theft from autos).

One analytic product that analysts believe is highly valued by front-line patrol officers is a map that identifies recently released offenders. As the following analyst explains,

> Our IT department created a data base a few years ago that actually pulls offenders, so
> that's each offender in our system that has a Known Offender number. So it pulls out that
> entity and it puts them into a report through a cue in COGNOS and it has their address.
> Their current address – the XY coordinate – so we can map it and then any addresses of
> crimes they've committed. So then we can throw it onto a map and you know, let's say that
> we had a couple of armed robberies in a couple of areas. We can pull up a radius around
> that and show every known offender that is living there now with that crime type Um …
> It's … it's amazing (I10).

Thus, crime analysts, through subjective and interpretive decision-making, pull information out of police records and street checks (which are themselves subjective narratives) and collate, synthesise, and analyse the data to construct 'intelligence' products. Through this sociotechnical work, objectivity is ascribed to the product, because it is believed that the analysis has 'taken the subjectivity out of it' (I21). As one analyst explains,

> I can now identify these hotspots … with certain confidence, statistically speaking. So I can
> now say that there is something going on there. So the risks … are greater in these areas
> than in the areas that are cold (I21).

These crime reports, as a Canadian police chief explains, provide '*analytical evidence*, our grounds to be working in the neighbourhood where we need to be'. (field notes) These products are used to '*suggest* where to patrol' (I13), and to encourage officers to 'do some directed patrol in their down time … and do some surveillance in that area' (I05). These reports, therefore, provide suggestions on where to go. They do not tell officers definitively, nor do they explain why problems exist there, but instead they draw attention to areas of concern and/or possible crime trends.

Crime reports and maps, we argue, have 'cognitive effects' that impact the policing of communities.[65] They 'project ideas, interpretations and representations of space … that reflect the conventions, norms and values underlying' the technologies and practices used to construct them.[66] For example, the technological platforms and data used to construct analytic products, as demonstrated earlier, are shaped by traditional police performance initiatives and practices which are not geared towards intelligence analysis but reinforce the police métier. The following interview excerpt with a crime analyst illustrates how her analysis is shaped by the norms, values, and practices of police management:

> … I try to keep track of our frequent flyers out of my division that I know of. Because as
> soon as they get out you know your stats are going up through the roof. Well that in turn is

> gonna affect the strategic intelligence meeting and your superintendent having to explain what's going on. And so I'm trying to cut off a lot of stuff from happening month over month by tracking those people or looking for those links. (I18)

The analyst's quote above illustrates how analysis is oriented towards the police métier as it is shaped by the norms and values of traditional policing practices. Thus, analytic products that are derived from street checks and police reports, we argue, 'sustain the validity of [police] practices because they are based on the same assumptions'.[67] In this way, analytic reports, which are to guide proactive policing, are directed at what Ericson referred to as 'ordering the street' by targeting resources on those identified as being out of order to put them back in order (1981). As a result, the analytic products constructed from police databases and technological platforms *reaffirm* traditional ways of knowing and policing. In this way, crime analysis is not being used for pre-emptive, pre-crime policing and accountability, but is instead being reappropriated for traditional policing practice.

Crime analysts synthesise, articulate, and visualise crime data for police. The analytic products produced by analysts do not tell police how to address the problem, or explain why it is happening. Instead, the information they provide is *analysed* and made *actionable* through the interpretive work of police managers and officers. As the following analyst explains,

> Typically it's not crime analysis that's being done, it's crime reporting. They're reporting things that have happened ... they're articulating, they're visualizing things that have already occurred. There's some value to that, but it's certainly not analytical. It's not analytical value. (I21)

Crime analysis, therefore, does not change or challenge traditional police practices or ways of knowing, but instead reaffirms it while changing the symbolic nature of policing.

Conclusion

By employing a social construction of technology framework and ethnographic methods, we have conducted an analysis that problematises, rather than reaffirms the police métier, by providing a 'sociologically grounded theory of policing as practice'.[68] We illuminate the tenuous place crime analysis, and by extension crime analysts, hold within contemporary policing in Canada. Our analysis draws attention to the way in which the technological frames of crime analysts run counter to traditional action-oriented practices of policing and ways of using information to make decisions.[69] By focusing on 'technological frames',[70] we demonstrate how definitional understandings of crime analysis, as well as the division of police labour and the occupational culture of policing, are embedded within analytic technologies that, in turn, facilitate and constrain the production of intelligence. Further, by being analytically attentive to both the sociotechnical context and cultures of policing, we have uncovered the ways in which crime analysis is oriented towards, while also reinforcing, the broader police métier.

As such, our study challenges many of the claims and rhetoric surrounding data-driven pre-crime policing. Our analysis, for example, identifies how organisational policies and technological platforms pose significant constraints on the type and amount of data accessible for analysis. Intelligence-led and predictive policing are 'premised on analysing large volumes of data using advanced technology and applying a methodical analytic process that generates defendable conclusions in a timely manner that can lead to a predicted outcome'.[71] While there is a growing literature base across North America concerning the adoption and utilisation of information technologies for the manipulation of intelligence data for intelligence-led and predictive policing,[72] much of the literature is theoretical or methodological in nature – often analysing the technologies, platforms, and analytic techniques in isolation from their organisational, cultural, and social contexts of use. Yet, as Bennett Moses and Chan argue, in order to assess the suitability and effectiveness of big data and algorithmic practices in policing requires an examination along three dimensions: technical (i.e. functionality and effectiveness of technologies and platforms), social (practitioner update and perspectives towards the technology), and normative (ethics and values of the user).[73] Our findings identify how the integration and utilisation of crime analysis are challenged along the technical, social, and normative dimensions of policing, which in turn, raise critical questions about the suitability and effectiveness of contemporary policing driven by algorithmic practices.

Further, our analysis sheds light on the often invisible and subjective labour of crime analysts that becomes hidden within the analytic technologies and algorithms they use.[74] Injustices, however, can be perpetuated when we do not understand how crime data are being collected, analysed, and interpreted.[75] Finally, our analysis demonstrates how crime analysis is shaped by and oriented towards the police métier,[76] which in turn raises concerns that the processes through which crime analysts police *through* flows of data create cognitive effects that can lead to technologically augmenting the policing of usual suspects.[77] Organisational understandings and perceptions of crime analysis *combined* with the analytic platforms utilised for analysis, have forced crime analysts to work within traditional police performance initiatives (i.e. crime reporting and crime counting) that *reinforce* and *technologically augment* reactive policing practice. Thus, crime analysis, and the practice of policing *through* flows of data, has changed the *symbolic* nature of policing while reaffirming traditional ways of knowing and policing.

Notes

1. FCW, "Boston Probe's Big Data."
2. Boba Santos, *Crime Analysis with Crime Mapping*.
3. Ericson, *Making Crime*; and O'Malley, *Risk, Uncertainty and Government*.
4. Cope, 'Intelligence-led Policing or Policing-led'.
5. Whitelaw et al., 'Community-based Strategic Policing'.
6. Sheptycki, 'Beyond Cycle of Intelligence-led'; and Coyne and Bell, 'Strategic Intelligence in Law-Enforcement'.
7. Bedford, 'Whitelists, Jurisdictional Reputation'.
8. De Lint et al., 'Controlling the Flow: Security, Exclusivity, and Criminal Intelligence in Ontario'.
9. Orr, *Ethnography of a Modern Job*; and Suchman, *Plans and Situated Actions*.
10. Amicelle and Jacobsen, 'Banking policing in UK and India'.
11. Amicelle et al., 'Questioning Security Devices', 294.
12. Ibid., 297.
13. Grove, 'Crowdmapping Security and Sexual Violence'
14. Manning, *Democratic Policing in a Changing World,*200
15. Ibid., 202; see also Sheptycki, 'Liquid modernity and the police *métier;* thinking about information flows in police organisation'.

16. Ratcliffe, 'Crime Mapping, Training Needs'.
17. Evans and Kebbell, 'The Effective Analyst'; Cope, 'Intelligence-led Policing or Policing-led'; Innes et al.,'Theory and Practice of Crime Intelligence', Manning, *The Technology of Policing*; Ratcliffe, 'Crime Mapping and Implications'; and Darroch and Mazerole, 'Organizational Factors Influencing Uptake'.
18. Gill, *Rounding Up Usual Suspects*.
19. Cope, 'Intelligence-led Policing or Policing-led', 200.
20. Ibid., 202.
21. Ibid., 198.
22. Chin et al., 'Analytical Process of Intelligence Analysis'; Boba Santos, *Crime Analysis with Crime Mapping*; and Prox and Griffiths, 'Introduction to Special Issue'.
23. See above 14.
24. Ibid., 106.
25. Perry et al., *Predictive Policing*, xix.
26. Sanders and Henderson, 'Police 'Empires' and Information Technologies."
27. Dunworth, 'Criminal Justice and IT Revolution'; Chan, *Changing Police Culture*; Chan, 'Police and New Technologies'; Hughes and Jackson, 'Technical, Social and Structural Factors'; Manning, 'Information Technology, Crime Analysis'; Manning, 'Theorizing Policing'; Manning, *The Technology of Policing*; Manning, 'Information Technology and Police Work'; and Sanders and Hannem, 'Policing the "Risky"'.
28. Chan, 'The Technological Game'; Sanders et al., 'Police Innovations'.
29. Sanders et al., 'Discovering Crime in a Database'.
30. Innes et al., 'Theory and Practice of Crime Intelligence', 54.
31. See above 12.
32. Daston and Galison, 'The Image of Objectivity', 98.
33. Sanders and Hannem, 'Policing the "Risky"'.
34. See above 30.
35. Perry et al., *Predictive Policing*, xix.
36. Corkhill, 'Evaluation a Critical Point'.; de Lint et., 'Controlling the Flow: Security, Exclusivity, and Criminal Intelligence in Ontario'.
37. Joseph and Corkhill, 'Information Evaluation'; Corkhill, 'Evaluation a critical point'; Marrin and Clemente, 'Improving Intelligence Analysis'.
38. Joseph and Corkhill, 'Information Evaluation'.
39. Bennett Moses and Chan, 'Big Data for Legal and Law Enforcement'.
40. Lefebvre, 'A Look at Intelligence Analysis'.
41. See above 38.
42. Innes et al., 'Theory and Practice of Crime Intelligence'.
43. Orlikowski, 'Using Technology and Constituting Structures'
44. Van den Scott et al., 'Reconceptualizing Users'.
45. Hughes and Jackson, 'Technical, Social and Structural Factors'.
46. Charmaz, *Constructing Grounded Theory*.
47. O. Reg. 3/99, s. 5 (1).
48. Cope, 'Intelligence-led Policing or Policing-led'; and Piza and Feng, 'Crime Analysts Evaluations'.
49. This is an important insight and one that requires further analysis. For example, what are the similarities and differences between the work and organisational fit of crime and intelligence analysts? What factors facilitate or impede the organisational adoption and utilisation of crime and intelligence analysis?
50. This realisation is worthy of further exploration in order to better understand the ways in which economic, political, and cultural contexts shape, facilitate, and impede crime and intelligence analysis.
51. Innes et al., 'Theory and Practice of Crime Intelligence'; and Manning, *The Technology of Policing*.

52. Lum et al., 'Limits of Technology's Impact', 23; and Bennett Moses and Chan, 'Algorithmic Prediction in Policing'.
53. We thank an anonymous reviewer for this important insight.
54. Bennett Moses and Chan, 'Big Data for Legal and Law Enforcement'; and Lum, Koper and Willis, 'Limits of Technology's Impact'.
55. Bennett Moses and Chan, 'Big Data for Legal and Law Enforcement', 653.
56. Oudshoorn and Pinch, *How Users Matter*.
57. Bijker, 'Theory of Sociotechnical Change'.
58. Waterloo Region Police Service website, http://www.wrps.on.ca/inside-wrps/corporate-planning-systems#UCR.
59. See above 14.
60. It is important to note, that depending on the size of the service, IT decisions can be based on an individual service needs (e.g. RCMP, Toronto and Ottawa Police Services or Vancouver Police Department) or on a network of services (e.g. PRIDE network which incorporates Waterloo, Brantford, Stratford and Guelph police services)
61. Bennett Moses and Chan, 'Big Data for Legal and Law Enforcement'; and Sanders and Sheptycki, 'Policing, rime, "Big Data"'.
62. Star, 'Invisible Work and Silenced Dialogues'; Star, 'Politics of Formal Representations'; an d Star and Strauss, 'Layers of Silences'.
63. Bennett Moses and Chan, 'Big Data for Legal and Law Enforcement'; and Cope, 'Intelligence-led Policing or Policing-led'.
64. See above 19.
65. Grove, 'Crowdmapping Security and Sexual Violence'; and Ratcliffe and McCullagh, 'Police Perceptions of High Crime'.
66. Amicelle et al., 'Questioning Security Devices'.
67. Manning, *Democratic Policing in a Changing World*, 202
68. See above 24.
69. Bennett Moses and Chan, 'Big Data for Legal and Law Enforcement'; Chan, 'The Technological Game'; and Cope, 'Intelligence-led Policing or Policing-led'.
70. See above 43.
71. Prox and Griffith, 'Introduction to Special Issue', 100.
72. Prox and Griffith, 'Introduction to Special Issue'; and Ratcliffe, 'Intelligence-led Policing'.
73. Bennett Moses and Chan, 'Big Data for Legal and Law Enforcement'.
74. See also Ibid.
75. Bennett Moses and Chan, 'Algorithmic Prediction in Policing'; Innes, Fielding and Cope, 'Theory and Practice of Crime Intelligence'; Cope, 'Intelligence-led Policing or Policing-led'; and Ratcliffe, 'Crime Mapping and Implications'.
76. Manning, *Democratic Policing in a Changing World*; alsoSheptycki, 'Theorizing the police intelligence division-of-labour; some further contributions to the pluralist perspective in policing intelligence'.
77. See above 33.

Acknowledgement

The authors wish to thank the guest editors and the insightful feedback provided by the anonymous reviewers. Further, they wish to thank Janet Chan, Lyria Bennett Moses, James Sheptycki, Crystal Weston, Debra Langan and Lisa-jo van den Scott for comments on earlier drafts.

Disclosure statement

No potential conflict of interest was reported by the authors.

Funding

This work was supported by an Insight Grant from the Social Sciences and Humanities Research Council of Canada #435-2016-1511.

Bibliography

Amicelle, A., C. Aradau, and J. Jeandesboz. "Questioning Security Devices: Performativity, Resistance, Politics." *Security Dialogue* 46, no. 4 (2015): 293–306. doi:10.1177/0967010615586964.

Amicelle, A., and E. Jacobsen. "The Cross-colonization of Finance and Security Through Lists: Banking Policing in the UK and India." *Environment and Planning D: Society and Space* 34, no. 1 (2016): 89–106. doi:10.1177/0263775815623276.

Bedford, K. "Letting the Right Ones In: Whitelists, Jurisdictional Reputation, and the Racial Dynamics of Online Gambling Regulation." *Environment and Planning D: Society and space* 34, no. 1 (2016): 30–47. doi:10.1177/0263775815595816.

Bennett Moses, L., and J. Chan. "Using Big Data for Legal and Law Enforcement Decisions: Testing the New Tools." *UNSW Law Journal* 37, no. 2 (2014): 643–678.

Bennett Moses, L., and J. Chan. "Algorithmic Prediction in Policing: Assumptions, Evaluation, and Accountability." *Policing and Society* (2016): 1–17. doi:10.1080/10439463.2016.1253695.

Bijker, W. *Of bicycles, Bakelites, and Bulbs: Toward a Theory of Sociotechnical Change*. Cambridge: The MIT Press, 1995.

Boba Santos, R. *Crime Analysis with Crime Mapping*. 3rd ed. Los Angeles: Sage Publications, 2013.

Brodeur, J. P. "High Policing and Low Policing: Remarks about the Policing of Political Activities." *Social Problems* 30, no. 5 (1983): 507–520. doi:10.2307/800268.

Chan, J. *Changing Police Culture: Policing in a Multicultural Society*. Melbourne: Cambridge University Press, 1997.

Chan, J. "The Technological Game: How Information Technology is Transforming Police Practice." *Criminal Justice* 1 (2001): 139–159.

Chan, J. "Police and New Technologies." In *Handbook of Policing*, edited by T. Newburn, 655–679. Cullompton: Willan, 2003.

Charmaz, K. *Constructing Grounded Theory: A Practical Guide Through Qualitative Analysis*. London: Sage Publications, 2006.

Chin, G., O. Kuchar, and K. Wolf. "Exploring the Analytical Processes of Intelligence Analysts." *CHI* (2009): 11–20.

Cope, N. "Intelligence Led Policing or Policing Led Intelligence?" *British Journal of Criminology* 44 (2004): 188–203. doi:10.1093/bjc/44.2.188.

Corkhill, J. "Evaluation a Critical Point on the Path to Intelligence." *The Journal of Australian Institute of Professional Intelligence Officers* 16, no. 1 (2008): 3–11.

Coyne, J., and P. Bell. "Strategic Intelligence in Law Enforcement: A Review." *Journal of Policing, Intelligence and Counter Terrorism* 6, no. 1 (2011): 23–39. doi:10.1080/18335330.2011.553179.

Darroch, S., and L. Mazerolle. "Intelligence-Led Policing: A Comparative Analysis of Organizational Factors Influencing Innovation Uptake." *Police Quarterly* 16 (2012): 3–37. doi:10.1177/1098611112467411.

Daston, L., and P. Galison. "The Image of Objectivity." *Representation* 40 (1992): 81–128. doi:10.1525/rep.1992.40.1.99p0137h.

De Lint, W., D. O'Connor, and R. Cotter. "Controlling the flow: Security, exclusivity, and criminal intelligence in Ontario." *International Journal of the Sociology of Law* 35 (2007): 41–58. doi:10.1016/j.ijsl.2007.01.001.

Dunworth, T. "Criminal Justice and the Information Technology Revolution." *Criminal Justice* 65, no. 2 (2000): 371–426.

Ericson, R. V. *Making Crime: A Study of Detective Work*. London: Butterworths, 1981.

Ericson, R. V., and K. D. Haggerty. *Policing the Risk Society*. Toronto: University of Toronto Press, 1997.

Evans, J., and M. Kebbell. "The Effective Analyst: A Study of What Makes an Effective Crime and Intelligence Analyst." *Policing and Society: An International Journal of Research and Policy* 22, no. 2 (2012): 204–219. doi:10.1080/10439463.2011.605130.

FCW. "The Business of federal technology: Boston probe's big data use hints at the future." Accessed July 12, 2013. http://fcw.com/articles/2013/04/26/big-data-boston-bomb-probe.aspx

Gill, P. *Rounding Up the Usual Suspects? Developments in Contemporary Law Enforcement Intelligence*. Aldershop: Ashgate, 2000.

Grove, N. "The Cartographic Ambiguities of HarassMap: Crowdmapping Security and Sexual Violence in Egypt." *Security Dialogue* 46, no. 4 (2015): 345–356. doi:10.1177/0967010615583039.

Hughes, V., and P. Jackson. "The Influence of Technical, Social and Structural Factors on the Effective use of Information in a Policing Environment." *The Electronic Journal of Knowledge Management* 2, no. 1 (2004): 65–76.

Hunt, P., J. Saunders, and J. Hollywood. *Evaluation of the Shreveport Predictive Policing Experiment*. RAND Corporation, 2014. www.rand.org.

Innes, M., N. Fielding, and N. Cope. "The Appliance of Science? The Theory and Practice of Crime Intelligence Analsyis." *British Journal of Criminology* 45 (2005): 39–57. doi:10.1093/bjc/azh053.

Joseph, J., and J. Corkill. "Information Evaluation: How One Group of Intelligence Analysts Go About the Task." *Australian Security and Intelligence Conference* (2011). http://ro.ecu.edu.au/asi/20.

Lefebvre, S. "A Look at Intelligence Analysis." *International Journal of Intelligence and Counter Intelligence* 17, no. 2 (2004): 231–264. doi:10.1080/08850600490274908.

Lum, C., C. Koper, and J. Willis. "Understanding the Limits of Technology's Impact on Police Effectiveness." *Policing and Society* (2016). doi:10.1177/109861116667279.

Maguire, M. "Policing by Risks and Targets: Some Dimensions and Implications of Intelligence-led Crime Control." *Policing and Society* 9, no. 4 (2000): 315–336. doi:10.1080/10439463.2000.9964821.

Maguire, M., and T. Johns. "Intelligence-Led Policing, Managerialism and Community Engagement: Competing Priorities and the Role of the National Intelligence-Model in the UK." *Policing and Society* 16, no. 1 (2006): 67–85. doi:10.1080/10439460500399791.

Manning, P. "Technology's Ways: Information Technology, Crime Analysis and the Rationalizing of Policing." *Criminal Justice* 1 (2001a): 83–103.

Manning, P. "Theorizing Policing; The Drama and Myth of Crime Control in the NYPD." *Theoretical Criminology* 5, no. 3 (2001b): 315–344. doi:10.1177/1362480601005003002.

Manning, P. *The Technology of Policing: Crime Mapping, Information Technology, and the Rationality of Crime Control*. New York: New York University Press, 2008.

Manning, P. "Information Technology and Police Work." In *Springer Encyclopedia of Criminology and Criminal Justice*, edited by D. Weisburd and G. Bruinsema, 2501–2513. New York: Springer, 2013.

Manning, P. K. *Democratic Policing in a Changing World*. Boulder: Paradigm Publishers, 2010.

Marks, M. "Researching Police Transformation: The Ethnographic Imperative." *British Journal of Criminology* 44, no. 6 (2004): 866–888. doi:10.1093/bjc/azh049.

Marrin, S., and J. D. Clemente. "Improving Intelligence Analysis by Looking to the Medical Profession." *International journal of Intelligence and Counter Intelligence* 18, no. 4 (2005): 707–729. doi:10.1080/08850600590945434.

McCulloch, J., and S. Pickering. "Pre-Crime and Counter-Terrorism: Imagining Future Crime in the War on Terror." *British Journal of Criminology* 49 (2009): 628–645. doi:10.1093/bjc/azp023.

Murray, N. "Profiling in the Age of Total Information Awareness." *Race & Class* 52, no. 2 (2010): 3–24. doi:10.1177/0306396810377002.

O'Malley, P. *Risk, Uncertainty and Government*. London: The Glasshouse Press, 2004.

Ontario Regulation 3/99. "Adequacy and Effectiveness of Police Services." Police Services Act. Accessed May 12, 2013. http://www.elaws.gov.on.ca/html/regs/english/elaws_regs_990003_e.htm

Orlikowski, W. J. "Using Technology and Constituting Structures: A Practice Lens for Studying Technology in Organizations." *Organization Science* 11, no. 4 (2000): 404–428. doi:10.1287/orsc.11.4.404.14600.

Orr, J. E. *Talking about Machines: An Ethnography of a Modern Job*. Ithaca, NY: ILR Press, 1996.

Oudshoorn, N., and T. Pinch, eds. *How Users Matter: The Co-construction of Users and Technology*. Cambridge: MIT Press, 2005.

Perry, W., B. McInnis, C. Price, S. Smith, and J. Hollywood. *Predictive Policing: The Role of Crime Forecasting in Law Enforcement Operations*. RAND Corporation, 2013. www.rand.org.

Piza, E. L., and S. Q. Feng. "The Current and Potential Role of Crime Analysts in Evaluations of Police Interventions: Results from a Survey of the International Association of Crime Analysts." *Police Quarterly* (2017): 1–28. doi:10.1177/1098611117697056.

Prox, R., and C. T. Griffths. "Introduction to the Special Issue." *Police Practice and Research* 16, no. 2 (2015): 99–107. doi:10.1080/15614263.2014.972611.

Ratcliffe, J. H. "Damned if You Don't, Damned If You Do: Crime Mapping and Its Implications in the Real World." *Policing & Society* 12 (2002): 211–225. doi:10.1080/10439460290018463.

Ratcliffe, J. H. "Crime Mapping and the Training Needs of Law Enforcement." *European Journal on Criminal Policy and Research* 10 (2004): 65–83. doi:10.1023/B:CRIM.0000037550.40559.1c.

Ratcliffe, J. H. "Intelligence-Led Policing." In *Encyclopedia of Criminology and Criminal Justice*, edited by G. Bruisma and D. Weisburd, 2573–2581. New York: Springer, 2013.

Ratcliffe, J. H., and M. J. McCullagh. "Chasing Ghosts? Police Perceptions of High Crime Areas." *British Journal of Criminology* 41 (2001): 330–341. doi:10.1093/bjc/41.2.330.

Sanders, C. B., A. Christensen, and C. Weston. "Discovering Crime in a Database: 'Big data' and the Mangle of Social Problems Work." *Qualitative Sociology Review* 11, no. 2 (2015a): 180–195.

Sanders, C. B., and S. Hannem. "Policing the "Risky": Technology and Surveillance in Everyday Patrol Work." *Canadian Review of Sociology* 18, no. 7 (2013): 389–410. doi:10.1111/j.1755-618X.2012.01300.x.

Sanders, C. B., and S. Henderson. "Police 'Empires' and Information Technologies: Uncovering Material and Organizational Barriers to Information Sharing in Canadian Police Services." *Policing and Society* 23, no. 2 (2013): 243–260. doi:10.1080/10439463.2012.703196.

Sanders, C. B., and J. Sheptycki. "Policing, Crime, 'Big Data'; Towards a Critique of the Moral Economy of Stochastic Governance." *Crime, Law and Social Change: An Interdisciplinary Journal* (2017). doi:10.1007/s10611-016-9678-7.

Sanders, C. B., C. Weston, and N. Schott. "Police Innovations, 'Secret Squirrels' & Accountability: Empirically Examining the Integration of Intelligence-led Policing in Canada." *British Journal of Criminology* 55, no. 4 (2015b): 711–729. doi:10.1093/bjc/azv008.

Sheptycki, J. "Beyond the Cycle of Intelligence-Led Policing." In *Beyond the Intelligence Cycle*, edited by M. Pythian, 99–118. London: Routledge, 2013.

Sheptycki, J. "Liquid Modernity and the Police Métier; Thinking about Information Flows in Police Organisation." *Global Crime* (2017): 1–17. doi:10.1080/17440572.2017.1313734.

Sheptycki, J. "Theorizing the Police Intelligence Division-Of-Labour; Some Further Contributions to the Pluralist Perspective in Policing Intelligence." *Policing and Society* (Forthcoming).

Star, S. "Invisible Work and Silenced Dialogues in Representing Knowledge." In *Women, Work and Computerization: Understanding and Overcoming Bias in Work and Education*, edited by I. Eriksson, B. A. Kitchenham, and K. G. Tijdens, 81–92. Amsterdam: North Holland, 1991.

Star, S. "The Politics of Formal Representations: Wizards, Gurus, and Organizational Complexity." In *Ecologies of Knowledge: Work and Politics in Science and Technology*, edited by S. L. Star, 8801–8818. Albany, NY: SUNY, 1995.

Star, S., and A. Strauss. "Layers of Silence, Arenas of Voice: The Ecology of Visible and Invisible Work." *Computer Supported Cooperative Work* 8 (1999): 9–30. doi:10.1023/A:1008651105359.

Suchman, L. *Plans and Situated Actions*. Cambridge: Cambridge University Press, 1987.

Van den Scott, L., C. B. Sanders, and A. Puddephatt. "Reconceptualizing Users Through Rich Ethnographic Accounts." In *Handbook of Science and Technology Studies*, edited by C. Miller, U. Felt, L. L. Smith-Doerr, and R. Fouche. 4th ed. Boston: The MIT Press, 2017.

Whitelaw, B., R. B. Parent, and C. T. Griffiths. *Community-Based Strategic Policing in Canada*. 6th ed. Toronto, ON: Thomson Nelson, 2014.

European border policing: EUROSUR, knowledge, calculation

Julien Jeandesboz

ABSTRACT

The article asks how we can make sense of the central role attributed to technology in border policing today and relates discussions of 'techno-' or 'technology-driven' (border) policing to the issue of knowledge. It examines EUROSUR, a set of measures for placing the external borders of the European Union under, 'real-time' surveillance. It argues that current understandings of knowledge in the border policing literature require conceptual specification to make otherwise unnoticed aspects of border policing amenable to empirical inquiry. To this end, the article foregrounds the notion of centres of calculation as a way to refine inquiries into policing as 'knowledge work'. It examines knowledge arrangements related to European border policing, showing how the understanding that border policing is concerned with and operates through flows is contingently and progressively built through processes of stabilisation, mobilisation and extension of social and material networks of actors, institutions and devices.

Introduction

The article examines the establishment of the European Border Surveillance System (EUROSUR), a set of measures aimed at placing the external borders of the European Union (EU) under constant, 'real-time' monitoring. EUROSUR is a computerised network for collecting, exchanging and analysing information for 'the surveillance of land and sea borders, including the monitoring, detection, identification, tracking, prevention and interception of unauthorized border crossings for the purpose of detecting, preventing and combating illegal immigration and cross-border crime and contributing to ensuring the protection and saving the lives of migrants'.[1] The European Parliament and the Council of Ministers of the EU decided on the establishment of EUROSUR in 2013, although it had been in development for a few years at that time already.[2] The contributions analysing EUROSUR foreground its 'high-tech' components, including the planned use of data fusion combining information from human sources and technological sources including radar, satellite and unmanned vehicles.[3] At stake here is in particular the way in which EUROSUR would contribute to the development of a 'common pre-frontier intelligence picture' (CPIP) for the purpose of conducting

---

I would like to thank the editors of this special issue and the two anonymous readers for sharing their insights on earlier versions of this contribution.

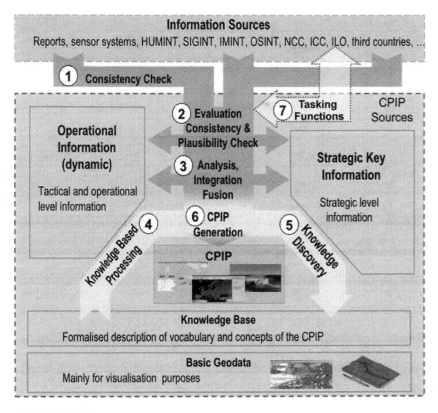

Figure 1. EUROSUR CPIP.
Seiffarth, 'The development of EUROSUR'.

cooperative border policing operations among the national authorities of EU Member States and Frontex, the EU's external borders agency. As Figure 1 illustrates, CPIP speaks to a technology-centred account of border policing, in that it embodies the ambition of fusing into a single visualisation information flowing from a variety of surveillance devices (CCTV, radars, drones, satellites) and human sources.

Given these features, it is tempting to frame the establishment of EUROSUR as a clear move away from existing practices of European border policing. The article argues however that for all its purported novelty, the development and eventual establishment of EUROSUR does not embody a clean break from an earlier situation that could be attributed to the availability of advanced technology, but an incremental and controversy-intense process through which existing sociotechnical configurations of European border policing transform. This claim is demonstrated through a focus on the issue of knowledge and how we conceive of (border) policing as knowledge work. Knowledge work has been characterised as a broad and underqualified notion in the policing literature.[4] The article thus further specifies that we should distinguish between how policing as knowledge work is done, that is how knowledge is generated by policing actors and made actionable, and how the production of knowledge is made possible in the first place, that is the production of the conditions that make the generation of policing knowledge and its rendering actionable possible. It is more specifically this second aspect that the examination of the establishment of EUROSUR speaks to.

To this end, the article deploys the notion of centres of calculation, initially developed by sociologists of science and engineering to move beyond the understanding of technoscience as driven by the 'ideas' of researchers and engineers.[5] The notion of 'centre of calculation' is at the same time descriptive and conceptual. It accounts for the way in which scientific knowledge is produced through processes of mobilisation, stabilisation and extension of networks and 'alliances' between materials and people and allows us to understand how knowledge thus becomes a source of social power. In the case of EUROSUR and European border policing, as the article demonstrates, this is the power to define policing as being concerned with flows rather than with territorial demarcations, and as unfolding through the handling of informational flows. In this regard, the article contributes to the special issue by affirming the sociotechnical constructedness of policing as an activity that takes place in/through flows.

The article unfolds as follows. The next section starts with a review of some of the claims in the contemporary literature on border policing, technology and knowledge. It outlines how we can refine our use of knowledge and knowledge work by distinguishing between inquiries into how knowledge is produced and rendered actionable and into how knowledge work is made possible in the first place. It further specifies the scope and limits of the notion of centres of calculation. The remainder of the article, in three substantial sections, proceeds to make sense of the establishment of EUROSUR in terms of the shaping of a European centre of calculation on border policing, studying how this involves processes of mobilisation, stabilisation and extension of sociotechnical networks of persons and materials.

European border policing, knowledge, calculation

European border policing

Contemporary efforts by state authorities to control cross-border movements of persons have attracted considerable attention among scholars of international relations, security and surveillance, law as well as policing.[6] This interest is spurred in part by the growing place that issues related to asylum, migration and their purported association with illicit activities have occupied in the public debate, particularly in Western states since the early 1990s and their 'securitisation'.[7] It is further nurtured by the increasingly transnational shape of practices and actors of social control invested in these issues. The cross-jurisdictional and 'networked' outlook of border and migration policing today is understood to depart from established conceptions of policing as a territorialised activity bound to and by the nation-state.[8] This interest, finally, is grounded in the notion that border policing today is less concerned with the conduct of criminal investigation and prosecution than with the monitoring and surveillance of specific individuals and groups combined with the exercise of extensive administrative powers of arrest, detention and deportation[9] and the way in which such practices involve a 'digitisation' of border policing, particularly in Europe and North America.[10]

Much of this discussion is of relevance when considering EU activities in the field of policing, which have consistently expanded since their inception in the late 1980s and early 1990s. The entry into force of the Maastricht treaty in 1992 established a 'third pillar' on justice and home affairs in EU policies, while the entry into force of the treaty of Amsterdam in 1999 constituted the Union as an 'area of freedom, security and justice' (AFSJ). The establishment of new EU-wide agencies and bodies is a helpful indicator of this expansion. The European Police Office (Europol) was established in 1992 as the European Drugs Unit and became a fully fledged office after 1999, the European Union Judicial Cooperation Unit (Eurojust) started its work in 2002, and in 2004, the European Parliament and the Council of Ministers adopted legislation to establish the European agency for external borders (Frontex). These judicial and policing bodies, however, do not display the investigative and coercive powers usually conferred upon 'traditional' law enforcement and judiciary services. 'European policing is a largely *informationalized* activity' notes Loader, whereby EU bodies are set up and called upon to collect, analyse, disseminate information, including in some cases personal data, and coordinate joint investigations and operations by national agencies or services, rather than to take operational matters in their own hands.[11] In fact, a study estimated that by the end of 2011, there were 25 computerised information sharing mechanisms functioning, in development or foreseen, to implement the AFSJ.[12] A number of those concern border policing and the control of cross-border movements of persons, in particular the Schengen Information System (SIS, now in its 'second generation'), rolled out in 1995, the database for registering the fingerprints of asylum seekers Eurodac rolled out in 2003, the Visa Information System (VIS) whose roll-out started in 2011, and EUROSUR whose deployment started in 2013. The information systems of EU policing agencies and bodies also involve the collection and exchange of information on border crossers and border crossings, although not systematically personal – the Europol Analytical Work Files for smuggling and trafficking activities, and the Frontex Information System with regard to the collection and aggregation of statistics on detection and interception of persons at the external borders.

European policing is in fact so 'informationalised' that this aspect has over time developed into a policy domain in its own right, dubbed 'management of large-scale IT systems'. In 2009, the EU Council of Ministers adopted an 'information management strategy for EU internal security',[13] and in 2010, the European Commission published an 'overview' document of information-management activities related to 'law enforcement and migration' which tellingly also comprises 'core principles that should underpin the design and evaluation of information management instruments in the area of freedom, security and justice', that is guidelines for the development of additional such instruments.[14] In 2011, an EU regulation established eu-LISA, the European agency for the Operational Management of large-scale IT systems, outsourcing activities and tasks which until then were conducted inside the European Commission's home affairs services, including the management of existing transnational databases such as the SIS or the VIS, and the development and deployment of new such devices, in particular the so-called smart borders systems.[15]

In this perspective, there is considerable resonance between conceptions of (border) policing centred on monitoring and surveillance, data collection, analysis and dissemination and scholarly accounts in terms of technology-driven policing and security. Interestingly, however, this resonance is a site of analytical tension rather than scholarly consensus. On the one hand, the increasing 'informationalisation' of (border) policing remains construed as 'both constituted by and dependent on an unprecedented development in technologies of surveillance and control'.[16] Claims made about technology in the security and policing literature as well as in the broader discussion in the social sciences on the effects of digital devices are thus often made possible by a certain discourse on technology, one that draws attention to particular devices – very centrally to 'high-tech' contraptions grounded in digital computing technology – that are framed in epochalist terms in the corresponding political and policy discourse.[17] On the other, the literature is prompt to point out that technological development in itself does not determine security and policing practice. The 'data derivatives' used for pre-emptive purposes in US and UK border policing, Amoore argues for instance, are *specific* rather than 'more advanced' ways of abstracting the profiles of individuals deemed to be problematic.[18] Lucia Zedner warns against 'techno-credulity – or blind faith in technological solutions to otherwise irresolvable problems', in dealing with questions of security, surveillance and policing.[19] In dealing with these tensions and working to circumvent such a discourse on technology, scholarly debates have increasingly gelled around the examination of policing and security practices as *sociotechnical*. As suggested by recent work on security devices, for instance, such devices are the outcome of 'struggles, controversies and translations between various actors, heterogeneous conceptions, and myriad interests, goals and values'[20] as much as they are the effect of technological innovation. They are therefore neither strictly social nor strictly technical, but a mesh of social and technical processes.

There are two ways in which such an approach can be implemented in studying border policing. We can look at 'the mentalities and practices of those working at the sharp end of border enforcement'.[21] Looking at the 'sharp end' of border policing is crucial to explore and understand issues of appropriation and resistance in the context of the *deployment* of specific devices.[22] Such a perspective can also be mobilised to examine how the introduction of particular devices gels with transformations in policing organisations.[23] Studying deployment, though, only yields a partial picture of border policing. Devices are not only deployed and used, they are also designed, and quite often the sites where they are designed can differ significantly from the sites where they are deployed.[24] The eu-LISA agency, for instance, is not a policing body but a service tasked with coordinating the design, development and roll-out of information systems. Understanding how devices are designed, the struggles and controversies involved in designing them, is then as important a research endeavour when it comes to examining contemporary (border) policing. In the context of European policing, this is all the more crucial if we are to give credit to Loader's claim that despite their low visibility and lack of operational remit, European (border) policing bodies constitute 'new sites of social power'.[25]

Policing as knowledge work and centres of calculation

The question that can be addressed by thinking not only about the deployment of policing devices but also about their design is how these sites are constituted, and accordingly what this social power consists of. Sheptycki follows earlier studies on detective and uniformed police work[26] in associating concerns with the collection, analysis and dissemination of information in transnational policing with 'knowledge production and management'.[27] In this sense, the focus of European bodies on knowledge work does not make them any less policing actors, although the more directly coercive aspects of police work are beyond their remit. Brodeur and Dupont however note that for all the success that the characterisation of police work as knowledge work has enjoyed among students of policing, the conceptualisation of 'knowledge' in this field has been left fallow.[28] They draw on the sociology of knowledge[29] to point out that the production of police knowledge has a very important and specific characteristic, which is the requirement that it be 'validated' in order to be actionable in a policing context.[30] We can add to this work of specification – in the double sense of analytical specification and of focusing on the specificities of policing knowledge – by pointing out that while the focus on how policing actors generate and act upon knowledge is certainly central, it should not be conducted at the expense of examining how these practices are made possible in the first place, that is of the production of the conditions that make the generation of policing knowledge and its rendering actionable possible.

This work of specification is achieved here by drawing on the notion of centres of calculation, developed in particular in relation to the interest in accounting for the formation of scientific centres of knowledge in science and technology studies (STS). Calculation is understood not only in a mathematical or computational sense but also as 'qualitative issues of group management, such as ranking, ordering, organizing and measuring'.[31] As a field, STS works with the assumption that science and technology are social activities: scientists and engineers are embedded with specific social spaces that are themselves enmeshed in society and are constantly engaged in struggles inside and outside these social spaces to support their ideas and view and gain access to resources needed to further them.[32] For STS, 'knowledge and technological artifacts are *constructed* [...] marked by the circumstances of their production'.[33] From the perspective of what would come to be known as Actor-Network Theory (A-NT),[34] the production of scientific and technological knowledge ('technoscience') is not only social but sociotechnical. It is conditioned upon the accumulation of human and material resources (including samples, maps, charts, data, figures) and their circulation through the constitution of vast networks of people and things, to the extent that the traditional image of science – that of the lone genius scientist coming up with breakthrough ideas and products by themselves – cannot be considered accurate.[35] The peculiar power of Western 'technoscience', accordingly, rests on the constitution of centres of calculation through the mobilisation of resources, the stabilisation of knowledge claims, and the further extension of knowledge networks.[36]

The best example to deploy the notion of centres of calculation may well be mapmaking. Latour discusses the case of French navigator Lapérouse landing on a shore of the East Pacific only known to him and to the economic and military centres of Western Europe as Sakhalin, without the means to determine whether this was an island or a continental peninsula.[37] It is only after interacting with the local populations and mobilising their knowledge that Lapérouse is able to establish that Sakhalin is indeed an island. As his expedition carries the best equipment available at the time, it is able to draw maps and put down astronomical measurements that stabilise the fact that Sakhalin is an island and the probable location of the strait between the island and the continent. This is because, as Latour puts it, 'the people who sent them away are not so much interested in their coming back as they are in the possibility of sending *other* fleets *later*'.[38] These maps, logbooks and measurements are indeed later brought back overland to France and Europe by an officer of Lapérouse's expedition. The information (the inscriptions, in Latour's vocabulary) brought back by the officer would subsequently serve as the basis for launching other expeditions, and expanding on this initial knowledge (by actually navigating the strait, which Lapérouse himself never got around to do).

For the purpose of unpacking the notion of centres of calculation, four observations are important here. The work done by Lapérouse's expedition, first, is enabled by the devices, including the equipment, techniques of measurement and drawing, that have been produced and packaged in Europe. Knowledge work, then, is not only a matter of individual genius or ideas but a sociotechnical process to which both material and human elements contribute. Second, the work of Lapérouse's expedition would ultimately only matter because the inscriptions produced through these devices are brought back and processed in Amsterdam, London or Paris. What happens at the 'sharp end' of knowledge work (here geographical, in our case policing), said differently, matters insofar as this knowledge work is embedded within a broader network of people and things connecting the 'sharp end' with centres of calculation. Third, the constitutive processes of centres of calculation – mobilisation, stabilisation and extension – can be conceived, to be more precise, both as processes involved in the constitution of centres of calculation and as 'overlapping strategies in the course of knowledge production'[39] enabled by centres of calculation. Mobilisation, stabilisation and extension in knowledge work are always ongoing processes, rather than simply sequential outcomes. Fourth, it is this process of accumulating, bringing and sending 'back' knowledge that is constitutive of the 'social power' of centres of calculation. 'Knowledge', as Latour writes,

> is not something that could be described by itself or by opposition to "ignorance" or "belief", but only by considering a whole cycle of accumulation: how to bring things back to a place for someone to see it for the first time so that others might be sent again to bring other things back.[40]

The notion of centres of calculation is thus useful for specifying further how and what can be studied under the heading of policing as knowledge work. Overall, this involves analysing European policing and border policing in particular in terms of the establishment and functioning of centres of calculation. We need to take into account not only the 'sharp end' of this work, the generation of knowledge and its rendering actionable, but also the embedding of this knowledge in networks of accumulation and circulation. The constitution of these networks through processes of mobilisation, stabilisation and extension is an integral part of inquiries into police work as knowledge work. The remainder of the article, accordingly, analyses how the establishment of EUROSUR can be understood in terms of the mobilisation, stabilisation and expansion of knowledge networks. In addition, we need to consider these networks in their social as well as technical dimension, as sociotechnical configurations where technology is not an external driver for change, but part of the internal processes through which these configurations shift over time. In the following sections, this outlook enables the article to show that for all its purported novelty, the development of EUROSUR does not embody a radical break due to the availability of advanced technology, but an incremental and controversy-intense process through which existing sociotechnical configurations of European border policing transform. Finally, centres of calculation cannot be dissociated from relations of power and are instrumental to their operation. This serves the examination of EUROSUR by emphasising that through the establishment of European arrangements, (border) policing becomes predominantly defined as being concerned with flows rather than territorial boundaries, and as operating through flows, through the collection and exchange of information among national and EU immigration and border policing authorities.

There can of course be questions about the relevance of using a notion developed in STS for examining policing practices. Notwithstanding the fact that this move mirrors past imports in policing studies from the sociology of knowledge, the approach to knowledge heralded by Latour and his colleagues has over time also evolved into 'a general social theory centred on technoscience, rather than just a theory of technoscience'.[41] In other words, STS/A-NT scholars have already done the labour of portability in order to take the notion of centres of calculation 'outside of the laboratory', so to speak. In discussing centres of calculation, Latour notes in this regard that

> we should not overlook the administrative networks that produce, *inside* rooms in Wall Street, in the Pentagon, in university departments, fleeting or stable representations of what is the state of the forces, the nature of our societies, the military balance, the health of the economy, the time for a Russian ballistic missile to hit the Nevada desert [...] In all cases you need to be hooked up to costly networks that have to be maintained and extended.[42]

Mobilisation: CIREFI data

The early weeks of 2010 saw the abolition of the Centre for Information, Discussion and Exchange on the Crossing of Frontiers and Immigration (CIREFI) and the transfer of its attribution to the EU's external borders agency FRONTEX. CIREFI had been established in December 1992 as a body of the Council of the EU adjunct to the Ad hoc Group on Immigration, staffed by representatives of EU Member State ministries of Interior, although its organisation and functions were only formalised in the conclusions of the Justice and Home Affairs Council of 30 November 1994.[43] These conclusions tasked CIREFI with three sets of responsibilities:

> [...] collate, using standard forms, statistical information concerning:
> a) legal immigration;
> b) illegal immigration and unlawful residence;
> c) facilitating of illegal immigration;
> d) use of false or falsified travel documents;
> e) measures taken by competent authorities, and draw up regular and occasional situational reports on this basis commenting on trends, developments and changes;
>
> [...] analyse the information compiled, draw conclusions and, when appropriate, give recommendations;
>
> [...] conduct exchanges of information on expulsion matters, particularly in respect of countries of destination, airports of departure or arrival, carriers, flight routes, fares, reservation possibilities, conditions of carriage, escort requirements and charter possibilities, as well as on problems in obtaining repatriation travel documents.[44]

What the CIREFI is set out to do, in other words, is to organise a flow of information on immigration and border control. Over the years and until its demise in 2010, CIREFI came to embody the knowledge work conducted on borders among EU and national authorities in charge of immigration and policing, to the extent that 'CIREFI data' has become a frequent shorthand for referring to the Centre's statistical products, among practitioners and academics alike.[45] The constitution and handling of 'CIREFI data', however, has also been central to a number of controversies during the Centre's lifetime. Controversies have ranged from the adoption of common definitions to categorise the data being generated through CIREFI to the format under which such data should be transmitted and circulated, from the possibility to disclose publicly this data to the possibility of adding new functionalities to the Centre's remit. In that sense, the work conducted in the framework of CIREFI was as much about how to mobilise knowledge as about its production.

The outlook and material support of 'CIREFI data', for one, was not clearly established from the moment members of the Centre started their meetings. Common definitions for the categories of information to be exchanged through CIREFI were only adopted in 1998.[46] In January 2000, the Portuguese Presidency of the EU circulated a note to other CIREFI delegations, pointing out 'certain limitations arising from the existence of distinct immigration regimes' and requesting further clarifications on the way in which national statistics were converted into 'CIREFI data'.[47] In July 2000, the subsequent French Presidency transmitted a note to CIREFI members expressing concerns over 'the practical arrangements for exchanging statistical and factual information on the current state of illegal immigration and immigration networks'.[48] In particular, it proposed

> using a standard format report containing statistical information, comparing data from previous months and the same period in the previous year in order to establish a "trend" (stability, increase or decrease) but also qualitative factual data which will enable a better assessment to be made of actual illegal immigration flows, the way they operate, and Member States' responses.[49]

This form was ultimately adopted at the end of 2000 (see Figure 2). Filled in by national authorities in charge of immigration and border policing, it became an established vehicle for the exchange of information within CIREFI.

Part of the controversies on 'CIREFI data' further stemmed from a brief provision introduced at the end of 1994 Council conclusions which established this body. The document notes that besides the regular meetings of CIREFI delegations in Brussels (as a rule of thumb, on a monthly basis), 'the national central units of the Member States concerned will exchange information directly at a multilateral level or bilateral level in cases requiring immediate action'.[50] In other words, the conclusions aimed to establish the principle that immigration and border policing authorities would not only exchange statistics, but that operational information on situations deemed to be worthy of immediate attention for them and their EU counterparts would also flow. Little follow-up occurred with regard this provision, until the Austrian Presidency introduced a standardised form in 1998. At the time, it was established that the form would be sent by telex to the general secretariat of the Council of Ministers in Brussels, which would then forward it to CIREFI contact points in national ministries of Interior (except in emergency situations, when national authorities would inform other contact points and the general secretariat concurrently).

The standard form was rapidly considered insufficient, because it did not create a binding commitment for national authorities to circulate information of interest for others. This point led to a proposal of the German Presidency, in the first months of 1999, for establishing an 'early warning system' (EWS) embodying such a commitment within CIREFI. The binding aspect of the German proposal proved controversial and was ultimately left aside. The EWS was formally launched by a Council Resolution adopted on 27 May 1999.[51] The EWS was expected to link the national central units of Member

THE POLICING OF FLOWS

**CIREFI/EXCHANGE OF INFORMATION ON THE CURRENT
ILLEGAL IMMIGRATION SITUATION**

– ASSESSMENT FORMAT FOR MIGRATION PRESSURE PER MEMBER STATE –

1.   **Statistical data and general trends (stability, increase, decrease)** for the period under consideration (one or two months depending on the interval between two meetings).

1.1.   Refusal of entry at all frontiers

1.1.1.   Land
1.1.2.   Air
1.1.3.   Sea

1.2.   Illegal aliens apprehended

1.3.   Applications for asylum at the frontier

1.4   Applications for asylum within the national territory

1.5.   Expulsions carried out

1.6   Comments

> *In each case please indicate the total number, and where appropriate draw attention to those nationalities for which a sharply altered trend has been observed. A comparison may also be made with the previous period if the delegation considers it necessary.*

2.   **Salient facts** (*information may be provided under the following headings as necessary*)

2.1.   Reminder of the particulars communicated via the early warning system and measures taken

2.2.   Principal investigations leading to the dismantling of illegal networks or workshops

2.3.   New operating methods and causes identified

2.3.1.   New itineraries detected
2.3.2.   Role of participants in the organisation of networks (travel agencies etc.)
2.3.3.   Use of fraudulent methods to obtain visas
2.3.4.   Use of false documents
2.3.5.   Other

Figure 2. Mobilisation (I): CIREFI 'standard form'.
Council of the EU, *Clarification of statistical data*, 5–6.

States in charge of CIREFI cooperation (immigration and border policing authorities in other words), with a particularly broad remit: convey 'first indications of illegal immigration and facilitator networks' as well as information on

> events and incidents which herald new developments in the field of illegal immigration and facilitating and which represent a threat such that immediate counter-measures are required, for example, concentrations of specific nationalities, perceptible changes in routes and methods, new types of large-scale travel documents forgery, doubling of the monthly figures for illegal immigrants stopped at an external land border with a neighbouring State or in air and sea traffic and large-scale facilitation, i.e. roughly groups of over 40 people.[52]

One may note in passing the rather blunt framing of the subject matter: undocumented movements of persons and facilitation are expressly stated as 'threats' requirement 'counter-measures'.

Just as with exchanges of statistical information however, the creation of EWS did not put an end to controversies. The German delegation tried to push ahead with making the exchange of 'ad hoc' information an obligation,[53] a move opposed among others by the French and UK representatives in CIREFI. In a January 2001 note, the French delegation' qualified such a move as 'extreme', pointing out that '[d]efective targeting of contact points [in Member State authorities] could be one of the major reasons for the failure of the EWS where the person concerned is not right at the centre of his country's border control arrangements'.[54] In a February 2001 note, the United Kingdom indicated it 'firmly believe[d] that the answer is in improving the current system rather than making it a mandatory requirement to use the system, which has many imperfections'.[55] The idea of making exchanges of information via the EWS mandatory was ultimately dropped with the new guidelines proposed by the UK delegation, adopted in April 2001.[56] It is however only in May 2001 that a standard form for the exchange of ad hoc factual information was adopted (Figure 3), and in December 2001 that a full list of CIREFI contact points was put together.[57]

With the adoption of the ad hoc information exchange form, CIREFI data experience a further shift. The scope of concerns moves from exchanging statistical, that is 'static' knowledge, to mobilising and ensuring the flow of operational, fluctuating knowledge. Furthermore, the focus of the framework for generating and mobilising knowledge outlined by the 'ad hoc exchange form' of Figure 3 shifts away from the 'fixed' concerns of the standard CIREFI form, which revolve around entry and (forced) exit from the territory and regulatory aspects to concerns with flows both across and inside the country (section 1 of the ad hoc form), means of transport or route. The ad hoc exchange form, in other words, is more about flow analysis than situational reporting. It exemplifies in its contrast with the standard form the move towards a conception of border policing that operates in, and through, flows.

'CIREFI data' shifted in two further ways in this regard until the Centre's demise. The first shift was the adjunction of the EU network of immigration liaison officers (ILOs) within the exchanges of factual information in the centre. The ILO set-up has its own trajectory, which would be too long to recount here.[58] It originates in measures adopted in the framework of EU police cooperation (the so-called Third Pillar of the Union) foreseeing the deployment of assistance missions to local agents in third country airports for controlling the passengers of flights to the EU[59] and in the Schengen framework on the deployment of 'document advisers' to third countries.[60] Throughout the end of the 1990s and early 2000s, a number of discussions took place around the deployment of officials from immigration and border police services of the EU Member States in third countries, usually for purposes of information gathering and provision of support to local authorities. The first deployment of this kind under the aegis of the EU was officially initiated in May 2001 and targeted the countries of the Western Balkans.[61] A legal instrument in the form of a Council Regulation was finally adopted in June 2003 to formalise the set-up.[62] It establishes that ILOs 'shall collect information for use either at the operational level, or at a strategic level, or both', the list of which largely overlaps with the operational knowledge to be exchanged via CIREFI and the EWS since it

RESTREINT/RESTRICTED
EU CIREFI
Ad hoc information exchange form

Date: ....

Reference number : ....
Subject: ....
Issuing authority: ....

1. **Place and date of detention**   or **suspected entry** ....
at the border (land , sea , air) ....
inside the country ....

2. **Nationality (nationalities)** of third-country nationals (ISO code): ....
(a) Number of persons: ....
(b) Comments: ....

3. Illegal border crossing **using facilitators:**   Yes   No
(a) Nationality (nationalities) and number of facilitators (ISO code): ....
(b) Comments: ....

4. **Means of transport:**   (a) on foot   (b) car   (c) minibus
                (d) bus/coach   (e) lorry   (f) aeroplane
                (g) passenger train   (h) goods train   (i) ship

Comments: ....

5. **Route:** coming from .... via .... to ....

6. **Travel or identity documents used**
6.1. **Type of document:**

ordinary passport	service passport	diplomatic passport	non-convention alien's identity document
Convention travel document (1951 Geneva Convention)	national identity document	residence permit	other

6.2. **Country in which travel or identity document issued (ISO code):** ....

7. **Visa used**
7.1. **Type of visa:**   airport transit   short stay
               transit   long stay

7.2. **Date and place of issue:** ....
7.3. **Country issuing visa (ISO code):** ....

8. **Type of forgery:**   (1) counterfeit   (2) falsification
                                    photograph substituted
                                    entries altered
                                    pages replaced
                    (3) stolen blank
                    (4) use of foreign official documents
                    (5) Undefined

9. **Number of suspicious documents:** ....

10. **Action taken:** ....

11. **For more information contact:** ....

Accompanying sheet: additional information

Figure 3. Mobilisation (II): CIREFI ad hoc information exchange form.
Source: Council of the EU 2001: 3

concerns issues such as: [...] flows of illegal immigrants originating from or transiting through the host country [...] routes followed by those flows [...] in order to reach the territories of the Member States [...] their modus operandi, including the means of transport used, the involvement of intermediaries, etc. [...] the existence and activities of criminal organisations involved in the smuggling of migrants [...] incidents and events that may be or become the cause for new developments with respect to flows of illegal immigrants [...] methods used for counterfeiting or falsifying identity documents and travel documents [...] ways and means to assist the authorities in host countries [...] ways and means to facilitate the return and repatriation of illegal immigrants to their countries of origin [...] legislation and legal practices relevant to the issues referred to above [...] information transmitted via the early warning system [of CIREFI].[63]

The ILO network came to be adjunct to CIREFI by means of the second shift in CIREFI data, which concerns its means of transmission. In November 2003, the European Commission followed on a request by the Council to propose the creation of a web-based system for the exchange of factual information. Until then, this information had been transmitted by fax or telex. The system, dubbed ICONet, was adopted in March 2005.[64] ICONet was not only a technical update on the means of exchange of information within CIREFI. It also enabled the transformation of CIREFI data by making it 'modular' and open-ended. The ICONet decision thus specifies that '[t]he elements for information exchange shall include at least the following: [...] early warning system [...] network of immigration liaison officers [...] information on the use of visas, borders and travel documents in relation to illegal immigration [...] return-related issues'.[65] With this last iteration of CIREFI data, the materialisation of immigration and border-related flows of knowledge shifts. Although the substance remains in many ways similar to what it had been in previous iterations – statistical and operational knowledge – the support for this exchange becomes further digitised, from telex transmission to online circulation.

Stabilisation: CIRAM

The work undertaken through CIREFI activities thus progressively inscribed the notion that EU immigration and border policing takes place in flows, that is in the exchange of first statistical/static, later operational/dynamic, knowledge, and that immigration and border policing is concerned with flows rather than with holding the border 'line' as such. This shift did not take place ineluctably, or in relation to technological break-throughs, but rather through successive controversies and related adjustments to the substantial and material outlook of the knowledge generated through the Centre.

CIREFI's demise in 2010 coincided with the redeployment of most of its activities through the EU's external border agency FRONTEX. Formally established in 2004 by Council Regulation 2007/2004,[66] FRONTEX is best known for the joint border control operations coordinated through it among EU Member State border agencies and services. These activities are said to be 'intelligence-driven', a process whose most visible (and only public) manifestation is the crafting of risk analyses under the aegis of the agency. Much like 'CIREFI data', 'FRONTEX risk analyses' have become a category of knowledge about EU external borders of its own since the agency's inception. Over time, they have even risen to public debate fame. In March 2011, for instance, among the turmoil caused by the North African uprisings, the reported figure of 20,258 Tunisian nationals being intercepted by European border control authorities in the Mediterranean supported British Prime Minister David Cameron's call for intervention in Libya.[67]

The practice of and stabilisation of knowledge work in European border policing through risk analysis predate the incorporation of CIREFI activities within FRONTEX and have a trajectory of their own. Without entering into a full examination of the genesis of the agency (Neal, 2009), it is useful to return to an anodyne episode in the process that eventually resulted in the establishment of FRONTEX, namely the short-lived ad hoc border centres initiative of 2002–2003. The ad hoc centres emerged from the controversy over proposals to establish a European corps of border guards following the entry into force of the Amsterdam treaty and in the context of EU reactions to the attacks of 11 September 2001. The controversy emerged following two initiatives supported by representatives from several Member States' ministries of Interior (Austria, Belgium, France, Germany, Spain) that considered the possibility of establishing an EU body in charge of controlling the Union's external borders with direct enforcement competences. Chiefly opposing this idea were the representatives of the United Kingdom's Home Office who 'agreed that more co-operation on external border issues was needed, but expressed reservations about the idea of creating a European Border Police Force'.[68] The May 2002 final report of the study group on a European border police reflects these tensions, by arguing in favour of a 'tertium genus' set-up, combining a central 'Council of national representatives' from Member States' border services with a network of operational centres.[69] Five ad hoc border centres were established on the basis of the latter: three focused on specific types of borders, a fourth one on issues of training,[70] and the fifth one became the EU's Risk Analysis Centre (RAC).[71]

Just as 'CIREFI data' were supported by the development of a set of devices such as standard information exchange forms, the workings of the RAC involved the manipulation of a specific format, the Common Integrated Risk Analysis Model (CIRAM). The RAC was in fact established to stabilise the use of CIRAM as a routine practice in exchanges among EU border control services. CIRAM, which is still in use at the time of writing, was developed under the aegis of the Finnish Frontier Guard between September and December 2002, that is before the establishment of the RAC. In a note to SCIFA of February 2003, the Finnish delegation presents the RAC as a measure rendered necessary by the drafting of CIRAM and commits for this purpose both a location for the centre (in the Finnish Frontier Guard headquarters in Helsinki) and staff, including the director, then-Lieutenant Colonel Ilkka Laitinen, who would later become the first executive director (2005–2015) of FRONTEX. The RAC was expected to include permanently detached experts from other Member States and to be backed by a 'support group' involving other temporary experts from Member States and from other EU bodies.

Just as with 'CIREFI data', furthermore, CIRAM aims both to organise into flows various items of knowledge related to border policing and to focus policing on flows. While the main document itself remains confidential, it is possible to rely on other available sources to document this point. As summarised in a note from the Finnish representatives in SCIFA, CIRAM is envisaged

> as a tool to be used mainly at strategic level [...] The CIRAM, based on a six-field matrix, brings together the aspects of criminal intelligence (threat assessment) and risk assessment, the latter focusing on the weaknesses of border management systems at the external borders of the European Union. As a conclusion of these two aspects, the CIRAM provides SCIFA+ with problem-oriented risk analyses, including concrete proposals for measures to be taken.[72]

Risk assessment as envisaged in the CIRAM framework bring together both general considerations related to the organisation of border control and punctual operational information. In addition to this 'threat assessment'/'risk assessment' combination, CIRAM also includes both factual and statistical information. Factual information is collated within the so-called Risk analysis formula of CIRAM (see Figure 4), while statistical data are put together via a specific CIRAM standard form, comprising a list of indicators (presented in Figure 5). The risk formula example displayed in Figure 4 is thoroughly articulated around the issue of flows: how they are 'pushed', 'pulled' and affected by a variety of factors, including in the countries through which these flows 'transit'. Likewise, the risk indicators outlined in Figure 5 qualify and quantify border policing arrangements according to how they organise flows of information (e.g. 'coverage' of border

EXAMPLE OF A RISK ANALYSIS FORMULA

(Member States' national contributions to the Risk Analysis Centre)

Push and Pull Factors

1. Please mention the current push factors in the main countries of origin of illegal immigrants entering your country (reasons why people want to leave their country):

A.	...
B.	...
C.	...

2. Please mention the current main pull factors for illegal immigrants entering your country (reasons why people want to go to your country):

A.	...
B.	...
C.	...

3. Please mention other current factors, if any, which may cause illegal migration to your country, e.g. in transit countries:

A.	...
B.	...
C.	...

Figure 4. Stabilisation (I): CIRAM risk analysis formula.

1. Length of external land and sea borders
2. Number of border crossing points at external EU borders
3. Number of deployed personnel involved in border checks/surveillance at the external borders
4. Estimated percentage of coverage of border checks
5. Estimated percentage of coverage of border surveillance (radar, fence, etc.)
6. Estimated percentage of checked all possible means of transportation (cars, lorries, trains, containers, etc.)
7. Number of deployed Liaison Officers in third countries dealing with immigration matters
8. Total number of passengers travelling via the external borders
9. Total number of performed border checks at the external borders
10. Number of detected false or falsified documents at the external borders
11. Estimated number of undetected false or falsified documents at the external borders
12. Number of refused entries/aliens/inadmissible at the external border crossing points
13. Number of apprehended facilitated aliens
14. Number of apprehended facilitators
15. Number of readmitted aliens to third countries
16. Number of removed aliens to third countries
17. Total number of asylum seekers in your country, not specifying between the borders
18. Number of apprehended aliens illegally present inside your country (= illegal immigrants); total number reflects the apprehended aliens illegally present in your country, along the external borders and inside the country

Figure 5. Stabilisation (I): CIRAM risk indicators.

surveillance, stages of deployment of ILO networks), and according to the characteristics of flows of persons. Indicators thus include the number of travellers crossing external borders, the proportions of these flows that involve irregular circulations, as well as outgoing flows (persons 'removed' to third countries).

Just as with 'CIREFI data', finally, the RAC/CIRAM set-up was also characterised by failures and controversies. Not all Member States committed permanent experts to this endeavour. A September 2004 note from the UK delegation to SCIFA also points out that the questionnaire-based collect of information is not considered to work effectively, and that the RAC 'has no harmonised statistical base from which to develop its analysis'.[73] The note also indicates some disagreements over the kind of analysis that the RAC should undertake. The UK representatives highlight in this regard that the frequency of CIRAM-based analysis could be increased, so as to provide elements beyond the objective of assessment. The RAC would in this perspective be called to examine the monthly compilations of 'CIREFI data' to 'assume a role regarding the prediction of future trends as part of the RAC's strategic function'.[74]

One of the key effects of the CIRAM/RAC set-up was to thus constitute a set of stable relations, both between different groups and organisations and between different types of knowledge work, to the extent that this set of relations would later be 'ported' to other settings. Some of the experts initially tasked with developing CIRAM were thus transferred to the RAC. With the establishment of FRONTEX, the RAC was itself transferred and became the Risk Analysis Unit of the agency, again with some members of this initial group of experts. In line with the notion of translation discussed previously, however, this second transfer also entailed a transformation, insofar as risk analysis (understood here as the heterogeneous practices of knowledge work outlined so far) was promoted from a component of the EU's activities in the field of border control to what the executive director of FRONTEX considers as 'the "engine" of FRONTEX activities'.[75] This is illustrated, of course, by the fact that himself was the director of the RAC prior to his posting to the agency. The compilation and drafting of risk analyses through FRONTEX also follow the pattern initiated through the CIRAM/RAC set-up. General overviews are currently provided on a quarterly basis as part of the activities of the FRONTEX risk analysis network (FRAN), which replaced the network of risk analysis contact points established through the RAC, as well as on a yearly basis. These analysis, incidentally, also make use of FRONTEX access to CIREFI data. So-called tailored analyses are also provided through the agency, focusing on a specific region (e.g. the Western Balkans) or issue (e.g. unaccompanied minors).

The development of FRONTEX risk analyses can be interpreted in two, complementary ways. First, these analyses contribute to enact baseline scenarios, cross-cutting views of what a 'normal' situation at the EU external borders look like. The quarterly risk analyses published through the FRAN provide a good example of this articulation. Each report opens with a presentation of key risk indicators such as the one presented in Figure 6.

The remainder of each of these quarterly risk analyses consists of statistical and at times narrative details of these indicators, grouped into a 'situational picture'. They examine current developments in relation, for instance, to 'seasonal expectations' about border crossings and establish whether contemporary trends reproduce or diverge from past trends. A 2012 instalment of these reports points out for instance that '[t]he border between Greece and Turkey is very likely to remain in 2013 among the main areas of detection of illegal border crossings'[76] or that '[t]he likelihood of large numbers of illegal border-crossings in the southern maritime border remains very high, either in the form of sporadic episodes similar to those reported in 2011 or in sustained flows on specific routes originating from Africa'.[77] Risk analysis here is as, if not more,

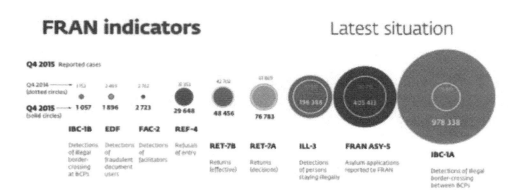

Figure 6. Stabilisation (II): Example of Frontex risk analysis network key indicators.
FRONTEX, *FRAN Quarterly: Quarter 4*, 6.

concerned with establishing trends defining the normal outlook of border control and border crossing as with predicting possible future disruptions of these patterns. These operations constitute what Neal calls 'an ongoing process of incremental normalization' of the external borders of the EU, in terms of how they are controlled and crossed, and how a 'normal' situation gets disrupted.[78]

Second, in line with the notion that they constitute instances of incremental normalisation, the practice of risk analysis enabled through FRONTEX constitutes a more systematic enactment of retroaction. CIREFI data embodied a certain reactive quality, particularly through the establishment of the EWS. The conception underpinning the EWS was that border control authorities should be able to change their behaviour in relation to certain specific events. FRONTEX risk analyses display a different quality: behavioural modification should not only be punctual, but structural, it should quite literally 'go with the flow' and adjust to changing patterns of circulation across borders. It is in this sense that the unfolding of CIRAM can be understood as a process of stabilisation of the network mobilised through the CIREFI set-up. As the next and final section of the article outlines, furthermore, it is also the stake of this changing quality of retroaction that constitutes the basis of a process of extension of the network of knowledge production constituted about and constitutive of contemporary European border policing.

Extension: CPIP

EUROSUR was officially named for the first time in a November 2006 communication from the European Commission on 'Reinforcing the management of the European Union's southern maritime borders'.[79] It was given a dedicated communication in the 'border package' adopted by the European Commission in 2008 and in 2011 was turned into a legislative proposal.[80] EUROSUR is at the same time a framework for organising border control activities among EU Member States and with selected third countries, and a computerised network for the collection, exchange and analysis of so-called surveillance information on EU external border areas. EUROSUR is simultaneously a network of National Coordination Centres (NCCs) expected to bring together the various national authorities in charge of border control and which are in most cases set up specially for the purpose of enrolment in this network with funding from the EU's external borders fund, and a communications network connecting said NCCs and FRONTEX, as well as with a set of 'surveillance tools' (satellites, unmanned aerial vehicles, radars and so on). How the system would work is basically by building 'pictures', consisting of statistics, incident reports as well as visualisations of the situation at the external borders of the EU. So-called situational pictures are enacted for each NCC as well as through FRONTEX, which is tasked with collating both the so-called European Situational Picture and the Common Pre-Frontier Intelligence Picture. The latter is collated through information obtained from third countries involved in EUROSUR and from EU immigration liaison officials, as well as observational data from surveillance applications. EUROSUR and the CPIP foreground electronic digital computing as an integrator of previous steps in the exchange of information and generation of knowledge on borders. EUROSUR and the CPIP, however, articulate both the communication system underpinning CIREFI data and the production process of FRONTEX risk analyses. In this sense, they constitute less a break in EU border policing, and more of an extension taking place within an existing sociotechnical configuration.

Discussions over the deployment of a surveillance system along EU external borders originated in the debates over the identification and control of so-called suspect vessels among representatives of national ministries of the Interior to the CIREFI in the early 2000s. These debates were spurred by the highly mediatised arrivals of boats carrying undocumented persons beaching on the shores of Italy, France, Greece and Spain – in particular, the arrival of the freighter *East Sea* with 900 Kurds on board near the French city of St. Raphaël on 17 February 2001. Discussions within CIREFI first led to a decision by the Belgian presidency to circulate a questionnaire collecting information from each delegation on how their respective Member States were affected by the issue and dealt with it.[81] Following this episode, the Council requested the Commission to launch a feasibility study on the surveillance of EU maritime borders. The study was conducted by Civipol Conseil, a semi-public body and sub-contractor to the French Ministry of Interior. The team responsible for putting together the 'Civipol study'[82] consisted of representatives from the French border police and national police, the Italian Guardia di Finanza, and the Spanish Guardia Civil. The report lauded the initiative launched in 1999 by the Spanish Ministry of Interior and under the responsibility of the Guardia Civil establishing the Sistema Integrado de Vigilancia Exterior (SIVE).[83] SIVE, the study noted, 'reduces a patera's chances of completing a crossing without being detected and inspected, either in the high seas or coastal waters, to 10%'.[84] The report recommended generalising the use of 'SIVE-type' systems. The priority areas for deploying such systems included the 'southern contact zone between Spain and Morocco' (essentially the Canary Islands region), the 'contact zone between Italy, Tunisia and Libya', and the 'contact zone between Greece and Turkey'.[85] The report further stressed the possibility of using what it calls 'new technologies', including the Galileo satellite network and unmanned aerial vehicles.

These findings were carried over a few years later in the BORTEC 'study on technical feasibility of establishing a surveillance system (European surveillance system)', tabled by FRONTEX in January 2007.[86] FRONTEX drafted the report with a 'Core Team' of experts representing the same organisations that had already been involved in the Civipol study, endorsing the approach as 'the EU approach towards the establishment of an Integrated Border Management System'.[87] BORTEC, however, no longer makes reference to 'SIVE-type' systems in the declassified version but advocates a 'system-of-systems' approach whereby the proposed surveillance system would operate by linking existing national systems and systems to be developed. This observation, incidentally, highlights that EUROSUR did not develop in linear fashion (from conception to implementation), but that just as with other parts of the calculation politics in European border policing recounted so far, it is a contingent outcome. Of further relevance to our understanding of these calculation politics, the design and materialisation of EUROSUR and the CPIP overlap partially with processes of mobilisation and stabilisation unfolding in relation to CIREFI and CIRAM, while already envisaging their extension.

There are in fact two ways in which EUROSUR and CPIP can be understood in terms of processes of extension of the knowledge work involved in European border policing that has been surveyed so far. First, they embody concerns with the organisation of policing as a flow, and with the embedding of these concerns in the very design of the various components of the EUROSUR 'system-of-systems'. This includes the very architecture of the NCCs that should serve as the nodes of the system. Figure 7 visualises the 'ideal' NCC according to the work of experts steered by the European Commission. The operations centre, that is the hub for all national border surveillance information and the point of connection with the European-wide network, is the literal centre of the schematics. Figure 8 recasts these individual hubs as parts of EUROSUR, thoroughly inscribing the notion that European border policing works in flows in the design of the system. Second, the figures further reflect how the designing of EUROSUR involves in large parts articulating pre-existing elements of the sociotechnical configuration underpinning European border policing, rather than a technological or organisation rupture or disruption. In particular, they display components of this configuration that have been mobilised and stabilised in the earlier iterations of CIREFI and CIRAM, such as risk analyses and ILO networks.

This does not mean, of course, that EUROSUR and CPIP are simply a reshuffling of pre-existing elements. Figure 9 documents what is currently envisaged as the step that should follow the deployment of EUROSUR and CPIP, namely the establishment of a 'common information sharing environment' (CISE) on EU external borders.

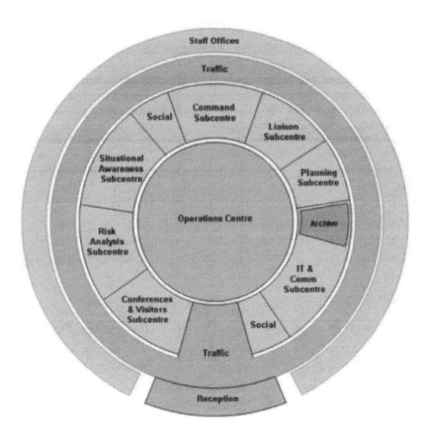

Figure 7. Extension (I): Schematics for EUROSUR NCC.
Seiffarth, 'The development of EUROSUR'.

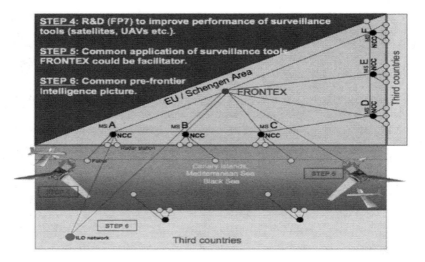

Figure 8. Extension (II): Visualisation of the EUROSUR and CPIP network.
Seiffarth, 'The development of EUROSUR'.

In the CISE perspective, EUROSUR is ensconced as one 'information layer' among several others, concerned in particular with the maritime domain, including vessel monitoring (VMS), maritime safety (Safeseanet) and maritime defence (Marsur, a project from the European Defence Agency involving the exchange of operational maritime information among European navies). The figure calls for two observations. First, the embedding of EUROSUR and CPIP within CISE furthers the design of European border policing as working

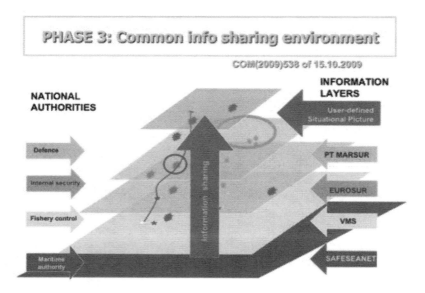

Figure 9. Extension (III): Design of the common information sharing environment.
Seiffarth, 'The development of EUROSUR'.

in, and through, flows. Second, the CISE is evocative for the ways in which we can further develop investigations into European border policing: by conceiving of changes and shifts in terms of the connection, or more accurately here of the 'layering' of previously autonomous sociotechnical configurations.

Conclusion

The article has sought to add to discussions of policing, technology and flows by focusing on the issue of knowledge. It has argued that current understandings of knowledge in the literature interested in contemporary efforts by state authorities to control cross-border movements of persons require further conceptual specification, in order to make otherwise unnoticed aspects of border policing work amenable to empirical inquiry. To this end, it has outlined the need to consider both the 'sharp end' aspects of policing work and the ways in which devices employed in policing practices are designed. It has, finally, foregrounded the notion of 'centres of calculation' as a way to account for the designing of these devices without considering technology as the driver or determinant of policing practices. Centres of calculation draw attention, first, to the meshing of material and ideational, social and technical, aspects in knowledge work in specific sociotechnical configurations and, second, to the fact that change in practices takes place within rather than outside of these sociotechnical configurations. Discussions on centres of calculation also offer a framework to organise such an inquiry, by distinguishing between processes of mobilisation, stabilisation and extension of knowledge work.

The concrete payoff of such a perspective lies in the finding, developed through the examination of the development of EUROSUR and the CPIP as specific devices of European border policing, that there is nothing self-evident or inevitable about the shift to understandings of policing as operating in and through flows. The notion that border policing is organised around and in terms of flows of information, embodied in EUROSUR and CPIP and to be furthered through the development of the CISE project, has solidified through incremental and controversial processes that originate in low-key efforts undertaken through the CIREFI to build statistical knowledge about external border crossing in Europe. The notion that border policing is concerned *with* and operates *through* flows is equally and progressively built through processes of stabilisation, mobilisation and extension of social and material networks of border control actors, institutions and devices. The article may convey the impression that these processes can be neatly isolated and that each is in turn conveniently embodied by a particular device (CIREFI, CIRAM, CPIP). On the one hand however, it is important to reiterate that one particular device does not end where another begins. 'CIREFI data' continued to circulate while CIRAM was being established and contributed to nurturing its functioning. Likewise, CPIP articulates, combines and meshes both (former) CIREFI data and CIRAM into an incrementally different configuration. On the other, 'centres of calculation' and concomitant notions of mobilisation, stabilisation are interpretive rather than representational tools. 'CIREFI data', for instance, was taken as a starting point in the presentation of findings because it is the first setting within which the objective of mobilising data on flows of persons crossing the external borders of EC/EU Member States is endorsed. There is room for further research here however, as the mobilisation of such data is understood to have predated, albeit not in such a systematic way, in the context of

European immigration enforcement cooperation in the 1980s (e.g. Bigo 1996). In the meantime, the findings generated through this approach speak to the 'anti-functionalist' analysis of criminal phenomena developed in policing studies and criminology, which have shown how policing actors contribute to the definition of crime and deviance rather than simply respond to such phenomena, including in order to justify existing powers and resources or the expansion thereof.[88]

This concluding section should also probe and take stock of the limits of both the approach deployed in the article and the findings it generates. The first limit concerns methods, and the issue deserves to be addressed in some details here because claims about methods are an essential part of the STS/A-NT literature where the notion of centres of calculation has gelled.[89] This literature's insistence on grasping technoscience as it is produced rather than conducting an ex-post analysis of specific devices or findings, on production rather than product, comes with the methodical requirement that researchers follow and 'shadow' engineers and scientists 'at the times and at the places where they plan a nuclear plant, undo a cosmological theory, modify the structure of a hormone for contraception, or disaggregate figures used in a new model of the economy'.[90] Yet, shadowing can be complicated by extraneous circumstances, when scholars want, as is the case of this article, to look at things that happened before their time and beyond the places that they can have access to. To circumvent these difficulties, the article has supported its claims by relying on archive work, that is the generation and examination of a corpus of documents, for the purpose of reconstructing the networks of mobilisation, accumulation and expansion through which EUROSUR was eventually produced. Empirically, documents, the ways and contexts in which they are produced, have been a staple of STS/A-NT scholars: Latour and Woolgar, for instance, have examined qualified scientific work as the practice and process of collating and circulating documents, conceived of as 'inscriptions'.[91] But this literature has also routinely relied on 'documentary shadowing' for demonstration purposes. This is the case of Latour's own account of Lapérouse's expedition, recounted earlier, as well as other classic texts of that literature such as John Law's examination of Portuguese imperial expansion in the fifteenth and sixteenth centuries.[92] The article, in turn, has used documents as both receptacles of traces left behind by processes of mobilisation, stabilisation and extension (and in this sense, engaged in the kind of 'ex-post' analysis criticised by Latour and others) and as inscription devices enacting a certain kind of knowledge work (as in, for instance, the case of the CIRAM).

As noted earlier, a second limit is that the findings presented here only illuminate a particular aspect of how issues of policing and flows relate to one another. The essential task at hand, particularly in the currently European and North American context where cross-border movements of persons are largely interpreted and framed as potentially threatening, is to relate the design, the conditions of possibility of knowledge work, with the frontline or 'sharp end' practices that generate knowledge and render it actionable. The analytical perspective offered by centres of calculation is a relational one, which offers the possible to engage with policing as a contentious and controversial matter, including for policing actors themselves, which is by no means advanced as a replacement for 'sharp-end' focused inquiries.

Looking at the establishment of EUROSUR through an examination of the question of knowledge in policing, lastly, could further inform discussions about the role of technology in contemporary forms of policing. The argument developed through the article speaks to a conception of the reliance on 'new' technical devices, especially digital computing, as unfolding within, rather that outside of, the sociotechnical settings enacting border policing. This constitutes a response to the tendency to qualify contemporary policing in terms of its reliance on technology – as 'technology-led policing' for instance[93] or as reflecting 'technologisation of [border] security'[94] rather than through considerations of how specific artefacts, devices or techniques become embedded in existing policing practices. Said differently, the article works to problematise technology beyond its understanding as an external factor driving change in the conception and conduct of (border) policing today. Devices such as the CPIP are always already entangled in social processes and social relations and do not affect policing practices from the 'outside'.[95] This is in part a descriptive requirement meant to counter-balance what Gary Marx called the 'techno-fallacies of the information age',[96] that is the misconceptions about artefacts, technical objects or devices used in policing, security and surveillance practices that may well be reproduced through the scholarly tendency to deliver 'high-tech theory',[97] not necessarily supported by, or conducive to, empirical investigation.

Notes

1. OJEU, *Regulation (EU) No. 1052/2013*, Art. 2(1).
2. Jeandesboz, "Beyond the Tartar Steppe."
3. Duez and Bellanova, "The Making (Sense) of EUROSUR"; Rijpma and Vermeulen, "Eurosur."
4. Brodeur and Dupont, "Knowledge Workers."
5. Latour, *Science in Action*; Jöns, "Centre of Calculation."
6. E.g. Leese and Wittendorp, *Security/Mobility*; Loftus, "Border regimes"; Pickering and Weber, *Borders, mobility and technologies*; Scherrer, Guittet and Bigo, *Mobilités sous surveillance*; Zureik and Salter, *Global surveillance*.
7. Huysmans, "Securitization of Migration."
8. Andreas, *Border Games*; Bigo, *Polices en réseaux*; Weber and Bowling, "Policing Migration."
9. Aas, "'Crimmigrant' bodies"; Weber and Bowling, "Policing Migration."
10. Amoore, "Biometric borders"; Broeders, "The New Digital Borders"; Brouwer, *Digital Borders and Real Rights*; Côté-Boucher, "The diffuse border."
11. Loader, "Governing European Policing," 297 (original italics).
12. Bigo et al., *New Legal Framework for Data Protection*, 34.
13. Council of the EU, *Information Management Strategy*.
14. European Commission, *Overview of Information Management*, 3.
15. Jeandesboz, "Smartening border security"; Leese, "Security/Facilitation Nexus."
16. Bonelli and Ragazzi, "Low-tech security," 478.
17. Amicelle, Aradau and Jeandesboz, "Questioning security devices"; Ruppert, Law and Savage, "Reassembling Social Science Methods."
18. Amoore, "Data Derivatives," 27.
19. Zedner, "The inescapable insecurity," 257.
20. Amicelle, Aradau and Jeandesboz, "Questioning security devices," 297; see also: Valkenburg and van der Ploeg, "Materialities between security and privacy"; Bourne, Johnson and Lisle, "Laboritizing the border."
21. Loftus, "Border regimes," 115.
22. Bonelli and Ragazzi, "Low-tech security"; Tanner and Meyer, "Police work."
23. Casella Colombeau, "Policing the internal Schengen border"; Prokkola, "Neoliberalizing border management."
24. Davidshofer, Jeandesboz and Ragazzi, "Technology and security practices."

25. Loader, "Governing European Policing," 293.
26. Ericson, *Making Crime*; Ericson, "The division of expert knowledge"; Manning, *Symbolic Communications*.
27. Sheptycki, "The Global Cops Cometh," 58.
28. See Endnote 4.
29. Specifically on Berger and Luckmann, *The Social Construction of Reality*.
30. Brodeur and Dupont, "Knowledge Workers," 23.
31. Crampton and Elden, "Space, politics, calculation," 681.
32. Sismondo, *Science and Technology Studies*, 11–12.
33. Ibid, 12 (original italics).
34. Callon, "Society in the Making"; Latour, *Science in Action*; Law, "Technology and Heterogeneous Engineering."
35. Latour, *Science in Action*, 165–166.
36. Jöns, "Centre of Calculation," 159.
37. Latour, *Science in Action*, 215–219.
38. Ibid, 217 (original italics).
39. See Endnote 36.
40. Latour, *Science in Action*, 220.
41. Sismondo, *Science and Technology Studies*, 81; see e.g. Law, *A Sociology of Monsters*.
42. Latour, *Science in Action*, 256–257.
43. OJEC, *Council Conclusions of 30 November 1994*.
44. Ibid, 50.
45. Kraler and Reichel, "Measuring Irregular Migration"; Poulain, Perrin and Singleton, *THESIM*.
46. Council of the EU, *Conceptual framework*.
47. Council of the EU, *Clarification of statistical data*.
48. Council of the EU, *Action plan*.
49. See Endnote 44.
50. OJEC, *Council Conclusions of 30 November 1994*, 51.
51. Council of the EU, *Council Resolution of 27 May 1999*.
52. Council of the EU, *Early warning system and rapid reaction*, 3.
53. Council of the EU, *Draft initiative by the Federal Republic*.
54. Council of the EU, *Optimising the early warning system*, 2.
55. Council of the EU, *Improvements to the CIREFI*, 1.
56. Ibid.
57. Council of the EU, *Early-warning system*.
58. Jeandesboz, "Les usages du voisin."
59. OJEC, *Joint Position of 25 October 1996*.
60. OJEC, *Decision of the Executive Committee*.
61. Council of the EU, *Adoption of Council conclusions*.
62. OJEU, *Council Regulation (EC) No 377/2004*.
63. See Endnote 44.
64. OJEU, *Council Decision of 16 March 2005*.
65. See Endnote 44.
66. OJEU, *Council Regulation (EC) No 2007/2004*.
67. Jeandesboz and Pallister-Wilkins, "Crisis, enforcement and control."
68. House of Lords, *Select Committee on European Union*, 11.
69. Study Group on a European Border Police, *Feasibility study*.
70. Council of the EU, *Border Guard Training*.
71. Council of the EU, *Risk Analysis Centre*.
72. Council of the EU, *Common Integrated Risk Analysis Model*, 2.
73. Council of the EU, *Risk Analysis Centre (RAC)*, 1–2.
74. See Endnote 44.
75. Laitinen, "Introductory talk."
76. FRONTEX, *General Report 2011*, 39.

THE POLICING OF FLOWS

77. See Endnote 44.
78. Neal, "Securitization and Risk," 353.
79. European Commission, *Reinforcing the management*, 8.
80. European Commission, *Examining the creation*.
81. Council of the EU, *Problem of ships*; Council of the EU, *Analysis of Member States' replies*.
82. Council of the EU, *Feasibility study*.
83. See Carling, "Migration control and migrant fatalities."
84. Council of the EU, *Feasibility study*, 27.
85. Ibid., 66.
86. Declassified version available in European Commission, *Impact Assessment*, 78–84.
87. See Endnote 44.
88. Cohen, *Folk Devils*.
89. I should like to acknowledge the comments of two anonymous reviewers, whose demands for clarification drew my attention to this point.
90. See Endnote 40.
91. Latour and Woolgar, *Laboratory Life*.
92. Law, "Technology and Heterogeneous Engineering."
93. de Pauw et al., *Technology-led policing*.
94. Ceyhan, "Technologization of security"; Kaufmann, "Security Through Technology?"
95. E.g. Zedner, "The inescapable insecurity."
96. Marx, "Rocky Bottoms," 83.
97. Bonelli and Ragazzi, "Low-tech security."

Disclosure statement

No potential conflict of interest was reported by the author.

Bibliography

Aas, K. F. "'Crimmigrant' Bodies and Bona Fide Travelers: Surveillance, Citizenship and Global Governance." *Theoretical Criminology* 15, no. 3 (2011): 331–346. doi:10.1177/1362480610396643.
Amicelle, A., C. Aradau, and J. Jeandesboz. "Questioning Security Devices: Performativity, Resistance, Politics." *Security Dialogue* 46, no. 4 (2015): 239–306.
Amoore, L. "Biometric Borders: Governing Mobilities in the War on Terror." *Political Geography* 25, no. 3 (2006): 336–351.
Amoore, L. "Data Derivatives: On the Emergence of a Security Risk Calculus for Our Times." *Theory, Culture & Society* 28, no. 6 (2011): 24–43.
Andreas, P. *Border Games: Policing the U.S.-Mexico Divide*. Ithaca: Cornell University Press, 2009.
Berger, P. L., and T. Luckmann. *The Social Construction of Reality*. London: Penguin Books, 1966.
Bigo, D. *Polices en réseaux: L'expérience Européenne*. Paris: Presses de Sciences Po, 1996.
Bigo, D. "Security and Immigration: Toward a Critique of the Governmentality of Unease." *Alternatives: Global, Local, Political* 27, no. 1 (2002): 63–92.
Bigo, D. "Internal and External Aspects of Security." *European Security* 15, no. 4 (2006): 385–404.
Bigo, D. "The (In) Securitization Practices of the Three Universes of EU Border Control: Military/Navy–Border Guards/Police–Database Analysts." *Security Dialogue* 45, no. 3 (2014): 209–225.
Bigo, D., S. Carrera, G. Gonzalez Fuster, E. Guild, P. De Hert, J. Jeandesboz, and V. Papakonstantinou. *Towards A New EU Legal Framework for Data Protection and Privacy*. Brussels: European Parliament (PE 453.216, 2011.
Bonelli, L., and F. Ragazzi. "Low-Tech Security: Files, Notes, and Memos as Technologies of Anticipation." *Security Dialogue* 45, no. 5 (2014): 476–493.
Bourne, M., H. Johnson, and D. Lisle. "Laboratizing the Border: The Production, Translation and Anticipation of Security Technologies." *Security Dialogue* 46, no. 4 (2015): 307–325.

Brodeur, J.-P., and B. Dupont. "Knowledge Workers or "Knowledge" Workers?" *Policing & Society* 16, no. 1 (2006): 7–26.

Broeders, D. "The New Digital Borders of Europe: EU Databases and the Surveillance of Irregular Migrants." *International Sociology* 22, no. 1 (2007): 71–92.

Brouwer, E. *Digital Borders and Real Rights*. Leiden: Martinus Nijhoff, 2008.

Callon, M. "Society in the Making: The Study of Technology as a Tool for Sociological Analysis." In *The Social Construction of Technological Systems: New Directions in the Sociology and History of Technology*, edited by W. E. Bijker, T. P. Hughes, and T. J. Pinch, 83–103. Cambridge, MA: MIT Press, 1987.

Carling, J. "Migration Control and Migrant Fatalities at the Spanish-African Border." *International Migration Review* 41, no. 2 (2007): 316–343.

Casella Colombeau, S. "Policing the Internal Schenge Borders – Managing the Double Bind between Free Movement and Migration Control." *Policing and Society* 27, no. 5 (2017): 480–493.

Ceyhan, A. "Technologization of Security: Management of Uncertainty and Risk in the Age of Biometrics." *Surveillance & Society* 5, no. 2 (2008): 102–123.

Cohen, S. *Folk Devils and Moral Panics: The Creation of the Mods and the Rockers*. 3rd ed. London: Routledge, 2002.

Côté-Boucher, K. "The Diffuse Border: Intelligence-Sharing, Control and Confinement along Canada's Smart Border." *Surveillance & Society* 5, no. 2 (2008): 142–165.

Council of the EU. *Conceptual Framework to Be Used in the Exchange of Data on Illegal Entry in International Cooperation*. Brussels: Council of the EU (9738/99), 1999.

Council of the EU. *Council Resolution of 27 May 1999 on the Creation of an Early Warning System for the Transmission of Information on Illegal Immigration and Facilitator Networks*. Brussels: Council of the EU (7965/99), 1999.

Council of the EU. *Action Plan to Improve the Control of Immigration*. Brussels: Council of the EU (10017/00), 2000.

Council of the EU. *Clarification of Statistical Data Gathering in CIREFI*. Brussels: Council of the EU (5581/00), 2000.

Council of the EU. *Early Warning System and Rapid Reaction System*. Brussels: Council of the EU (9803/00), 2000.

Council of the EU. *Adoption of Council Conclusions Concerning the Creation of a Network of National Immigration Liaison Officers to Help Control Immigration Flows through the Western Balkans Region*. Brussels: Council of the EU (8684/01), 2001.

Council of the EU. *Draft Initiative by the Federal Republic of Germany for the Adoption of a Council Resolution on Member States' Obligations to Transmit Information on Illegal Immigration and Facilitator Networks Pursuant to an Early Warning System*. Brussels: Council of the EU (13165/1/00 REV1), 2001.

Council of the EU. *Early-Warning System for the Transmission of Information on Illegal Immigration and Facilitator Networks - List of Contact Points*. Brussels: Council of the EU (9728/3/01), 2001.

Council of the EU. *Improvements to the CIREFI Early Warning System*. Brussels: Council of the EU (8049/01), 2001.

Council of the EU. *Optimising the Early Warning System*. Brussels: Council of the EU (5545/01), 2001.

Council of the EU. *Problem of Ships Carrying Illegal Migrants*. Brussels: Council of the EU (13766/01), 2001.

Council of the EU. *Analysis of Member States' Replies to the Questionnaire on Ships Carrying Illegal Migrants*. Brussels: Council of the EU (5976/02), 2002.

Council of the EU. *Border Guard Training*. Brussels: Council of the EU (12570/1/03), 2003.

Council of the EU. *Project on the Common Integrated Risk Analysis Model (CIRAM)*. Brussels: Council of the EU (5622/03), 2003.

Council of the EU. *Risk Analysis Centre*. Brussels: Council of the EU (7396/03), 2003.

Council of the EU. *Feasibility Study on the Control of the European Union's Maritime Borders – Final Report*. Brussels: Council of the EU (11490/1/03), 2003.

Council of the EU. *Risk Analysis Centre (RAC): Information Analysis*. Brussels: Council of the EU (12208/04), 2004.

Council of the EU. *Draft Council Conclusions on an Information Management Strategy for EU Internal Security*. Brussels: Council of the EU (16637/09), 2009.

Crampton, J. W., and S. Elden. "Space, Politics, Calculation: An Introduction." *Social & Cultural Geography* 7, no. 5 (2006): 681–685.

Davidshofer, S., J. Jeandesboz, and F. Ragazzi. "Technology and Security Practices: Situating the Technological Imperative." In *International Political Sociology*, edited by T. Basaran, D. Bigo, E.-P. Guittet, and R. B. J. Walker, 205–227. London: Routledge, 2016.

de Pauw, E., P. Ponsaers, K. van der Vijver, W. Bruggeman, and P. Deelman, eds. *Technology-Led Policing*. Antwerp: Maku, 2011.

Duez, D., and R. Bellanova. "The Making (Sense) of EUROSUR: How to Control the Sea Borders?" In *EU Borders and Shifting Internal Security: Technology, Externalization and Accountability*, edited by R. Bossong and H. Carrapico, 23–44. New York: Springer, 2016.

Ericson, E. *Making Crime: A Study of Detective Work*. Toronto: Butterworths, 1981.

Ericson, E. "The Division of Expert Knowledge in Policing and Security." *British Journal of Sociology* 45, no. 2 (1994): 149–176.

European Commission. *Reinforcing the Management of the European Union's Southern Maritime Borders*. Brussels: European Commission (COM(2006) 733), 2006.

European Commission. *Examining the Creation of a European Border Surveillance System*. Brussels: European Commission, (COM(2008) 68), 2008.

European Commission. *Examining the Creation of a European Border Surveillance System: Impact Assessment*. Brussels: European Commission (SEC(2008) 151), 2008.

European Commission. *Overview of Information Management in the Area of Freedom, Security and Justice*. Brussels: European Commission (COM(2010) 385), 2010.

FRONTEX. *FRONTEX General Report 2011*. Warsaw: FRONTEX, 2012.

FRONTEX. *FRAN Quarterly: Quarter 4, October-December 2015*. Warsaw: FRONTEX, 2015.

House of Lords. *Select Committee on European Union: Twenty-Ninth Report*. London: The Stationery Office, 2003.

Huysmans, J. "The European Union and the Securitization of Migration." *Journal of Common Market Studies* 38, no. 5 (2000): 751–777.

Jeandesboz, J. "Les usages du voisin: Genèse, enjeux et modalités des politiques de voisinage de l'Union européenne." PhD diss., Sciences Po, 2011.

Jeandesboz, J. "Beyond the Tartar Steppe: EUROSUR and the Ethics of European Border Control Practices." In *A Threat against Europe? Security, Migration and Integration*, edited by J. P. Burgess and S. Gutwirth, 111–132. Brussels: VUB Press, 2011.

Jeandesboz, J. "Smartening Border Security in the European Union: An Associational Inquiry." *Security Dialogue* 47, no. 4 (2016): 292–309.

Jeandesboz, J., and P. Pallister-Wilkins. "Crisis, Enforcement and Control at EU Borders." In *Crisis and Migration: Critical Perspectives*, edited by A. Lindley, 115–135. London: Routledge, 2014.

Jöns, H. "Centre of Calculation." In *The SAGE Handbook of Geographical Knowledge*, edited by J. A. Agnew and D. N. Livingstone, 158–170. London: Sage, 2011.

Kaufmann, S. "Security through Technology? Logic, Ambivalence and Paradoxes of Technologised Security." *European Journal of Social Research* 1, no. 1 (2016): 77–95.

Kraler, A., and D. Reichel. "Measuring Irregular Migration and Population Flows - What Available Data Can Tell." *International Migration* 49, no. 5 (2011): 97–128.

Laitinen, I. *Introductory Talk to the Joint Parliamentary Meeting Initiated by the European Parliament and the Parliament of Finland: "From Tampere to the Hague"*. Brussels: European Parliament, 2006. October 2-3.

Latour, B. *Science in Action: How to Follow Scientists and Engineers through Society*. Harvard: Harvard University Press, 1987.

Latour, B., and S. Woolgar. *Laboratory Life: The Construction of Scientific Facts*, Princeton: Princeton University Press, 1986.

Law, J. "Technology and Heterogeneous Engineering: The Case of Portuguese Expansion." In *The Social Construction of Technological Systems: New Directions in the Sociology and History of*

Technology, edited by W. E. Bijker, T. P. Hughes, and T. J. Pinch, 111–134. Cambridge, MA: MIT Press, 1987.

Law, J., ed. *A Sociology of Monsters: Essays on Power, Technology and Domination*. London: Routledge, 1991.

Leese, M. "Exploring the Security/Facilitation Nexus: Foucault at the 'Smart' Border." *Global Society* 30, no. 3 (2016): 412–429.

Leese, M., and Wittendorp S., eds. *Security/Mobility: Politics of Movement*, Manchester: Manchester University Press, 2017.

Loader, I. "Governing European Policing: Some Problems and Prospects." *Policing & Society* 12, no. 4 (2002): 291–305.

Loftus, B. "Border Regimes and the Sociology of Policing." *Policing and Society* 25, no. 1 (2015): 115–125.

Manning, P. K. *Symbolic Communications: Signifying Calls and the Police Response*. Cambridge, MA: The MIT Press, 1988.

Marx, G. T. "Rocky Bottoms: Techno-Fallacies of an Age of Information." *International Political Sociology* 7, no. 1 (2007): 83–110.

Neal, A. W. "Securitization and Risk at the EU Border: The Origins of FRONTEX." *Journal of Common Market Studies* 47, no. 2 (2009): 333–356.

OJEC. *Council Conclusions of 30 November 1994 on the Organization and Development of the Center for Information, Discussion and Exchange on the Crossing of Frontiers and Immigration (Cirefi)*. Brussels: Official Journal of the European Communities (C 274/50, 19.9.96), 1996.

OJEC. *Joint Position of 25 October 1996 Defined by the Council on the Basis of Article K.3 (2) (A) of the Treaty on European Union, on Pre-Frontier Assistance and Training Assignments*. Brussels: Official Journal of the European Communities (L 281/1, 30.10.96), 1996.

OJEC. *Decision of the Executive Committee of 16 December 1998 on Coordinated Deployment of Document Advisers (Sch/Com-Ex (98) 59 Rev.)*. Brussels: Official Journal of the European Communities (29.9.2000), 2000.

OJEU. *Council Regulation (EC) No 377/2004 of 19 February 2004 on the Creation of an Immigration Liaison Officers Network*. Brussels: Official Journal of the European Union (L 64/1, 2.3.2004), 2004.

OJEU. *Council Regulation (EC) No 2007/2004 Establishing a European Agency for the Management of Operational Cooperation at the External Borders of the Member States of the European Union*. Brussels: Official Journal of the European Union (L 349/1, 25.11.2004), 2004.

OJEU. *Council Decision of 16 March 2005 Establishing a Secure Web-Based Information and Co-Ordination Network for Member States' Migration Management Services (2005/267/EC)*. Brussels: Official Journal of the European Union, (L 83/48, 1.4.2005), 2005.

OJEU. *Regulation (EU) No. 1052/2013 of the European Parliament and of the Council of 22 October 2013 Establishing the European Border Surveillance System (Eurosur)*. Brussels: Official Journal of the European Union (L 295/11, 6.11.2013), 2013.

Pickering, S., and L. Weber, eds. *Borders, Mobility and Technologies of Control*. Dordrecht: Springer, 2006.

Poulain, M. *THESIM: Towards Harmonised European Statistics on International Migration*, edited by N. Perrin and A. Singleton. Louvain-la-Neuve: Presses universitaire de Louvain, 2006.

Prokkola, E.-V. "Neoliberalizing Border Management in Finland and Schengen." *Antipode* 45, no. 5 (2012): 1318–1336.

Rijpma, J., and M. Vermeulen. "Eurosur: Saving Lives or Building Borders?" *European Security* 24, no. 3 (2015): 454–472.

Ruppert, E., J. Law, and M. Savage. "Reassembling Social Science Methods: The Challenge of Digital Devices." *Theory, Culture & Society* 30, no. 4 (2013): 22–46.

Scherrer, A., E.-P. Guittet, and D. Bigo, eds. *Mobilités sous surveillance: Perspectives croisées UE-Canada*. Montreal: Athéna, 2010.

Seiffarth, O. "The Development of the European Border Surveillance System (EUROSUR)". Presentation at the 2010 Security Research Conference, Oostende, 22 September, available from: http://www.belspo.be/EU2010/end/SRC10/presentations/Day1_Seiffarth.pps (accessed March 2016), 2010.

Sheptycki, J. "The Global Cops Cometh: Reflections on Transnationalization, Knowledge Work and Policing Subculture." *The British Journal of Sociology* 49, no. 1 (1998): 57–74.

Sismondo, S. *An Introduction to Science and Technology Studies*. 2nd ed. Malden, MA: Wiley-Blackwell, 2010.

Study Group on a European Border Police. *Feasibility Study for the Setting-Up of a "European Border Police" - Final Report*. Rome: Italian Ministry of Interior, 2002.

Tanner, S., and M. Meyer. "Police Work and New 'Security Devices': A Tale from the Beat." *Security Dialogue* 46, no. 4 (2015): 384–400.

Valkenburg, G., and I. van der Ploeg. "Materialities between Security and Privacy: A Constructivist Account of Airport Security Scanners." *Security Dialogue* 46, no. 4 (2015): 326–344.

Weber, L., and B. Bowling. "Policing Migration: A Framework for Investigating the Regulation of Global Mobility." *Policing and Society* 14, no. 3 (2004): 195–212.

Zedner, L. "The Inescapable Insecurity of Security Technologies?" In *Technologies of InSecurity: The Surveillance of Everyday Life*, edited by K. F. Aas, H. O. Gundhus, and H. M. Lomell, 257–270. New York: Routledge-Cavendish, 2009.

Zureik, E., and M. B. Salter, eds. *Global Surveillance and Policing: Borders, Security, Identity*. Cullompton: Willan, 2005.

Liquid modernity and the police *métier*; thinking about information flows in police organisation

James Sheptycki

ABSTRACT

This paper focuses attention on the police *métier* in order to understand the internal organisation of the typical multifunctional urban police service in the UK, Europe and North America. It shows how the modern police organisation has been fundamentally imagined, even if often only at a subconscious level, as the embodiment of machine-like political-legal rationality. The paper observes how 'liquid modernity' has affected machine-thinking in police organisation. Understanding what is going on inside 'the police' is crucial to making sense of how they configure in broader networks of security governance

Introduction

In recent years police agencies in North America, the UK and Europe have come to embrace the terminology of 'intelligence-led policing'.[1] According to a report published by the US Department of Justice:

> To implement intelligence-led policing, police organizations need to re-evaluate their current policies and protocols. Intelligence must be incorporated into the planning process ... Information sharing must become a policy, not an informal practice.[2]

The report indicated that 'effective intelligence operations can be applied equally well to terrorist threats and crimes in the community ... officers "on the beat" are an excellent resource for gathering information on all kinds of potential threats'.[3] However, due to lack of co-ordination and an absence of common polices and terminology for gathering, collating and exchanging relevant information, this vision of things to come was said to be problematic. In order to correct the problem

> ... fundamental changes are needed in the way information is gathered, assessed, and redistributed. Traditional, hierarchical intelligence functions need to be reexamined and replace with cooperative, *fluid* structures that can collect information and move intelligence to end-users more quickly.[4]

New theorists of policing and security governance have imagined information flows across a nodal landscape of networked governance.[5] Clifford Shearing and Monique Marks argue that, under conditions of liquid modernity, the police *qua* 'Police' need to

THE POLICING OF FLOWS

adapt to the new situation.[6] Consequently, police and community security intelligence partnerships that aim to democratise the governance of police intelligence have been promulgated.[7] Zygmunt Bauman used the notion of 'liquid modernity' to describe the social, political and economic changes at the dawn of the twenty-first century.[8] He observed that the characteristic force of modernisation was the pursuit of order – the need to domesticate, categorise and rationalise the world so as to make it controllable, predictable and secure. Equally Bauman observed, modernity brought with it constant technological innovation and social change. For Bauman, liquid modernity is a twenty-first-century condition characterised by the continuing failure to rationalise a world experiencing escalating change. According to him, this condition manifests in endemic uncertainty, heightened insecurity, massive social upheaval and gross inequity, and he quotes the novelist Arundhati Roy saying 'the elite, somewhere at the top of the world, pursue their travels to imagined destinations [while] the poor stay caught in a spiral of crime and chaos'.[9] Bauman discerns that tough control responses to the insecurities of liquid modernity only seem to make matters worse. One important question that organisation theorists ask has to do with what it is like to work inside major social institutions in liquid modern times.[10] What is going on inside the modern police institution as it adapts to the plurality of security arrangements in its task environment?

This paper describes the internal organisational work-world of the typical multifunctional police service found in many cities in the contemporary period. It shows how modern police organisation has been imagined as a machine and how the machine metaphor has evolved over time. Echoing Peter Manning, I will argue that police organisation gains practical coherence as a result of the police *métier*.[11] Describing the internal organisation of the police offers another view of liquid modernity and one that has crucial implications for theories of nodal governance. Democratic police legitimacy has long rested on organisational claims concerning, *inter alia*: bureaucratic rationality, the rule of law and effective policing based on the doctrines of minimal force and policing by consent.[12] Despite the paucity of the machine metaphor for describing police organisation, it percolates through the language of police governance. Because 'the police are like social litmus-paper, reflecting sensitively the unfolding exigencies of a society', the way these organisations adapt internally to liquid modern times has wide implications.[13]

The machine model and the formation of the police *métier*

Accepting for the purposes of this discussion the proposition that the establishment of the London Metropolitan Police in 1829 set the standard for the archetypal modern police, then the centrality of the machine model in imagining police organisation was clear from the start. This is evident in the two commissioners Robert Peel had appointed – Colonel Charles Rowan (of the Light Brigade) and Mr. Richard Mayne (a Barrister) – for the job of establishing the first police of the metropolis.[14] These two men exemplified military and legalistic modes of bureaucratic organisational thinking. In this they were no different than many others involved in the process of state-building and police institution-building in Europe during the post-Napoleonic era.[15] Weber's notion of the bureaucratic 'iron cage' is another way of depicting machine-like organisation of a rational-legalistic authority structure such as the modern state.[16] As with the state more generally, being a central pillar of modern governance the police have been consistently imagined in terms of machine organisation. This explains the emphasis on drill, discipline and training by rote learning in the British police up until the 1970s.[17] The machine metaphor of police and state was essential in imagining how the mechanisms of liberal democracy could hold them to account and thereby render them legitimate.

Municipal police institutions established in the United States took their cue from the Peelian model.[18] According to Albert Reiss, by the end of the nineteenth century these organisations had become so beholden to the 'machine politics' endemic in most US cities that they were in profound need of reform.[19] Pioneers of the police reform movement, such as O.W. Wilson and August Vollmer, aimed to organise policing along the lines of scientific management.[20] Evidence of machine-thinking is everywhere present in this discourse which emphasised measurement of workload distribution based on calls for service. The mantra of professional policing was the efficient management of personnel through bureaucratic design and it evaluated success based on measurable outcomes such as number of arrests and legal citations, and the rapid response to calls for service. The subsequent evolution of police institutions during the twentieth century saw the gradual shift from fixed-point system of walking beat patrol to radio-dispatched car patrol and so-called fire-brigade policing, but machine-thinking remained prevalent regardless.[21]

Much of twentieth-century professional police discourse conjures the image of policing institutions as rank-structured bureaucracies wherein the instructions issued by (sometimes charismatic) senior officers are carried out in machine-like fashion by subordinates in a 'chain-of-command'.[22] In spite of obvious differences between policing and factory work, police managerialism can be heard echoing the tenants of Fredrick Taylor, Elton Mayo and the avant-garde of scientific management.[23] In Manning's words, police are a 'mass-produced service delivery system' which possesses and holds in reserve slack personnel resources that can be mobilised in the event of emergency.[24] In Taylorism, managerial control of worker's behaviour is ensured through the employment of objective information about work operations and work performance and the craft knowledge of workers – 'rules of thumb' – are deemed inefficient. In policing, 'managing for results' consists in systematically collecting and reporting on streams of data measuring individual and unit activity and effectiveness in crime control, traffic law enforcement and the enhancement of public tranquility in a never-ending 'management cycle'.[25]

Police organisation can be highly complex and need not, despite the formal rationality depicted in organisational charts, exactly conform to the machine-like expectations of a rank-structured bureaucracy. Nevertheless, so-called senior managers and mid-level managers do their best to try to make it so, for example, by paying attention to key performance indicators (KPIs). People inside police organisations have played the 'numbers game' since the nineteenth century and the production of police statistics is central to the manufacture of the façade of formal bureaucratic rationality. According to Malcolm Young, in the police organisation 'the detection rate is of vital concern, and a succession of poor [statistical] returns in the monthly or quarterly detection figures can break an ambitious detective inspector … [thus] a stream of "hard facts" and objectified crime statistics are produced'.[26] In Mike Chatterton's view, police officers have a contradictory and complex attitude towards management 'paperwork'; they routinely disparage it while at the same time they 'treat it as important and use it to promote their own ends'.[27] While the police organisations he studied were *laissez faire* by present standards, as Mollie Weatheritt contemporaneously recorded, the tighter routines of target-setting, tasking and deployment now commonly exhibited in the 'intelligence-led' policing organisation were already being established.[28]

Gradually over time the interactions between police management, front-line officers and the technological infrastructure of police organisations forged what Peter K. Manning refers to as the police *métier* – a set of habits and assumptions focused on the trope of 'crime' that 'envisions only the need to control, deter and punish the visible and known contestants'.[29] The *métier* built up during the course of the twentieth century is that of an authoritatively co-ordinated, legitimate organisation employing practices aimed at tracking, surveillance and arrest and it remains ready to apply force, up to and including fatal force, in pursuit of the organisational goal of 'reproducing order', 'making crime', 'policing risk society' and 'governing insecurity'.[30] The police *métier* is orientated around the ability to muster coercive force and undertake systematic population surveillance. Its bearers crucially influence the broader policing web.[31] Manning observed that the theatrical core of the *métier* lies in police patrol work and the work of detectives, and that the occurrence of crime and disorder – 'the incident' – is its 'sacred centre'.[32] Primary police socialisation concerns the mastery of a set of tactics that are about asserting authority, taking control, closing 'the incident' in some fashion and returning to service while producing an adequate account for the purposes of bureaucratic organisation. Managing the flow of police work according to the organisational principles of the machine has ingrained in generations of police officers a ritualised and repetitive mode of thinking about resource allocation based on rewarded activities like issuing citations and arresting offenders and the unconscious assumptions embedded in the police *métier* are such that it makes perfect sense that the measure of police success can be found in police statistics. Police statistics are, for those who compile them, a positive achievement of the panoptic power they represent. The police *métier* provides the impetus for both informal and non-rational police practice and communications as well as for formal management and it configures the flow of information and the production of KPIs.

The police *métier* shapes understandings and assumptions about where disorder happens in the city, how it is generated, by which groups of people and during what hours, days and months of the year. Police records sustain the validity of the practices because they are based on these same assumptions. Institutionalised rewarded activities epitomise the police *métier*. Work is performed on the basis of institutional inducements. Academics publish articles and compete for research funding because they are pro-moted on the basis of their success in doing so. Likewise, *mutatis mutandis*, police perform their work according to rewarded activities such as issuing traffic citations, apprehending suspects, undertaking street checks of suspicious persons and other interventions in places known for the potential for disorder. The KPIs that police are induced by seldom, if ever, include problem-solving, developing community partner-ships or preventing crime through social capacity-building. If such KPIs do exist, they are considered marginal to the more important symbolic activities of routine street checks, criminal apprehension and other activities that are concerned with surveillance, crime control and maintaining social order on the street. There is great variety in police organisation, but despite the shifting fads and fashions found among police profes-sionals there remains a 'fundamental mindset'.[33] The police *métier* is what allows policing to be maintained as a coherent set of practices over time, despite the tides and currents of change that surround it. The police *métier* then refers to occupational assumptions and subconscious premises embedded in technical routines and practices, and it is analytically distinct from the formal organisation that is always transforming. It points to the assumptive world in which the formal organisation operates where taken-for-granted and deeply held understandings about the true nature of the work reside.

Police information flows and the paucity of the machine model

Police scientific management conceives of humans only in terms of organisational needs, a point of view that many, if not all, people are likely to resist. James Q. Wilson called it 'the bureaucracy problem' in *Varieties of Police Behavior*. According to him the problem was how senior command could get the front-line police worker to do the right thing when the evidently special property of police organisation is that discretion increases as one moves *down* the hierarchy.[34] Actually, the situation is even more complicated. In a formally rank-structured bureaucracy such as the police organisation, as a matter of protocol, power is said to be concentrated at the top of the hierarchy. However, in practice responsibility for decisions is pushed down the line as far as possible. The displacement of responsibility for operational decisions onto subordinates relieves senior management of knowledge about entangling details thereby removing the potential for blame when things go wrong. This disassociation puts pressure on middle ranking supervisory personnel to protect the organisation, their bosses and themselves and to return 'good results' in a timely fashion, while avoiding 'trouble'. Credit flows up the structure and is most often appropriated by the highest ranking officer involved in successful projects. The person who thus appropriates credit redistributes it as it seems advantageous to his or her position (and to the image of the organisation) and it is partially bound by internal perceptions of fairness. These fluid relationships have been explained in terms of the gulf between 'street cops' and 'management cops'.[35] For front-line operational patrol officers, police organisation can be a punitive bureaucracy that is as dangerous to their careers as it is capricious. Sergeants and other mid-ranking officers mediate their own precarious positions in relation to 'command-level' personnel who view rules as tools to keep the troops in line.[36]

Information flows in the police organisation concern knowledge that is considered socially dirty and dangerous.[37] Since policing is a 'tainted occupation' and the police are 'the fire it takes to fight fire' police knowledge (i.e. 'intelligence') can burn its handlers.[38] Decisions to circulate information in the police organisation involve assessing the possibility of both 'in the job trouble' and 'on the job trouble'. The latter is anything in the external environment that compels police to undertake action and former refers to 'blow back' from within the police bureaucracy when things go wrong. The need to 'provide cover' and 'protect your back' is a stubborn feature police work. This is especially true for detectives involved in serious and organised crime investigations where the use of covert methods and informants is key.[39] Often the safest way to communicate 'the dirt' is to do so informally and off the record. 'One reason for the oft-noted tendency of patrolmen to form cliques, factions and fraternal associations', J. Q. Wilson observed, is to 'defend officers … because the administrator, if he is a strong man, is "out to get us" and, if he is a weak one, is "giving way before outside pressure"'.[40] Inbuilt tensions and conflicts of interest affect the flow of information. Cooperation, as illustrated by the many examples of shift sergeants and other supervisory personnel colluding with front-line officers in the manufacture of formal accounts, is one adaptation.[41] The centrality of street stories and the importance of keeping secrets in the police occupation undercut rationalised machine-thinking but it is redolent of the police *métier*.[42]

Managing the flow of 'human intelligence' presents enormous organisational difficulties because of its low visibility.[43] Police work is enabled by information-gathering, analytical and investigative tools and techniques including covert surveillance, tasked criminal informants, 'bugging' and visual surveillance devices, closed-circuit television, financial tracking capabilities, and a vast range of computer facilities, packages and databases.[44] Enormous quantities of information (dirty data) exists at what might best be called a 'pre-investigative stage' in the intelligence process and it forms the basis of decision-making for tactical priority and strategic agenda setting in intelligence-led policing.[45] According to Martin Innes, detectives assemble information into a form of knowledge cognisable as either intelligence or evidence.[46] The former has a 'projected internal career', the latter a 'projected external career'.[47] In other words, the flows of police intelligence information are strictly internal, whereas information as evidence flows to outside audiences. Perhaps not surprisingly, the amount of information in police hands frequently 'outstrips the organisational capacity to act upon it', consequently 'an important form of action in intelligence-led policing systems is in fact no action'.[48] With decisions based on 'dirty data', the tendency to secretiveness and a high degree of informalism in the backstage areas known only to organisational *habitués* is significant.

Police organisations are not rationally structured in the way that organisational charts suggest because they are in a constant state of reform.[49] According to Christopher Giacomanionio, police 'organizations retrench or grow, acquire new technologies, connect with new partners, cycle through priorities, remove old leaders and get new ones, redesign organizational charts and hierarchies, outsource or disregard certain tasks while expanding into novel spheres of activity'[50] and otherwise are 'transformed'.[51] Information flows in the police organisation are shaped in irrational ways due to ongoing and perpetual modifications of informational processes. Edward R. Maguire calls it 'functional differentiation'.[52] He notes that police organisations tend to become more elaborate over time because they embrace reforms that increase structural complexity but not those that call for decreases. For example, most North American police departments have a 'hold-up squad' specialising in incidents involving armed robbery, and they also typically have drug squads, anti-gang units, vice squads and special patrol groups who in practice 'hunt' on the same territory for much the same 'quarry' as the hold-up squad. Police managers struggle to ensure open information sharing among these various specialist units. However, the organisational incentive is for special units to 'buffer' themselves, which among other things means to hoard information as a means to protect organisational turf.[53] Information is shared outside of the small group only informally, strategically and parsimoniously (if at all) and this is another important reason why police organisation is not fully rational and machine like.

Machine model thinking shapes beliefs about police action and accountability. From a perspective outside the police organisation, there is a basic belief that administrative prescriptions and the 'rule of law' mechanistically hold police accountable. For example, many civilians seem to believe that when the Chief of Police issues an order – for example, to end the practice of 'street checks', to 'proactively arrest' in all occurrences of domestic violence and sexual assault, or to clamp down on speeding in school zones – front-line officers will comply as night follows day. For police insiders, machine model thinking is reflected in the beliefs of some officers about the police ability to issue commands on the basis of legal policy, rules and regulations. With machine model thinking, 'police subculture' is something to be cajoled and manipulated by police managers and is usually a term used to denote problematic 'rank-and-file' resistance to rational management decisions.[54] The trouble is, the police organisation is not a machine. Capable of coming together into units, squads or teams that *sometimes* behave with military precision, the organisation is fluid. It is held together by a myriad of formal and informal rules, rational and non-rational beliefs and it retains organisational coherence by being oriented to the police *métier* not because of machine rationality. Despite the paucity of the machine model, it nevertheless persists as a feature of the police *métier*, often only at a subconscious level. To remind the reader, the *métier* is an aspect of police professionalism and its defining feature involves the use of surveillance and coercion in the maintenance of a putative social order.

Liquid modernity and the police *métier*

In the final decade of the twentieth century, new computer technologies gave rise to the new 'cybernetic model' of thinking about police organisation. The term cybernetic is often used in a rather loose way to mean any system of organisational control that depends on technology. Cybernetics is a way of thinking about organisation, which is imagined as a machine – electronic, neural, economic and social. The cybernetic picture of information flows within police organisations is highly complex involving closed-system intelligence 'cycles', with 'inputs', 'outputs' and 'processes'. Cybernetic models are never simple machines because they attempt to build in features designed to compensate for those factors that filter, divert and block the flow of system information, features intended to enable managers to achieve increased automation.[55]

The cybernetic model is another variation of machine-thinking. This is nowhere more evident than it is with CompStat. David Weisburd and others observed that despite the possibilities that computerisation holds for problem-solving, the CompStat model served ultimately to 'maintain and reinforce the "bureaucratic" or "paramilitary" model of police organization'.[56] CompStat policing was linked to 'zero tolerance'.[57] The theory of zero-tolerance is known well enough – that is, by focusing on 'quality of life offences' and 'low-level' street disorder, and using strong, coercive police powers against them, more serious types of disorder and crime will be prevented from occurring.[58] The machine-logic of CompStat aimed to ensure that front-line personnel were active in enforcing against low-level disorder and maintaining an intense focus on traditional police 'symbolic assailants'.[59] CompStat and other variations of intelligence-led policing using advanced computer technologies resulted in the super-quantification of police work. Weisburd *et al.* concluded that, 'American police agencies have adopted CompStat enthusiastically more because of its promise of reinforcing the traditional hierarchical

THE POLICING OF FLOWS

model of police organization than for its efforts to empower problem solving in police agencies'.[60]

At the beginning of the twenty-first century

> ... although computers have been used by police services for more than two decades to store information, their miniaturisation combined with the explosion of the Internet have made possible the dematerialisation of the police station. Mobile Data Computers permit the retrieval of information from police databases and the lodging of reports from police cars, which can also exchange text messages with each other. Files can also be updated from the field, sparing police officers unnecessary return visits to their station.[61]

This is the harbinger of what we might call the 'uberisation of urban policing' with all of the techno-fallacies that implies.[62] Police now view the world largely through screens: patrol cars with their 'mobile data terminals', intelligence analysts with their intelligence maps and charts, and senior managers with their computerised 'executive dashboards'. Police view through screens a 'hyper-reality' and thereby decide how to apply coercion and surveillance in social situations where coercion and surveillance are deemed necessary and legitimate according to internally generated organisational metrics displayed on screens.

As surveillance experts long practiced in the application of panoptic power, police are now subject to synoptic power.[63] Ericson's and Haggerty's landmark book *Policing the Risk Society* was an early indicator of the effects when police system surveillance includes also surveillance on those whom the system depends to undertake surveillance. They record reactions to the growing complexity of police 'knowledge work' observing that the instruction, policy and operational manuals – like the information systems themselves – are 'large complex and confusing'. As a result, according to one police manager they quote, people in such positions 'preferred crisis management rather than long term planning'. Operational and policy manuals 'articulate the administrative structure of reporting' and provide police organisations with 'the imagery of rationality', but they are not very useful in the context of day-to-day police work, where the 'rule of thumb' prevails.[64] Yet, rulebooks form the basis of the promotional examinations:

> ... against a background of increasingly intense competition for promotion in police organizations, they [management manuals] are therefore useful for deselecting those who have difficulty with the formats and thinking associated with administrative rules".[65]

They are also useful in the event that something goes wrong, since 'every officer violates administrative rules every day ... the question becomes one of using the rules to discipline an officer who has been found wanting'.[66] In 'The result', they conclude

> ... is a perpetual sense of everyone's part of being out of control. The organization is experienced as a juggernaut. There is an endemic feeling of insecurity that is derived from a feeling of never having enough knowledge and from a reflexive awareness that there are always systemic faults that can be ameliorated by better communication rules formats and technologies.[67]

Observation has revealed that the functionality of police technology is more often assumed than demonstrated, while constant technological innovation creates the feeling of frenetic organisational change. When new, sophisticated technologies are acquired, extensive, expensive and time-consuming training is required. Constant software and hardware 'upgrades' mean this is an endless process.[68] In organisations which count on 'results' deficiencies in training encourage pragmatic solutions and 'work arounds', which usually chime with the police *métier* and often involve patterns of informal communication that circumvent formal ones and thereby undercut the putative formal rationality of the organisation. Studies in Canada and Australia reveal structural disconnections between the technological solutions and the actual police work.[69] There is a gap between the 'infostructure' and the 'infoculture' – between all of the technological apparatus of contemporary policing knowledge work and what the users of the technology think they know. Hughes' and Jackson's upbeat conclusion was that

> ... while information systems and information technologies have a role to play in knowledge management strategies, without human expert interpretation these systems are merely tools that harvest information rather than create knowledge ... [thus] knowledge creation will not result from investment in technology itself, but from additionally investment in specific people skills that can make best use of the information assisted by the technology.[70]

Despite the rapid pace of change, proponents of intelligence-led policing believe in rationalisation of police knowledge management and that a fluid organisational situation suspended in the gulf between the infoculture and the infostructure can be managed for something approaching optimal efficiency and effectiveness.[71] Nevertheless, there are number of organisational pathologies that have been named in the professional lexicon of police intelligence expertise.[72] Police intelligence professionals worry about lack of crucial information and the ability to put it together. The solution to these worries is 'compulsive data demand' and 'defensive data concentration', which is when human agents attempt to compensate for various knowledge gaps by intensification of information acquisition and assemblage. Sometimes this results in 'data duplication', where information is held in separate 'information silos', and either the system as a whole, or parts of it, can suffer from 'information overload'. Constant technological change, with system software and hardware upgrades, contributes further to this organisational complexity by elaborating a 'digital divide' which creates 'functional disconnections' in information flows and thereby generates 'institutional friction' and non-optimal outcomes. This is often due to the generation of 'noise' which arises because, in the cybernetic intelligence system, intelligence outputs are interpretations of information inputs, which are myriad, potentially endless and inevitably often enough of dubious provenance. The flow of outputs can generate 'false positives', 'false negatives', as well as the suffering from recurrent problems of 'blind spots', 'linkage blindness' and the continuing perception of 'knowledge gaps'. Institutional thinking of this quality can easily result in police misapplication of coercion and surveillance, attendant unforeseen consequences and thereby contribute to the amplification of insecurity.

What the police do is inevitably fluid because it is in response to unpredictable demands emanating from the task environment. Inside the police, organisational processes are fluid but evidence of machine-thinking predominates even if misrecognised. To its participants the organisation gains coherence and meaning, despite its obvious flaws, in relation to the police *métier*. Cybernetic modelling of internal police intelligence flows imagines connections to other agencies in the form of inter-institutional security

THE POLICING OF FLOWS

partnerships, but this image is predicated on machine-thinking and seldom acknowledges the actual fluidity of police internal organisation. Whatever else is achieved, the transformative logic of police organisation always includes fundamental operating procedures concerning surveillance and coercion. When the police collaborate in the governance of security they do so on the basis of their *métier*.

Intelligence flows, plural security partnerships and the police *métier*

Plural policing and security partnerships are shaped by the available mentalities and technologies.[73] Across the police sector, 'police agencies have started to cooperate on common enemies such as counterfeiters, arms smugglers, and manufacturers of false documents [and so] law enforcement has laid the foundation for successful cooperation against terrorists as well'.[74] The police *métier* shapes the internal flow of police institutional expert knowledge. From this perspective, security governance is less concerned with social justice and more concerned with the justifiable application of coercion and surveillance in the governance of uncertainty. Contemplating the internal flows of information that constitute police organisation brings new understanding to the crisis of liquid modern times. What goes on inside 'the police' changes when some people live behind walls, hire guards, drive armoured vehicles and carry mace or handguns. With nodal governance, the social fragmentation of liquid modernity leaves 'the police' as specialists in the exercise of forceful high-level social control of regional and transnational crime, public order, counterterrorism and security functions while policing in local communities is increasingly left over to networks of security providers competing in the cash nexus. In policing intelligence there is a high a degree of uncertainty and the ever-present possibility of unknown unknowns.[75] Policing practice is fraught with moral hazard and the urge to try to mechanise the flow of information as a means to accountability is understandable, but the belief that machine-thinking can bring the police to account misses the *métier*. In a world where accurate knowledge is in short supply, the formalities of security sector governance often fail to create real certainty and provide cover for organisational actors when things go wrong.

Radical thinking about strategic priority setting in intelligence-led policing has been critical of the language of risks, threats and harms reified as objective indicators justifying police action. As Kira Vrist Rønn points out, these are normative concepts, like tastiness and prettiness. She is critical of the belief that police intelligence analysts 'are superior in terms of interpreting the criminal environment', since a 'problem arises when what is measured is not easily defined and values are in dispute'.[76] Rønn recommends a 'participatory approach' to intelligence that draws on a variety of perspectives in order to measure intelligence-led policing outcomes. The approach she envisages includes focus group interviews, Delphi studies and other similar research methods that draw in other actors besides police technocrats. The narrow version of relevant information flow in intelligence-led policing is that it is for and by organisation experts steeped in the police *métier*. A broad democratic approach to intelligence gathering brings in the values, interests and interpretations of a broader mix of community stakeholders. Rønn argues that a democratic approach contributes to more reliable and accurate priority setting within police organisations. The general idea is of a balanced approach that incorporates the expert knowledge of intelligence analysts and police officers equally alongside that of community members, crime victims, academic experts and others, which aims to increase the reliability of strategic intelligence priority setting and the measurement and evaluation of specific tactical interventions. This offers a conceptual bridge between the language of intelligence-led policing to other professional police discourses like community and problem-oriented policing.[77] Democratic influence is achieved by changing the inputs to the internalised flows of intelligence-led policing and thereby the expectations of projected outputs. Democratic participation in governing internal police intelligence flows would ensure 'accountability and reasonability of the decision-making process related to setting police priorities'.[78] Whether new models for the democratic governance of police intelligence will succeed in significantly altering the police *métier* has yet to be demonstrated, but they seem to harbour elements of machine-thinking.

The continuing prevalence of the machine-thinking within the police *métier* is reinforced by the feeling that social order needs to be enforced by strong measures like scientific rationality, rule of law and zero-tolerance enforcement, which needs to get efficiently with minimal economic cost. Organisationally speaking this is practically difficult since the police are in a perpetual state of flux, so an additional concern to lubricate the flow of intelligence has been injected into the discourse. The continuing influence of machine-thinking in contemporary intelligence-led policing is a paradox as is the currently imagined ends of policing – securing a social order that has become liquid. Recognising that the encroachment of the police *métier* into the broader governance of security results in restricted freedom, privacy invasion, discrimination, social exclusion and is self-defeating, it would perhaps be better to prioritise absorbent value questions that are non-rational, for example, concerning human rights, social well-being, psychological prosperity and communal solidarity.[79] The merely sceptical view is that the collaborative dream of achieving social justice through plural networks of security pays insufficient attention to the difficulty of doing so under liquid modern conditions in which the continuing failure to rationalise a world experiencing escalating change results in intensifying insecurity. The continuing failure to rationalise and control uncertainty by police means – to subject liquid modernity to the disciplines of the police *métier* – conjures up the image of King Canute commanding the tide with a sword.

Notes

1. Aepli et al., "Decision Making in Policing"; Devroe et al., *Tides and Currents in Police Theories*; Gill et al., *Intelligence Theory*; McCue, *Data Mining and Predictive Analysis*; Mastrofski, "Making Sense of CompStat"; and Ratcliffe, *Intelligence-Led Policing*.
2. Peterson, *New Intelligence Architecture*, vii.
3. Ibid., vii.
4. Ibid., vii – emphasis mine, JS.
5. Shearing and Johnston, *Governing Insecurity*.
6. Shearing and Marks, "New Police in the Liquid 21st Century,"
7. Delpeuch and Ross, *Democratic Governance of Police*; Renn "Democratizing Strategic Intelligence?"; and Sheptycki, "The New Human Security Paradigm."
8. Bauman, *Liquid Times*; and Bauman and Lyon, *Liquid Surveillance*.

9. Bauman, *Liquid Times*, 8
10. Clegg and Baumeler, "From Iron Cages to Liquid Modernity."
11. Manning, *Democratic Policing.*
12. Reiner, *The Politics of the Police,* 71–77.
13. Reiner, "Policing a Postmodern Society," 762.
14. Reiner, *Politics of the Police,* 43
15. Bayley, "Police Function, Structure, and Control"; Bayley, "Comparative Organization of the Police"; and Liang, *Rise of Modern Police.*
16. See note 10 above.
17. Reiner, *The Politics of the Police,* 80.
18. Miller, *Cops and Bobbies.*
19. Reiss, "Police Organization."
20. Fogelson, *Big-City Police*; and Walker, *Critical History of Police Reform.*
21. Dupont, "Technological Errors of the Past," 34-37.
22. Bordua and Reiss, "Command, Control and Charisma."
23. McLaughlin, *New Police*; and Ritzer; "'McDonaldization' of Society."
24. Manning, "Information Technologies and the Police," 354–55.
25. Butler, *Police Management,* 13 & 187.
26. Young, *Inside Job*, 255–256.
27. Chatterton, "Managing Paperwork," 107.
28. Chatterton, "The Supervision of Patrol Work"; Chatterton, "Assault Charges"; and Weatheritt, *Innovations in Policing.*
29. Manning, *Democratic Policing,* 105–106.
30. Ericson, Crime in an Insecure World.
31. Brodeur, *Policing Web.*
32. Manning, *The Technology of Policing,* 81–82
33. Sklansky, *Police Professionalism.*
34. Wilson, *Varieties of Police Behavior.*
35. Reuss-Ianni, *Two Cultures of Policing.*
36. Manning and van Maanen, *View from the Street*; Moskos, *Cop in the Hood*; and Van Maanen, *Working the Street.*
37. See note 26 above.
38. Bittner, *Functions of Police*, 6–8.
39. Billingsley et al., *Informers.*
40. See note 34 above, 73.
41. van Maanen, "Working the Street"; and Manning, *Police Work.*
42. Jackall, *Wild Cowboys*; and Jackall, *Street Stories.*
43. Gill et al., *Intelligence Theory.*
44. Maguire, "Policing by Risks and Targets"; and Maguire and John, "Intelligence, Surveillance and Informants."
45. Ratcliffe and Sheptycki, "Setting the Strategic Agenda."
46. Innes, *Investigating Murder.*
47. Travers and Manzo, *Law in Action.*
48. Innes and Sheptycki, "From Detection to Disruption," 13.
49. Bayley, "Comparative Organization of the Police," 539.
50. Giacomantonio, *Policing Integration*, 21.
51. See also, Henry and Smith, *Transformations in Policing.*
52. Maguire, *Organizational Structure in American Police*; Maguire, "Iron Cage of Rationality"; and Maguire and Uchida, "Explaining Police Organizations."
53. See note 50 above.
54. Loftus, *Police Culture.*
55. Gill, "Cybernetic Model," esp. 303–304.

56. Weisburd et al., "Reforming to Preserve," 422; Haggerty and Ericson, "Surviellant Assemblage"; Haggerty and Ericson, "Militarization of Policing"; Hills and Berger, "Paramilitary Policing Juggernau'"; and McCulloch, *Blue Army*.
57. Greene, "Zero Tolerance and Policing."
58. Bowling, "Zero Tolerance or Crack's Decline?"
59. Manning, *Police Work*, 498; Manning, *The Technology of Policing*.
60. Weisburd et al., "Reforming to Preserve," 450.
61. Dupont, "Policing in the Information Age," 37.
62. see also Leman-Langlois, *Technocrime, Policing and Surveillance*; and Marx and Corbett, "Technofallacies in Electronic Monitoring."
63. Doyle et al., *Eyes Everywhere*.
64. Ericson and Haggerty, *Risk Society*, 348–349.
65. Ibid., 349.
66. Ibid.
67. Ibid., 447.
68. Aepli et al., *Decision Making in Policing*.
69. *Giacomantonio, Policing Integration, 127*; Hughes and Jackson, "Information in a Policing Environment," 66–77; Sanders and Hannem, "Policing 'the Risky'"; Sanders and Henderson, "Police 'Empires'."
70. Hughes and Jackson, "Information in a Policing Environment," 67.
71. Ratcliffe, Intelligence-Led Policing; and Stainer, "Organizational Pathologies in Police Information Sharing."
72. Sheptycki, "Organizational Pathologies."
73. Johnston and Shearing, *Governing Security*, 28–30.
74. Bayer, *Blue Planet*, ix.
75. Higgins, "Intelligence collection," 85.
76. Renn, "Democratizing Strategic Intelligence," 57–59.
77. Bullock, "Community, Intelligence-led Policing"; Bullock *Citizens, Community and Crime Control*; Sheptycki, "Human Security Paradigm'; see: Sheptycki, "The Raft of the Medusa," for a meditation on the likely consequences of the failure to democratise intelligence-led policing.
78. see notes 76, 62 above.
79. Ericson, "Uncertainties of Risk Management."

Acknowledgements

Research for this paper was made possible by Social Sciences and Humanities Research Council of Canada Insight grant number 435-2013-1283. The author would like to thank Karine Coté-Boucher, Samuel Tanner and the other participants at the workshop on New Perspectives on Policing Flows, held at the Université de Montréal, 12–13 November 2015 and Marleen Easton, Stanny De Vlieger and Arne Dormaels and the other participants in the workshop on Information Flows in Policing, organised by the Centre for Policing and Security at the University of Ghent on 27 September 2016. Their insights and thoughts have been invaluable in shaping this paper for publication.

Disclosure statement

No potential conflict of interest was reported by the author.

Funding

Research for this paper was made possible by Social Sciences and Humanities Research Council of Canada Insight grant number 435-2013-1283.

Bibliography

Aepli, P., O. Ribaux, and E. Summerfield. *Decision Making in Policing: Operations and Management*. Paris: EPFL Press, 2011.

Bauman, Z. *Liquid Times; Living in an Age of Uncertainty*. Cambridge: Polity Press, 2007.

Bauman, Z., and D. Lyon. *Liquid Surveillance; A Conversation*. Cambridge: Polity Press, 2013.

Bayer, M. D. *The Blue Planet; Informal International Police Networks and National Intelligence*. Washington, DC: US Government Printing Office, 2010.

Bayley, D. "Police Function, Structure, and Control in Western Europe and North America: Comparative and Historical Studies." In *Crime and Justice*, edited by M. Tonry, Vol. 1, 109–143. The University of Chicago Press, 1979.

Bayley, D. "Comparative Organization of the Police in English Speaking Countries." In *Crime and Justice* Vol. 15 *Modern Policing*, edited by M. Tonry, 509–545. The University of Chicago Press. 1992.

Billingsley, R., T. Nemitz, and P. Bean. *Informers: Policing, Policy Practice*. Cullhompton: Willan, 2000.

Bittner, E. *The Functions of Police in Modern Society*. Chevy Chase, MD: National Institute of Mental Health, 1970.

Bordua, D. J., and A. Reiss. "Command, Control and Charisma." *American Journal of Sociology* 72, no. 1 (1966): 68–76. doi:10.1086/224261.

Bowling, B. "The Rise and Fall of New York Murder: Zero Tolerance or Crack's Decline?" *British Journal of Criminology* 39, no. 4 (1999): 531–554. doi:10.1093/bjc/39.4.531.

Brodeur, J.-P. *The Policing Web*. Oxford: Oxford University Press, 2010.

Bullock, K. "Community, Intelligence-Led Policing and Crime Control." *Policing and Society* 23, no. 2 (2013): 125–144. doi:10.1080/10439463.2012.671822.

Bullock, K. *Citizens, Community and Crime Control*. Basingstoke: Palgrave Macmillan, 2014.

Butler, A. J. P. *Police Management*. London: Gower, 1984.

Castells, M. *The Information Age: Economy, Society and Culture 1996-1998, 2000-2004 editions*. Oxford: Blackwell, Vol. 1 *The Rise of the Network Society* (1996, 2nd ed. 2000) Vol. 2 *The Power of Identity* (1997 2nd ed. 2004); Vol. 3, *End of the Millenium* (1998, 2nd ed. 2000), 1996-2004.

Chatterton, M. "The Supervision of Patrol Work under the Fixed Points System." In *The British Police*, edited by S. Holdaway. London: Edward Arnold, 1979.

Chatterton, M. "Police Work and Assault Charges." In *Control in the Police Organization*, edited by M. Punch. Cambridge, MA: MIT Press, 1983.

Chatterton, M. "Managing Paperwork." In *Police Research: Some Future Prospects*, edited by M. Weatheritt. 107–138. Aldershot: Avebury; Published in Association with the UK Police Foundation, 1989.

Clegg, S., and C. Baumeler. "From Iron Cages to Liquid Modernity in Organizational Analysis." *Organization Studies* 31, no. 12 (2010): 1713–1733. doi:10.1177/0170840610387240.

Delpeuch, T., and J. E. Ross. *Comparing the Democratic Governance of Police Intelligence*. Northampton, MA: Edward Elgar, 2016.

Devroe, E., P. Ponsaars, L. G. Moor, J. Greene, L. Skinns, L. Bisschop, A. Verhage, and M. Bacon, eds. *Tides and Currents in Police Theories*, *Journal of Police Studies*, No. 25. Antwerpen: Maku, 2012.

Doyle, A., R. Lippert, and D. Lyon. *Eyes Everywhere; The Global Growth of Camera Surveillance*. London: Routledge, 2013.

Dupont, B. "Technological Errors of the Past in Perspective." In *Policing the Lucky Country*, edited by M. Enders and B. Dupont, 34–48. Annadale, NSW: Hawkins Press, 2001.

Ericson, R. V. *Making Crime; A Study of Police Detective Work*. Toronto: Butterworths, 1981.

Ericson, R. V. *Reproducing Order, A Study of Police Patrol Work*. Toronto: Toronto University Press, 1982.

Ericson, R. V. "The Division of Expert Knowledge in Policing and Security." *The British Journal of Sociology* 45, no. 2 (1994): 149–175. doi:10.2307/591490.

Ericson, R. V. "Ten Uncertainties of Risk-Management Approaches to Security." *Canadian Journal of Criminology and Criminal Justice* 48, no. 3 (2006): 345–356. doi:10.3138/cjccj.48.3.345.

Ericson, R. V. *Crime in an Insecure World*. Cambridge: Polity, 2007.

Ericson, R. V., and K. D. Haggerty. *Policing the Risk Society*. Oxford: Clarendon, 1997.

Fogelson, R. M. *Big-City Police*. Cambridge, MA: Harvard University Press, 1977.

Giacomantonio, C. *Policing Integration; The Sociology of Police Co-ordination Work*. London: Palgrave Macmillan, 2015.

Gill, P. "Making Sense of Police Intelligence? The Use of a Cybernetic Model in Analysing Information and Power in Police Intelligence Processes." *Policing and Society* 8 (1998): 289–314. doi:10.1080/10439463.1998.9964793.

Gill, P., S. Marrin, and M. Phythian. *Intelligence Theory: Key Questions and Debates*. London: Routledge, 2008.

Greene, J. R. "Zero Tolerance and Policing." In *The Oxford Handbook of Police and Policing*, edited by M. D. Reisig and R. J. Kane, 172–197. Oxford: Oxford University Press, 2014.

Haggerty, K. D., and R. V. Ericson. "The Militarization of Policing in the Information Age." *Journal of Political and Military Sociology* 27 (1999): 233–255.

Haggerty, K. D., and R. V. Ericson. "The Surveillant Assemblage." *British Journal of Sociology* 51, no. 4 (2000): 605–622. doi:10.1080/00071310020015280.

Henry, A., and D. J. Smith, eds. *Transformations in Policing*. Aldershot: Ashgate, 2007.

Higgins, O. "The Theory and Practice of Intelligence Collection." In *Strategic Thinking in Criminal Intelligence*, edited by J. H. Ratcliffe, 85–107. Annandale, NSW: The Federation Press, 2009.

Hills, S., and R. Beger. "A Paramilitary Policing Juggernaut." *Social Justice* 36, no. 1 (2009): 25–40.

Hughes, V., and P. Jackson. "The Influence of Technical, Social and Structural Factors on the Effective use of Information in a Policing Environment." *The Electronic Journal of Knowledge Management* 2, no. 1 (2004): 65–76.

Innes, M. *Investigating Murder; Detective Work and the Police Response to Criminal Homicide*. Oxford: Clarendon, 2003.

Innes, M., and J. Sheptycki. "From Detection to Disruption: Intelligence and the Changing Logic of Police Crime Control in the United Kingdom." *International Criminal Justice Review* 14 (2004): 1–24. doi:10.1177/105756770401400101.

Jackall, R. *Wild Cowboys, Urban Marauders and the Forces of Order*. Cambridge, MA: Harvard University Press, 1997.

Jackall, R. *Street Stories: The World of Police Detectives*. Cambridge, MA: Harvard University Press, 2005.

Kraska, P. B. *Militarizing the American Criminal Justice System; The Changing Roles of The Armed Forces and the Police*. Boston: Northeastern University Press, 2001.

Leman-Langlois, S. *Technocrime, Policing and Surveillance*. London: Routledge, 2013.

Liang, H.-H. *The Rise of Modern Police and the European State System from Metternich to the Second World War*. Cambridge: Cambridge University Press, 1992.

Loftus, B. *Police Culture in a Changing World*. Oxford: Clarendon, 2009.

Maguire, E. R. *Organizational Structure in American Police Agencies; Context, Complexity and Control*. Albany, NY: Sate University of New York Press, 2003.

Maguire, E. R. "Police Organizations and the Iron Cage of Rationality." In *The Oxford Handbook of Police and Policing*, edited by M. D. Reisig and R. E. Kane, 68–98. Oxford: Oxford University Press, 2010.

Maguire, E. R., and C. D. Uchida. "Explaining Police Organizations." In *Criminal Justice Theory: Explaining the Nature and Behavior of Criminal Justice*, edited by E. R. Maguire and D. E. Duffe, 2nd ed., 81–115. London: Routledge, 2015.

Maguire, M. "Policing by Risks and Targets: Some Dimensions and Implications of Intelligence-Led Crime Control." *Policing and Society* 9, no. 4 (2000): 315–336. doi:10.1080/10439463.2000.9964821.

Maguire, M., and T. John. "Intelligence, Surveillance and Informants: Integrated Approaches." London Home Office: Police Research Group – Crime Detection and Prevention Series Paper 64, 1995.

Manning, P. K. "Information Technologies and the Police." In *Crime and Justice* Vol. 15 *Modern Policing*, edited by M. Tonry. Chicago: Chicago University Press, 1992.

Manning, P. K. *The Technology Of Policing: Crime Mapping, Information Technology, and The Rationality of Crime Control*. New York: New York University Press, 2008.

Manning, P. K. *Democratic Policing in a Changing World*. Boulder: Paradigm Publishers, 2010.

Manning, P. K. *Police Work; The Social Organization of Policing*. Prospect Heights, IL: Waveland Press, (1997)[1977].

Manning, P. K., and J. van Maanen, eds. *Policing a View from the Street*. Santa Monica, CA: Goodyear, 1978.

Marx, G., and R. Corbett. "Critique: No Soul in the New Machine: Technofallacies in the Electronic Monitoring Movement." *Justice Quarterly* 8, no. 3 (1991): 399–414. doi:10.1080/07418829100091111.

Mastrofski, S. D. "Making Sense of CompStat: How Popular Police Reform Works and Doesn't Work." In *Prospects and Problems in an Era of Police Innovation; Contrasting Perspectives*, edited by D. Weisbburd and A. Braga. Cambridge: Cambridge University Press, 2005.

McCue, C. *Data Mining and Predictive Analysis; Intelligence Gathering and Crime Analysis*. 2nd ed. Amsterdam: Elsevier, 2014.

McCulloch, J. *Blue Army: Paramilitary Policing in Australia*. Melbourne: Melbourne University Press, 2001.

McLaughlin, E. *The New Policing*. London: Sage, 2007.

Miller, W. R. *Cops & Bobbies: Police Authority in New York City & London, 1830-1870*. Chicago: University of Chicago Press, 1977.

Moskos, P. *Cop in the Hood: My Year Policing Baltimore's Eastern District*. Princeton: Princeton University Press, 2008.

Peterson, M. *Intelligence-Led Policing: The New Intelligence Architecture*. Washington, DC: National Institute of Justice, NIJ 210681, 2005.

Ratcliffe, J., and J. Sheptycki. "Setting the Strategic Agenda." In *Strategic Thinking in Criminal Intelligence*, edited by J. Ratcliffe. 194–210. Annadale, NSW: The Federation Press, 2004.

Ratcliffe, J. H. *Intelligence-Led Policing*. Cullhompton: Willan, 2011.

Reiner, R. "Policing a Postmodern Society." *The Modern Law Review* 55, no. 6 (1992): 761–781. doi:10.1111/mlr.1992.55.issue-6.

Reiner, R. *The Politics of the Police*. 4th ed. Oxford: Oxford University Press, 2010.

Reiss, A. J. "Police Organization in the Twentieth Century." In *Crime and Justice* Vol. 15 *Modern Policing*, edited by M. Tonry. 51–97. The University of Chicago Press1992.

Reuss-Ianni, E. *The Two Cultures of Policing; Street Cops and Management Cops*. New Brunswick, NJ: Transaction Books, 1983.

Ritzer, G. "The "McDonaldization" of Society." *The Journal of American Culture* 6, no. 1 (1983): 100–107. doi:10.1111/jacc.1983.6.issue-1.

Ronn, K. V. "Democratizing Strategic Intelligence?' On The Feasibility of An Objective, Decision-Making Framework When Assessing Threats and Harms or Organized Crime." *Policing* 7, no. 1 (2012): 53–62.

Sanders, C. B., and S. Hannem. "Policing "The Risky": Technology and Surveillance in Everyday Policework." *The Canadian Review of Sociology/Revue Canadienne de sociologie* 49, no. 4 (2012): 389–410. doi:10.1111/j.1755-618X.2012.01300.x.

Sanders, C. B., and S. Henderson. "Police 'Empires' and Information Technologies; Uncovering Material and Organizational Barriers to Information Sharing in Canadian Police Services." *Policing and Society* 23, no. 2 (2013): 243–260. doi:10.1080/10439463.2012.703196.

Shearing, C. and Johnston, L. Governing Security; Explorations in Policing and Justice. London: Routledge, 2003.

Shearing, C., and M. Marks. "Being a New Police in the Liquid 21st Century." *Policing* 5, no. 3 (2011): 210–218. doi:10.1093/police/par035.

Sheptycki, J. "Organizational Pathologies in Police Intelligence Systems: Some Contributions to the Lexicon of Intelligence-Led Policing." *The European Journal of Criminology* 1, no. 3 (2004): 307–332. doi:10.1177/1477370804044005.

Sheptycki, J. "Policing, Intelligence Theory and the New Human Security Paradigm." In *Intelligence Theory; Key Questions and Debates*, edited by P. Gill, S. Marrin, and M. Phythian, 166–187. London: Routledge, 2008.

Sheptycki, J. "The Raft of the Medusa; Further Contributions Towards a Constabulary Ethic." *Cahiers Politiestudies*, Special Issue: Policing in Europe no. 16 (2010): 39–56.

Sklansky, D. A. *The Persistent Pull of Police Professionalism*, New Perspectives in Policing Series. Cambridge MA: Harvard Kennedy School of Government, 2011.

Stainer, I. P. "Contemporary Organizational Pathologies in Police Information Sharing: New Contributions to Sheptycki's Lexicon of Intelligence In Policing." unpublished PhD Thesis, London Metropolitan University, 2013. uk.bl.ethos.590116

Travers, M., and J. F. Manzo. *Law in Action: Ethnomethodological and Conversation Analytic Approaches to Law*. Milton Park: Ashgate, 1997.

Van Maanen, J. "Working the Street: A Developmental View of Police Behavior." In *The Potential for Reform of Criminal Justice*, edited by H. Jacob, 83–130. Beverly Hills, CA: Sage, 1974.

Walker, S. *A Critical History of Police Reform*. Lexington, MA: Lexington Books, 1977.

Weatheritt, M. *Innovations in Policing*. London: Croom Helm, in association with the UK Police Foundation, 1986.

Weisburd, D., S. D. Mastrofski, A. M. McNally, R. Greenspan, and J. J. Willis. "Reforming to Preserve: Compstat and Strategic Problem Solving in American Policing." *Criminology and Public Policy* 2, no. 3 (2003): 421–456. doi:10.1111/cpp.2003.2.issue-3.

Wilson, J. Q. *Varieties of Police Behavior*. Cambridge, MA: Harvard University Press, 1968.

Young, M. *An Inside Job*. Oxford: Clarendon, 1991.

Zuboff, S. *In the Age of the Smart Machine; The Future of Work and Power*. New York: Basic Books, 1988.

International flows, political order and social change: (in) security, by-product of the will of order over change

Didier Bigo

ABSTRACT

International flows have been the focus of many research questions. Every school of thought on international relations covers them. However, the importance attributed to international flows concerning the international as an order, system, specific location and its changes is, in itself, subject to variation. One must be familiar with these positions to have a relevant understanding of how contemporary thought is organised with regard to forms of surveillance and the control of flows of information, capital, people, as well as logics of encoding, interception and the countermeasures that are expressed in and through these flows.

International flows have been the focus of many research questions. Every international relations school of thought covers them. However, the importance attributed to international flows in relation to the international as an order, system or specific location and its changes is, in itself, subject to variation. One must be familiar with these theoretical positions to have a relevant understanding of how contemporary thought is organised with regard to forms of (in)security, surveillance and controls of flows of information, capital, people, as well as logics of encoding, interception and the countermeasures that are expressed in and through these flows. The conception regarding order is de facto central as the background of the discourse and conceptualisation of (in)security in addition to its relation to legitimation of coercive and preventive measures.[1] International relations theories inspired by political science, despite strong divides between realist and liberal transnationalist visions, have been always characterised by this primacy of order over flows and changes, therefore privileging justification of security over freedom, privacy and even democracy. The permeability to discourse of state of exception or permanent emergency is a by-product of this primacy of order as the ultimate goal of politics. This does not come as a surprise as the aim of any strand of political science has been to sustain order as a way of living together inside specific state boundaries homogenising internally and differentiating externally. Stability has been the key word of this reasoning. On the other hand, international political economy, global geography and international political sociology have reversed the primacy between order and flows regarding what is the most legitimate way of life. In such approaches, order is not considered as a natural way of living or a specific achievement for international life, but instead as a constraint that blocks changes. Far too often, questions of order and security have been intellectually disconnected and forms of (in)securitisation and preventive coercion have been justified as if they were the only way to achieve 'order' under a maximum security strategy. This has created a rise in violence perpetrated by state organisations in the name of security, protection and prevention of their population against forms of dissent and escalation of violence attacking civilians. The very definition of politics by Carl Schmitt is a symptom of this justification of the state coercion against changes that can destabilise it. Change expressed by violence is unacceptable. Not only for war, but for any forms of local violence, including crime or even irregular stays of travellers. This has even affected the legitimacy of some liberal regimes who have been tempted to use exceptional measures and states of emergency to use a coercion which is not regulated in detail, and a discourse that justify restrictions on freedom and privacy. State organisations have justified the use of violence to their populations by stating that the survival of democracy depends on the restoring of 'order', even if this implies collaboration with authoritarian regimes. This justification has generally been accepted by the majority, despite human rights voices insisting on the dangers of these policies. This paper will not address the unfortunate consequences of these policies, which are well known.[2] With a more ambitious goal, this article seeks to challenge the premise upon which order is envisioned as a sign of peace, stability and protection, instead of positioning order as a problem in and of itself. I will therefore analyse in the first part the elements underpinning the reasoning that security is a priority because life needs order at the world scale to exist and expand. This first part requires a deconstruction of the idea that global flows are recent or simply the product of technologies and 'progress' of interdependence unheard of in the past. Flows are not destabilising a natural order of things as most international treaties seem to suggest. They are not 'disorder' or 'chaos'. On the contrary, all flows, including large-scale movements of persons at the world scale, are normal. In the second part, I develop an alternative vision sustained by economy and sociology, which insists that these flows and changes are the norm. The search for order and the idea that the state is the natural way of managing society, as opposed to an exceptional one, are instead framed as systems of justification used by some groups to assert their (illegitimate) primacy and legitimate their dominant position in society.

The realist story of governmental order assumes that order equates normality and considers that order and survival trump freedom and equality. This process occurs via a cynical understanding which pretends to be a 'reality' of life. The liberal transnationalist approach has tried to challenge this vision by insisting on the necessity of global governance to organise collaboration between different actors to create the emergence of an order based on the structural heterogeneity of flows. However, this debate has often been reduced to a simplistic question regarding border, identity, order and the survival or death of the state. In fact, the deregulation of political authorities has never meant the end of the state but a new arrangement of private and public authorities to manage flows in a way that achieves a dominant order. Only critical approaches have challenged the very idea of 'order' by focusing on the factors that constitute flows and why it is important to enhance freedom for change to happen. Using the metaphor of spring to speak of change is therefore more adequate than opposing chaos to a stable

THE POLICING OF FLOWS

order, the latter of which resembles winter more than summer. Thus, if one wants to reduce inequality and violence in the long term, analysing the structure of flows and their relationship to politics and fields of power is key to develop an alternative argument regarding war, global crime, (in)security, surveillance and suspicion in our contemporary society.

Flows and globalisation, a recent development due to technology?

From the start, one must take distance from established common sense whereby evolutions in academic theories are said to result from and reflect societal and political evolutions at the international level. For example, we are not gradually moving from a world of states, accurately depicted by realist authors, to a world of global flows, better described by liberal and transnationalist authors. International flows – understood as the mobility of goods, capital, information, technologies, services and people – are not a recent trend that depend on the diminution of the time to travel and the increased speed at which we travel. The conditions of 'globalisation' were not created with the end of the Cold War, which would have liberated them 'by taking them out of the freezer' of socialist states. Global flows were not born out of Thatcherite liberalism or the Treaty of Rome and its developments. They are not even the product of contemporary capitalism or developments in information technologies, despite their effective increase in terms of speed and volume of flows changing their everyday social use. Neither are they, as some authors increasingly argue, the result of a longer process which has reduced transportation time due to the democratisation of access to civil aviation, large passenger ships and the creation of banking products for capital and the radio for information, that emerged from the First World War. Still, the turn of the twentieth century seems the most significant in retrospect, since the speed at which these flows are circulating has accelerated so much that some authors consider this quantitative change to be a structural change.[3]

By definition, flows have always crossed city or state borders; they were not initially intrastate and later interstate. They are not the extension of an 'internal' entity through the crossing of 'external' borders. From a long-term perspective, cross-border interstate flows are an ambiguous indicator due to the increase in the number of borders following decolonisation, especially when compared to colonial and imperial contexts. The intensity, speed and number of actors involved in flows of production, finance, information, technology and people have varied throughout the ages, though certainly not in a linear fashion. In certain periods, conditions were ideal for the flow of ideas, capital or people over great distances, whereas in other time periods conditions were less optimal. City-states with multiple borders often communicated better than certain regions in empires. During the colonial period, there were regional 'integrations' between the North and the South, which no longer occur.[4] The contemporary era has undoubtedly a specificity which is to fill space by symbolically unifying the planet though satellite technology (think of the first image of earth seen from the moon), and by creating financial software powerful enough to trade across the globe for credit and speculation operations automatically using the differential hours where stock markets open and close. Although the global reach of internet and telephone technologies has been exaggerated as many regions have no real coverage, communication methods have nonetheless reduced global distances. The contemporary era has also witnessed a great deal of tourism. Furthermore, many people migrate to work in regions other than where they were born, whether it by choice or necessity (migrants and refugees). Numerous works describe this increase in flows.[5] However, flows and contemporary globalisation are two separate debates – the latter, although important, depends on the approach taken to reflect on flows, order, change and political authority.

Therefore, it is important to look beyond the discourse on technological innovation and the inevitability of the digitised post-Internet world in which only one option exists: adapt to the increasing speed of flows and the creation of a virtual world that will result in a loss of privacy and fewer liberties due to the ubiquity of surveillance. In this discourse, surveillance has become easy and commonplace; all it takes is 'a simple click'. Privacy then becomes an old-fashioned idea, and transparency within the state and global companies is the best strategy of adaptation. The argument of 'inevitability' can even take several forms, whether it is a private company trying to get us to like and purchase their products or intelligence agencies inviting themselves on to our computers without our consent to extract our index of 'normality' and compare it with their criteria for suspicious, radical, dissident, extreme or unusual characteristics. Many activists who support online 'community' values, or the right to be anonymous, 'loiter' and 'surf' the Web have fought this discourse on adapting behaviour and being compliant, and they have been right to do so. However, in this article, we want to go a step further by focusing on the underpinning elements of the concept of 'flows' itself. By firstly challenging the idea that flows should be thought of as the disruption of a natural order of states and/or markets, I develop an alternative view whereby flows are the signs of inevitable social change that are opposed by conservative interests. Flows are first, and order is second.

Flows and state, order and change: a doxa of 'order' resisting critiques

Here, the terminology of international flows is another name for social and political change. Flows signify an intellectual challenge to the idea that geographic borders established at some point by political authorities fulfil a certain atemporal need for order, balance and stability. Flows and changes occur in every era and are the 'material' that create history.

As Yosef Lapid pointed out, a process philosophy, such as Rescher's philosophy, is necessary to simultaneously reflect on the passing of time and spaces of territories and networks.[6] Perceiving international flows as a phenomenon that emerged during the modern or contemporary era is therefore a display of ingenuousness and a lack of anthropological perspective. Thinking about the crusades, forms of colonisation and imperial or neo-imperial governance, for example, show us that, firstly, the world has never been in a state of stasis, with political authorities successfully controlling the exchange of ideas, people, goods and capital. Secondly, there is a correlation between the creation of states and the acceleration of flows. Opposing these flows and states only makes sense if we accept a straightforward vision of the state as a principle of, a more or less timeless, dominant political order that would, itself, regulate the movement of individual, social and even global practices through the state system.[7]

THE POLICING OF FLOWS

If we substitute this essentialism and nominalism with a more sociological and anthropological perspective, it would be more sensible to recognise that world history is the history of these changes, of flows that have been encouraged or restricted by political authorities and their diplomatic or violent tactics, through economic activities in cities and the development of technologies over the long term. These flows have helped construct political authorities, states, borders and the mobilities that cross them. These movements and mobilities are what determine the conditions under which an international system, which inherently wants to be 'organised', is or is not capable of adapting to these dynamics, almost regardless of symbolic pretentions to 'control'. Thus, we must repudiate the idea of the confinement of populations inside a given territory. In the long term, even the most authoritative regimes have not been able to sustain themselves and protect themselves from troubling flows simply through the use of violence, immobility, conservatism and the construction of walls intended to prevent escape (or entrance). Walls have indeed generated discriminatory and violent practices. However, they, first and foremost, served a symbolic function as a reminder of territorial political order and have fallen before ever acting as a mechanism of defence. Political regimes establish their chains of obedience on networks of people, not on natural territories.

Similar to international demography and international political economy, the historical sociology of global state trajectories and its continental or regional variations undermine narratives that give priority to a world where states control all aspects of their territory and populations, and are the only ones capable of developing production and agreeing on an order based on nearly intangible border lines that can only be crossed with their permission.[8] This legal model of the world was established quite late as a colonial system for sharing various continents. A history of passports, identity and identification cards, visas and other international instruments determining the right of passage between states shows that it was only in the nineteenth century and in a select few nation states that this system became more or less effective in governing effectively metropolitan territories.[9] Of course, the fact that this was mostly possible, and was conducted this way over long periods, fluctuating between economic protectionism, political authoritarianism and free markets and institutions, marked our political imaginations along with the politicians governing us. It gave credibility to this vision of an international order controlled by states and states alone. It created a narrative on international law and international relations generating the political science rhetoric from that period. However, a long global sociological history reveals the profound Eurocentrism of this vision, which can only find refuge in the legal terminologies and definitions of the state as a historical constant that hide its unfree nature and presents itself as the example to follow.[10]

Nevertheless, at the expense of a history of governmental practices of mobility, this history of order and stability via a balance of power, based on legal terminologies and definitions, is the dominant one, despite critiques. It imposed itself as a 'doxa' and does not need to be said or to be believed. This one-sided evolutionist history – presented in both traditional and transnationalist narratives from the field of international relations as well as, more generally, from political science – is an underpinning element, which emerges rarely while guiding our representations of order and change, of what is good and what is evil or dangerous, of what is security and what is freedom, of what is civilised and what is barbaric, of what is modern and what 'failed' to attain this status.

We all know this story. We learned it when we were children. It was instilled in us as an explanation of the state, which inevitably speaks through us and justified itself.[11]

So, let us take a step back for a moment and distance ourselves from this neo-Kantian linearity about the universalisation of European liberal modernity, whose mission was passed on and successfully accomplished by the United States. Let us return to the diversity of domination practices in given spaces alongside the ability of populations to move, to 'escape', to resist and to contest their authorities. Let us consider Europe for what it is on the global scale and more closely analyse the other major regions of the world.

By doing this, one realises that change always comes first and that order, in particular international order as an identical reproduction of the previous situation, is a particular obsession of authorities from the Holy Roman Empire, which wanted to fuse *potestas* and *auctoritas* to establish an 'immobile' world, to resemble a city of God, which is itself always orderly. This fusion of *potestas* and *auctoritas* is of uttermost importance in the indefinite prioritisation of order over change, and conservation over transformation, but it is a 'local obsession', which is not necessarily part of the diverse political philosophies developed in India, China and Asia in general, or even Africa.[12] This priority of order over flows that structures our thinking, including the most contemporary authors, and often makes us Westerners view flows as dangerous, risky and threatening, is a central problem of misconception at the core of our logic. Instead of seeing them as a constant of the interaction between societies, a necessity that requires harmony so that order can always accompany change, it is possible to think of them as heterogeneities, which have no intention, and no goal to become 'enemies' as soon as they cross the erected borders. Take, for instance, the way Western societies and their outposts in the Southern hemisphere (Australia, New Zealand) associate migration with infiltration of a fifth column or circumventing states' strategies, and consider any movement like a wave that must be channelled to maintain order and stability. This allows us to see that this conception of order is a caricature and often far from a serious reflection on global social change and transformation, though still prominent in the way we continue to view migrants as an intrusion from a stranger's body trying to penetrate our own political body, or as 'aggressors' threatening the common good, which is defined by the people of that territory. We will come back to these relationships between order, border and identity that structure the way we think about flows.[13] But, at this point, it is appropriate to note that the grammar of the political order and the manner by which the discipline of international relations narrates flows, glorifies territorial maps, instantaneousness, immobility, homogeneity, uniformity, purification, sedentariness, and associates borders with safe barriers and obstacles to change, while dismissing movement, liquidity, flows, multiplicity, magma, nomadism and the border as an area of exchange and opportunities. Therefore, a logical conservativism is often superimposed over a political one.[14]

The state's management of flows: the realist story of governmental order

As so often the case, Raymond Aron has been the author who best highlighted the conservatism fostered by the narrative of flows and the state as separate entities by clearly taking this stance. His support for realism in international relations makes flows and changes an integral part of the argument. He, like many authors, against Sartre

THE POLICING OF FLOWS

existentialist freedom, believes that an authority correcting human nature is essential for social order and peace. Therefore, Aron argues that a reasonable policy taking into account the dynamic nature of societies and the movement of people through the preservation of the state is the best strategy to maintain order by avoiding the worst of global war, but without promising peace. In his preface to *Peace and War: A Theory of International Relations*, that he was writing for the republication of his work just before his death, he insisted on the validity of his analytical model of the contemporary world, which gives priority to state and interstate order, making the analysis of flows and change secondary.[15] He categorically dismissed arguments about increases in the number of players on the international scene, which would mitigate the role of the state and, thereby, the realist argument. He acknowledged that the increase of interactions between micro-actors was more and more visible and relevant in terms of description, but considered that it does not justify a paradigm shift that would be in favour of an 'international society'. For him, analyses must take into account transnational, international and supranational phenomena. But these phenomena are not a system and therefore do not create an organised totality, a whole – a society. They do not produce 'order', and consequently, they are heterogeneous and have a meaning only as a factor inside the interstate system which is based on the fear of death and its horizon for any individual and collectivity. Most of our contemporary political imaginary is still based on this assumption and organised the fears of the security professionals that just one foreigner crossing irregularly a border will endanger security and will justify to connect even more the dots, i.e. to reinforce surveillance of all travellers. For Aron, the strength of state border control does not come from his own will of sovereignty, but from an interstate system, which is based on a shared primacy of order, because the system, even unjust, protects us from death; death which is logically more important than assuring wealth and justice. This is why, for him, survival always trumps happiness and equality as a value. State and interstate systems, political order, public safety and individual survival are inseparable.

Starting from significantly different premises than Hans Morgenthau and Kenneth Waltz, Raymond Aron *in fine* comes nevertheless to the same conclusions. As long as an international society has not discovered regulatory mechanisms other than the state, and its national state form in particular, there is no conceivable alternative. Individual people have no right to move freely. Since it is heterogeneous, movement must be 'governed'; civilian society must be 'structured', 'nationalised' and 'democratised'. One can imagine a future of democratic states ensuring public peace through a stronger UN, but we cannot let 'change' guide us. Change is chance, and chance is not politics. Allowing flow to move freely is not an option as this would be revolutionary or, even worse, anarchic in the political sense. Raymond Aron's narrative has stayed with us, as the most eloquent and explicit narrative of this western doxa. It has been almost unchallenged for its core argument against a politics of freedom and equality, except maybe by another French author, not Jean Paul Sartre in this case, but Michel Foucault.

Michel Foucault has in his own way studied this ideal regulatory mechanism that Aron was summarising in his philosophy. Without arguing for or against Aron and political science, Foucault explained the genealogy of this reasoning and how this specific narrative of survival is in fact obliged to conclude that 'society must be defended' because order is necessary to its development.[16] He enlightened how this defence of order versus heterogeneous flows justified a certain type of governmentality where a form of liberal order has to be preserved in the name of society, where people have to be (self) governed via conducts of conducts, and where flows have to be channelled through market logics. Security neoliberal mechanisms limiting the freedom of movement but based on it are therefore superimposed to the more traditional mechanisms and dispositifs of sovereignty and discipline. They create the illusion of free choices under the diversity they encourage. By managing human bodies through a biopolitical logic and populations by using statistics that try to create an emergent order from heterogeneity itself through the identification of correlations, such restrictions on mobility soften the potentiality of violence of sovereignty and discipline without eliminating them. The emerging order of neoliberal logic replaces natural order, but order is necessary.

The genealogy methods that Foucault employed succeeded to show the efficiency of that liberal governmentality juggling risk and flexibility while 'managing' flows. This is why Foucault became so popular and is still a source of inspiration for critique.[17] In this regard, there are hardly any major contrasts between the realist narrative and the so-called transnationalist or liberal-institutionalist narrative; only strategic questions concerning 'good governance'. Of course, continuity between the two visions is hidden, and only the visible debate is omnipresent in international relations manuals. It presents as a radical opposition those who are the defenders of state and borders and those who are in favour of global markets, associated supposedly with no-border advocates. This main controversy is framed around management of flows to oppose proponents of the state and those who support a borderless world, nationalists versus cosmopolitans, people who promote borders versus those who discourage them, those who support regulation and those who support freedom of movement. However, we will see that, if such a debate exists, it is important to look elsewhere because behind the epithets of this 'war' surrounding the state and its role, there is only a shadow play producing the same management narrative and often pursuing a differential management of illegalities through an apparent preventive regulation which believes it can anticipate risks.

Market deregulation by political authorities: the false debate on the end of the role of states and the consecutive rise of global flows

Keohane and Nye were among the first to re-examine the critique of the sociology of dependence and Marxism from a liberal perspective by casting a doubt on the priority of survival over values of justice and development. They expressed concerns that a 'fixist' approach, centred on state policies and the interstate system alone, would end up destroying, instead of liberating, the forces that help produce the capital fuelling states and societies. They insisted on the urgent need to liberalise, to let flows evolve, whether it be capital, goods, information or even people whose movement creates wealth through consumption. Along with others, they placed emphasis on the role of international organisations in regulating business and economic activities as well as the importance of sharing ideas generated in non-governmental organisations. They invented the idea of governance to go beyond government by states and called for closer 'collaboration' between governments in regional groupings. They called on states to relinquish some of their 'self-interest' and security principles by creating international organisations, which could help create bridges across borders. They pointed out that good management required this acceleration of flows producing growth, and that it should bring together a wide variety of actors: international and regional organisations, states, but also major companies and non-governmental organisations, in order to prevent borders from being barriers, or obstacles to flows.[18] As they clearly indicated, they never intended to challenge the role of the state, allowing it to become just another chapter in history books. However, they wanted to see greater management and less coercive behaviour (minimally in Western democratic zones). Since states are far from going extinct, they must adapt to increased flows, promote them and integrate them into their processes.

The programme of these transnationalist liberal authors sought to 'preserve' the growth of flows of capital, information, goods and services and therefore support globalisation and technical progress by channelling them though institutions better suited to manage such flows and processes, even if it offends the hegemonic intentions of some overly controlling governments. They stressed the advantage for the self-interest of the most powerful states and governments, such as the United States, to share a little bit more hard power with negotiating partners by sometimes accepting to compromise. Such a trade-off would permit dominant states to remain nevertheless in a position of soft hegemony which would allow them to determine the level of their concessions and to guide their partners' conduct. While leaving open the possibility of losing small games, dominant players can define the very rules to the game and ultimately win in the long term. James Rosenau followed the same line of thinking, but adjusted the theory to a more in-depth approach of sovereignty. He especially highlighted turbulence created by the increased number of sphere of authorities and the difficulty of maintaining traditional forms of obedience since, according to Rosenau, governments are increasingly evaluated like companies regarding their performance. Therefore, sovereignty is not always an asset and can become a constraint due to some of its rigid characteristics (bound by sovereignty). Territoriality is no longer a significant advantage in a period of network control. The smaller players are also 'free' actors of sovereignty, he stressed. If these micro-actors built a network, they support flows and become nodes. In France, Bertrand Badie transplanted Rosenau's hypotheses, and as a form of provocation spoke of the end of territories and the emergence of an age of responsibility replacing sovereignty.

However, like Rosenau, he always emphasised the role of states as the basic structure for democracy and as the foundation for the regulation and distribution of flows, thus refusing to join the no-border groups criticising the coercive and inefficient nature of states.[19] Debates on the resistance of states against globalisation or, more precisely, the role of governments in the making of globalisation was certainly a strong moment of mobilisation of International Relations (IR) scholars as well as of think tanks and international institutions looking to exchange best practices of good government. However, there was hardly any substantial discussion on what the concept of flows meant in relation to change or on what the notion of governance implies in its relationship with the governmentality of conduct and with politics.

The supposed debate that opposed realists and transnationalists on the end of states, overwhelmed by transnational flows, never actually occurred. Still, these groups did carry out tactical attacks to stigmatise the other's claims and arguments using recent history, such as the end of bipolarity or 9/11, to undermine each other. However, there was a broad consensus on the proper management of flows, with states playing a key role. Aron's policy and conservative logic is still as pertinent as it was in 1984, because in fact, liberal transnationalists never attacked it. They just wanted to manage sovereignty differently.

Therefore, it is not in the debate between realists and transnationalists that we will find the key to understanding an analysis of change separate from order, also called an analysis of flows. If there is a debate on the concept of flows and change, it has more to do with the emergence of a different analysis of the economy and sociology of change and order than with traditional political science and international relations approaches which have avoided discussion of change and its fluid, liquid manifestations on its own.

International and global political economy: flows determine political authorities

Unlike liberal institutionalists and transnationalists, Susan Strange took a more subversive stance on the dialectical interplay between flows and states and how they are properly managed by revisiting the fundamentals of power structures, forms of social change and the role of governments. Instead of opposing states and flows, or trying to analyse them dialectically, she emphasised the constitutive ambiguity of these terms and the dualities they generate; dualities which lead to false solutions and problems that do not actually exist but worry many professionals all the same. According to Strange, the opposition between the market and the state, which she referred to in her first work, is less important than the possibility of the state's retreat from spheres of authority in the fields of production, credit, information and knowledge, and ultimately security. Therefore, the key element is not the pseudo opposition between states and markets but the fungibility of categories of politics and economy.[20] Her significant body of works seemed to have increasingly stressed our lack of conceptual apparatuses regarding globalisation and, more crucially, social and economic change and its relationship with politics. With her fellow researchers from Warwick, Susan Strange presented the role of bankers as 'unelected politicians' and not as specific agents of economic power to show that they were making crucial decisions affecting the lives of millions of people while marginalising elected politicians, whose political life is reduced to the acquits of symbolic politics in matter of security and border control spectacle.

They insisted on the lack of democracy that affects how power is structured on a global level, often allowing transnational elitist professional groups to control the political realm beyond what is visible and official because they have a particular 'technique' or 'expertise'. She also discussed the fundamental logic of management of change by bureaucratic groups and the emergence of parallel forms of political power, which became more or less institutionalised without having to acquire legitimacy beyond their own duration. This critical International Political Economy (IPE) approach analysed the structures of the G8, WTO, European Union, as well as gatherings of major investment banks and even mafias all as examples of these (unelected) politicians which go beyond the state because they are part of everyday processes of change, that some

THE POLICING OF FLOWS

prefer to silence instead of admitting that they cannot control or manage heterogeneous flows.[21]

Along the same lines of critique of liberal transnationalism, the idea to develop a global political economy (GPE) was present, even before Susan Strange and Robert Cox's works. Cox also suggested that there is a lack of theorisation about 'order' in the political science-tradition of international relations that explains the naturalisms, essentialisms and dualisms that characterise the all systems of thought in IR, be they realist or liberal transnationalists.[22] He used the concept of flows well before others and did not like the idea of categorising them as if they were products organised on the shelves of a small store. He set a research agenda for how a globalised sociology must view change as a principle and not order. For him, this was the absolute basic principle if one wanted to be called a critical scholar. Such an author must question the structure and history of flows and analyse how they relate to the hegemony and historic trajectories of social constructs that give rise to specific types of states or political and social order(s). He was also critical about the confrontation between actors in terms of the material (as well as ideational) capacities of these various political structures that not only comprise different forms of states (liberal or illiberal) but also affect the forms of power that straddle between the public and private spheres, the state politicians and the unelected politicians of the market, the central and the peripheral places. For Cox, change therefore relates to flows and social forces that must be interpreted through their relationship with the production and the forms of global order that try to adjust to the flows, even when they claim to control these flows. This method and way of thinking suggest the necessity to explore the origins, nature and development of these historical structures that determine a configuration of power on a given scale and at a given period. This is the only way one can see the formation of a doxa privileging an unquestioned order and the established dualisms that this specific doxa combines and reproduces in order to limit questions to 'problem-solving theories'.

In his critical approach, Robert Cox draws from Gramci, but also Charles Tilly and Norbert Elias, in order to redefine issues concerning long-standing historical knowledge and to question the way social change is configured by different flows of people, capital and information. It is central to understand the present as a knick-knack, that is as something non-reducible to a predictable pattern from the past because of its very specific configuration or field of power, but which is nevertheless tied to interdependent systems applicable to various levels (territoriality, network, network of networks). This sociogenesis creates the possibility to better appreciate the creation of collective identities and their permanent changes, therefore deconstructing the illusion of their permanence.[23] In this same line of thought, Stephen Gill has demonstrated how what he called the elite of the Trilateral Commission operated as an 'organic intellectual' forging the neoliberal ideology with the Washington Consensus.[24] A sociology of contemporary globalisation is thus a sociology of the social forces that has created and fuelled it. This is, firstly, the product of a comparative approach to variations in the different socio-historical trajectories of forms of political authorities (elected or unelected); secondly, this is the product of transnational fields of power that cross over territorial borders, national societies, and often take the form of solidarities organised around specific institutional habitus(es) or specific practical know-how and recognition of a specific knowledge – that is what I have termed transnational guilds.

Before analysing the evolution of crime and police practices in this context, it is important in this line of thought to first understand who benefits from the 'knowledge of crime'. Likewise, one must identify which social and professional groups have an interest in (in)security and how so-called new forms of crime, such as cybercrime, mimic older forms of crime, unquestionably transforming them but without radically changing their dynamics, and by increasingly following criminal developments and the new intransigence that lead to effective changes in practices.[25] The transnationalisation and enlargement of professional organisations fighting cybercrime, as well as inner logics of competition in this 'new' space, are just as helpful in understanding current politics regarding the cyber as are the innovations in cybercrime that make regulation a 'necessity', such as the practices of techno-gifted criminals or new fields of remote crime that operate like botnets. As opposed to focusing separately on the actions of criminals or of cybersecurity professionals,[26] it is the relation between these two opposing 'set of actors' and their trajectories of opposition which explain change and the structuration of an 'order'.

Global political geography and post-colonial studies: avoiding the territorial trap, networks and waves as descriptors of heterogeneous flows

Like the sub-discipline of critical International Political Economy set up by Susan Strange, Robert Cox and Stephen Gill, a Global Political Geography based on post-colonial and subaltern studies is now emerging, joining the historical sociology of globalisation in an effort to make change, networks and flows – not order – central. This new challenge, more external to traditional political science, has finally obliged specialists of International Relations to defend why they were continuing, despite evidence, to base their reasoning on the primacy of world order, and therefore of security, with the very same premises as before, i.e. that order comes first and is natural, or that order may be emerging from chaos and change, but change cannot be let to develop, it needs to be controlled in order for politics to exist to reinforce the stability of the power of the moment in a specific place.

John Agnew has been one of the first to specify various forms of spatiality of power and has highlighted what he called a 'territorial trap' into which political scientists and political theorists working on the idea of 'sovereignty' as an absolute have fallen.[27] He has concretely shown how the assumption that sovereign states require clearly defined and closed, or constantly controlled, borders did not reflect effective practices. He demonstrated the need to transfer the sovereignty of the political body identified as the sovereign person to another 'person', that is the people or the nation. It is thus at the symbolic level of identity that our conception of a naturalised and homogenised space working through borders that separate an inside from an outside can be understood. Referring to the work of Rob Walker on a critique of sovereignty not as an answer but as a question that modernity has not solved, he has clarified how the concept of flows is analysed as a transgression, because it crosses borders, connecting the inside with the outside.[28] If the aim of 'sovereign states' is to differentiate borders and to create uniformity inside in order to build 'one' people, populations flows are therefore perceived as chaos, or disorder. Stemming from these first two assumptions, the state border becomes a whole (meaning to prevent overflow and to homogenise) that

THE POLICING OF FLOWS

contains the political body of a uniform container in which nation, people and society are almost identical. Disparities in social and political forces and the different 'scales' in which they deploy, are therefore, deemed to be hierarchised vertically, as being either below or above the state. And as such local or global are being implicitly dangerous, especially if they refer to people on the move. This is why, if we want to understand the conditions of (in)security dynamics surrounding the mobility of people and the control of borders, they must be associated with the way state and international priorities have established the normality of flows as abnormal phenomenon in order to standardise the exceptionalisation of a European state as a universal model.[29]

Indeed, mechanisms of policing flows that want to be 'smarter' by structuring rather than stopping flows are not more effective. They are just slightly less visible as they focus less on combating surrounding dangers and risks and more on knowing about the private lives of those they are supposed to protect. This reveals a more 'liquid' representation of the world, making borders appear mobile and porous, that is a crossing point and not a barrier or fixed location. The concept of 'wave', as in an 'undulation' – which was developed in the hard sciences, medicine and art – now has a place in geography and international relations. We are replacing the networks of networks that multiply almost infinitely with a graphic representation of liquidity and field effects that considers limits and entanglements.

Thinking about the representation of the world as moving networks has intensified and has had some theoretical and political consequences.[30] Change is now perceived and the temporal stasis of order is put into perspective through such representations. However, as it is important to be wary of the supremacy of representations of political order and the mapping of states, it is also crucial to be cautious of the opposite – that is the tendency to think globalisation as a whole-in-the-making, instead of an intensification of disjunctures, which rejects reflection on the various boundaries that transnationalisation is making.

An International Political Sociology will therefore refute both the international order argument as well as the globalisation whole-in-the-making argument, instead preferring to explore the concepts of limits, lines and their non-circular topologies like a Moebius strip.[31] In this approach, a political anthropological research on international sociology may become possible as a transdisciplinary project based on a refutation of the political science doxa of order and a promotion of a political project of multiple universes (pluriverses) living in shared, but not necessarily common, spaces.

In practice, questioning the territorial trap means to analyse why there is a logical necessity to begin a map by tracing state borders to express the political on earth. Political authorities claiming to speak in the name of a state still want to capture and secure flows, at least in a political spectacle, to guarantee that people remain blind to all these limits which are not territorial borders but which are related to uncontrolled changes. They need the 'fiction' of a 'State' as a principle of unity. Otherwise, they will not be able to create the map and the imaginary world they have mapped out. Seeing like a state is the way by which it is still possible to see the world as a politician and to be credible; but often this means to see the world in a bubble or circle which creates a closure against any sort of flows traversing these so-called closures (be they walls or locks managing flows).

Therefore, many questions about sovereignty, state capacities to decide, organisation of war and economy are more or less transformed into a politics of 'policing', which is ultimately seen as a politics of ordering the world again, as a politics of maximum security re-creating the imaginary stasis of an order without any disorder or changes.

Conclusion: the by-product of the primacy of order over flows: a politics of global policing that produces more violence

Policing preventively to have a secure world has become the alpha and omega of politics, not only for the political spectacles of the professionals of politics, that is those elected to be spokespersons of the 'prince', but also for the unelected politicians that want to manage flows of capital, information, people and say they can prevent the flows to overflow by predicting their trajectories. The terminology of prevention became the key word of politics, especially after 2001, but this prevention is anticipation and often a fantasy about a dystopic future that leads to the so-called action of a prevention which may be de facto a first blow generating escalation of violence. This reasoning is applied to any form of violence beyond war and ends up being a generalised suspicion of every human being that changes, especially when he moves, travelling physically or in his mind.

Detecting, capturing and securing flows through methods other than territory and borders are therefore the most important techniques of policing. Despite its absolute marginality in terms of number of people dying if compared to domestic accidents, terrorism emerges as the key problem to resolve by counterterrorist measures that want to transform security into a technological surveillance maximum, total and global, as if the world could be fixed by controlling and predicting flows, limiting changes to the minimum, and restoring order.[32] In this sense, the narrative of a global counterterrorism effort establishing worldwide interstate collaboration against a microscopic and often personal, undetectable enemy intensified the fear of flows in general and the flows of people in particular: migrants, refugees, but also tourists travelling through airports and border crossings.[33]

Faced with these politics of terror, fear and trepidation whereby a metaphysical order legitimises transforming every change into potential danger, is it nonetheless possible to reverse reasoning, to think of individual and collective identities outside the prism of states and political authorities aiming to capture and secure them?

This implies our own intellectual 'decolonisation' and the learning of philosophies that do not oppose order and change, that do not make change subordinate to order by including opposites in a hierarchy that maintains the state's presence as order, even when there is mention of its dissolution and potential to disappear. This suggests an opening to multiplicity and uniformity that cannot be conveyed through a diagram of forces. This implies thinking of liquidity, rhizome or lines of flight and their forms of power. These are, without a doubt, the only ways be emancipated from forms of governmentality implemented by political authorities and state territorial technologies to manage flows. However, as mentioned above, this does not imply adhering to a neo-Kantian universalising project, which casts Eurocentric values into a predetermined future where the meaning of democracy, identity, religion or tradition would be known. One way to avoid desparing that the doxa of order will always be at the centre

THE POLICING OF FLOWS

153

of our philosophy is to continue the work of Zygmunt Bauman in critical approaches of international political sociology when discussing security, crime and surveillance. Some works have now engaged with this alternative.

Reflecting on flows and change: liquidity and/or lines of flight

In his voluntarist sociology, Zygmunt Bauman has been the most important sociologist who systematically placed priority on change and flows, therefore taking an unorthodox approach by viewing order, stasis and prediction as sources of the problem of politics, and never as their solutions. He has described the various aspects of the liquefaction of modernity and the mechanisms that dominant actors use to themselves escape state boundaries, such as the frequent formation of transnational professional elite groups, characterised by their capacity to capitalise on their access to flows of capital, information and people on a global level, while the dominated actors are trapped at a local level.[34]

His way of presenting the forces and social practices that structure these flows, by separating them from the permanent referents of the territorial state and political order, makes him one of the most important authors regarding the renewed analysis of society and social human, political and moral interactions. He may have been a bit too quick to use managerial metaphors and took a risk by not considering limits concerning the opposition of a solid modernity with a post-modern liquefaction. However, his attempt to view change as a priority over order allows him to present 'citizen' alternatives open to the foreigner and without a state referent. This does not prevent him from considering government practices that various social groups, other than political authorities, use by mocking or copying them. For globalisation, he tries to think beyond the elite and make associations between contemporary globalisation, restructuring social forces and change.

Prised by institutions, freedom of movement is revealed as a global distinction between those who have the luxury of access to the flows of capital, goods, information, services and people and those who are powerless beyond their reach and may either be required to leave despite their desire to stay or, inversely, are required to stay in spite of their wish to leave their city or village because of their lack of means or for fear that the elected or unelected political authorities will deny them visas.[35]

Some International Political Sociology authors have already criticised Bauman's over generalisation. They discuss Bauman's assumption that the wealthy can choose and escape surveillance, highlighting that even they are subject to controls and anticipations.[36] The reconfiguration of logics of distinctions between the globalised elite and elites trapped in the national context, as well as their relationships with elected and non-elected political authorities, on one hand, and the people, on the other, is not unidirectional. Post-modern liquidity does not necessarily offer the possibilities that democratisation would allow through generalisation and universalisation. Ethics will not replace politics.

Violence and surveillance are also liquid. They adapt to this need for the 'freedom of movement' to the perspective of distance, the acceleration of flows and the need to manage them in real time or the anticipation (forecast, prevention, simulation) that these last characteristics imply. Contemporary violence reconnects with mechanisms of mimetic rivalry and vengeance on a large scale. It also challenges us, as geographic proximity no longer determines fellowship or even friendship. Geographic proximity can develop and intensify animosity while simultaneously conjuring uncertainty about perpetrators and targets, therefore generating anxiety or a widely felt sense of uneasiness. As asked by Michel Serres, what do authorities do when faced with such a non-territorial 'atlas'? Not very much. Public authorities insist on their necessity and play on symbols. They try to mobilise other authorities to channel anger and violence that have taken on these fluid-like characteristics. They are deployed using various forms of 'remote policing', managing the mobility of people and anticipating their movements (profiling, using databases and software allowing them to anticipate future events and risky or unwanted individuals) instead of controlling them at borders. Faced with the fear of small numbers, described by Arjun Appadurai, risk is exasperated where majorities are afraid of minorities and of becoming a minority on another level or in another flow. In a context where distance has been eliminated, including for violence, and where territory no longer distinguishes friend and foe, the hyperbole of the catastrophic scenario haunts the political imagination – the only 'solution' being a technocratic belief in the ability of 'new' technologies to anticipate and predict human behaviour. This is even more powerful than surveillance based on suspicion. Yet, the twin of the uncertainty of violence is not only the product of the transnationalisation of (in)security professionals. Suspicion is also at the core of all individual networks that appreciate this kind of surveillance for the reassurance that it provides, in particular with regard to forms of external and institutional control. Self-surveillance and permanent monitoring coexist with profiling, therefore forging bonds and resistances differentiating the chains of commands and forms of allegiance that territory no longer follow. This leads to a series of tensions between possible emancipation, ban-opticon programme flowing through networks, voluntary servitude and resistances.

Flows and change can be considered outside the contexts of the state and the borderless world. However, this does not mean that we can overlook ethical and political ideas on the opportunities and risks that this implies, on liberties and rights of individuals and on the various uses that are created by the social forces at work. The changes taking place multiply the possibilities, but this does not indicate to us how they relate to certain ideals, such as democracy, equality or justice, no more than it teaches us about the strategic uses of these ideals by certain powers, including the way they establish their definitions. Power apparatuses are as rhizomatic as the flows they contain and the elected and non-elected, public and private political authorities have incorporated an excess of methods to control the change and liquidity of territorial apparatuses for quite some time. They have hardened the lines that now take the form of a Klein bottle or a torus.[37] The people inside are oblivious to such exertions of control because they do not see the borders, even though they are structured by them. Illusions of daily resistance near the coffee machine do not challenge the apparatuses that adapt to change.

Gilles Deleuze has nonetheless proposed viewing changes that lead to emancipation as lines of flight, different from the hard and flexible lines of apparatuses and resistances.[38] For Deleuze, lines of flight never return to the same spot. They do not determine a future; they determine a becoming. This reflection on emancipation, resistances, temporality and becoming are subjects that researchers working in international political sociology are becoming even more engaged in.[39] This becoming that opposes the claims of a predictive policing science to a perfect future that pretends to predict human behaviour and anticipate it through the use of mathematical algorithms and the processing speed of computers

THE POLICING OF FLOWS

highlights, on the contrary, the irreducibility of chance, the capacity to change the opinions of individuals at the last minute, and the possibility to escape an inevitable outcome. If the latter are indeed there as actions from the past, they are never an unyielding chain from which there is only one possible future. It is from this force, from this multiplicity of futures, from the political imagination that makes these other futures possible and from the coincidences related to the clash of multiple histories that we should take our inspiration.

Notes

1. Bigo, "Globalized-in-Security."
2. Bigo, "Globalisation and Security,"
3. Régis et Pascal Lamy, *Histoire de la mondialisation.*
4. Held et al., *Global Transformations.*
5. Pour un débat sur la mondialisation voir Zaki Laidi, "L'etat Mondialise (the Globalized State)."; Beck, *Pouvoir Et Contre-Pouvoir À L'ère de La Mondialisation*; Hardt and Negri, "Globalization and Democracy."; Hudson and Slaughter, *Globalisation and Citizenship.*
6. Albert et al., *Identities, Borders, Orders.*
7. For a strong critique see Lacroix, "Ordre Politique Et Ordre Social."
8. Wallerstein, "The Rise and Future Demise of World-Systems Analysis."; Foucher, *Fronts Et Frontières*; Pasha, *Colonial Political Economy.*
9. Noiriel, *Etat, Nation Et Immigration*; Torpey, *The Invention of the Passport Surveillance.*
10. Hindess, "The Liberal Government of Unfreedom."
11. Bourdieu, "Esprits D' Etat."
12. Chakravorty Spivak, *A Critique of Postcolonial Reason.*
13. Albert et al., *Identities, Borders, and Orders.*
14. Dumont, *Essais Sur L'individualisme.*
15. Aron, *Paix Et Guerre Entre Les Nations.*
16. Foucault et al., *Society Must Be Defended.*
17. Bonditti et al., *Foucault and the International.*
18. Keohane and Nye, *Power and Interdependence.*
19. Badie and Bertrand. La *fin Des territoires*, Cohen, La *Résistance Des Etats.*
20. Strange, *States and Markets.*
21. Strange "The Limits of Politics."; Strange et al., *Authority and Markets.*
22. Cox, *Production, Power and World Order.*
23. Tilly, *Identities, Boundaries, and Social Ties*; "Political Identities in Changing Polities." ; Elias, La *Dynamique* de *L'occident.*
24. Gill, *Power and Resistance in the New World Order.*
25. Mulone and Tanner, "Les Acteurs Privés De La Sécurité Transnationale Et Leurs Victimes".
26. Dupont, "Private Security Regimes."
27. Agnew, "The Territorial Trap."
28. Walker, *Inside/Outside.*
29. Bigo, "Security and Immigration."; Scott, *Seeing Like a State*; Foucault et al., *Les Anormaux.*
30. Castells, La *Société En Réseaux*; Musso, *Réseaux Et Sociétés.*
31. Bigo, "The Moebius Ribbon of Internal and External Security."
32. Bigo et al., *Illiberal Practices of Liberal Regimes.*
33. Côté-Boucher et al., "Border Security as Practice."
34. Bauman, *Liquid Love*; Distributed in the USA by Blackwell Pub., 2003); *Liquid Times.*
35. Bauman *Freedom.*; Bauman *Globalization.*
36. Lyon and David, Theorizing surveillance.
37. Bigo, "The Moebius Ribbon of Internal and External Security." op cit.
38. Deleuze and Guattari, *Mille Plateaux.*
39. voir les travaux du collectif COLLECTIVE C.A.S.E., "Critical Approaches to Security in Europe."

Disclosure statement

No potential conflict of interest was reported by the author(s).

Bibliography

Agnew, J. "The Territorial Trap: The Geographical Assumptions of International Relations Theory." *Review of International Political Economy* 1, Spring ((1994)): 53–80. doi:10.1080/09692299408434268.

Albert, M., D. Jacobson, and Y. Lapid. *Identities, Borders, Orders: Rethinking International Relations Theory. Borderlines; V. 18*. Minneapolis: University of Minnesota Press, 2001.

Appadurai, A. *Fear of Small Numbers: An Essay on the Geography of Anger. Public Planet Books.* Durham: Duke University Press, 2006.

Aron, R. *Paix Et Guerre Entre Les Nations*. Paris: Calmann Lévy, 1984(1962).

Badie, B. *La fin des territoires : Essai sur le désordre international et l'utilité sociale du respect*. Paris: Fayard, 1995.

Bauman, Z. *Liquid Love: On the Frailty of Human Bonds*. Cambridge: Polity press.

Bauman, Z. *Freedom. Concepts in Social Thought*. Minneapolis: University of Minnesota Press, 1988.

Bauman, Z. *Globalization: The Human Consequences. European Perspectives*. New York: Columbia University Press, 1998.

Bauman, Z. *Distributed in the USA by Blackwell Pub*. Malden, MA: Polity Press, 2003.

Bauman, Z. *Liquid Times: Living in an Age of Uncertainty*. Cambridge: Polity Press, 2007.

Beck, U. *Pouvoir Et Contre-Pouvoir À L'ère De La Mondialisation*. Alto. Paris: Aubier, 2003.

Bigo, D. "Security and Immigration: Toward a Critique of the Governmentality of Unease." *Alternatives* 27, no. 1_suppl, Feb (2002): 63–92. doi:10.1177/03043754020270S105.

Bigo, D. "Globalisation and Security." Chap. 204-213 In *The New Blackwell Companion to Political Sociology*, edited by E. Amenta, K. Nash, and A. Scott. London: Blackwell, 2011.

Bigo, D., L. Bonelli, E. Guittet, C. Olsson, and A. Tsoukala. *Illiberal Practices of Liberal Regimes: The (In)Security Games. Liberty and Security*. London: Roultledge, 2007.

Bigo, D. "The Moebius Ribbon of Internal and External Security." In *Identities, Borders, Orders*, edited by M. Albert, D. Jacobson, and Y. Lapid, 91–116. Minneapolis: University of Minnesota Press, 2001.

Bigo, D. "Globalized-in-Security: The Field and the Ban-Opticon." In *Muslims in Europe and in the United States: A Transatlantic Comparison*, edited by N. Sakai and J. Solomon. Harvard: Center for European Studies, 2006.

Bonditti, P., D. Bigo, and F. Gros, eds. *Foucault and the International*. CERI: Palgrave: New York,2017.

Bourdieu, P. "Esprits D' Etat : Genèse Et Structure Du Champ Bureaucratique." In *Raisons Pratiques Sur La Théorie De L'action*, edited by Pierre Bourdieu. Paris: Seuil, 1994.

C. A. S. E. Collective "Critical Approaches to Security in Europe: ANetworked Manifesto." *Security Dialogue* 37, no. 4 (2006): 443–487. doi:10.1177/0967010606073085.

Castells, M. *La Société En Réseaux : L'ère De L'information*. Paris: Fayard, 1998.

Cohen, S. *La Résistance Des Etats. Les Démocraties Face Aux Défis De La Mondialisation. L'épreuve Des Faits*. Paris: Le Seuil, 2003.

Côté-Boucher, K., F. Infantino, M. B. Salter, K. Côté-Boucher, F. Infantino, and M. B. Salter. "Border Security as Practice: An Agenda for Research." *Security Dialogue* 45, no. 3 (2014): 195–208. doi:10.1177/0967010614533243.

Cox, R. W. *Production, Power and World Order. Social Forces in the Making of History (Selected Chapters)*. New York: Columbia University Press, 1987.

THE POLICING OF FLOWS 157

Deleuze, G., and F. Guattari. *Mille Plateaux. Collection "Critique"*. Paris: Editions de minuit, 1980.

Dumont, L. *Essais Sur L'individualisme. Une Perspective Anthropologique Sur L'idéologie Moderne.* Paris: Le Seuil, 1985.

Dupont, B. "Private Security Regimes: Conceptualizing the Forces that Shape the Private Delivery of Security." *Theoretical Criminology* 18, no. 3 (2014): 263–281. doi:10.1177/1362480614527303.

Elias, N. *La Dynamique De L'occident*. Paris: Calmann-Lévy/Presses Pocket, 1990.

Foucault, M., F. Ewald, A. Fontana, V. Marchetti, and A. Salomoni. Collège de France. *Les Anormaux : Cours Au Collège De France (1974-1975)*. Hautes Études. Paris: Gallimard Seuil, 1999.

Foucault, M., M. Bertani, A. Fontana, F. Ewald, and D. Macey. *Society Must Be Defended : Lectures at the Collège De France, 1975-76*. 1st ed. New York: Picador, 2003.

Foucher, M. *Fronts Et Frontières. Un Tour Du Monde Géopolitique*. 2nd ed. Paris: Fayard, 1991.

Gill, S. *Power and Resistance in the New World Order*. Palgrave: New York, 2003.

Hardt, M., and A. Negri. "Globalization and Democracy." In *Implicating Empire. Globalization & Resistance in the 21st Century World Order*, edited by S. Aronowitz and H. Gautney, 109–122. New York: Basic Books, 2003.

Held, D., A. J. McGrew, D. Goldblatt, and J. Perraton. *Global Transformations*. Cambridge: Polity Press, 1999.

Hindess, B. "The Liberal Government of Unfreedom." *Alternatives* 26, no. 2 (2001): 93–111. doi:10.1177/030437540102600201.

Hudson, W., and S. Slaughter. *Globalisation and Citizenship: The Transnational Challenge. Abingdon Oxon*. New York: Routledge, 2007.

Keohane, R. O., and J. S. Nye. *Power and Interdependence. Scott, Foresman/Little, Brown Series in Political Science*. 2nd ed. Glenview, Ill.: Scott, Foresman, 1989.

Lacroix, B. "Ordre Politique Et Ordre Social. Objectivisme, Objectivation Et Analyse Politique." In *Traité De Science Politique, Sous La Dir*, edited by M. Grawitz and J. Leca, 469–565. Paris: PUF, 1985.

Laidi, Z. *L'etat Mondialise (The Globalized State)*. Paris Grasset, 2003.

Larner, W., and W. Walters. *Global Governmentality: Governing International Spaces*. London: Routledge, 2004.

Mulone, M., and S. Tanner. "Les Acteurs Privés De La Sécurité Transnationale Et Leurs Victimes: Quels Recours Possibles?" *Criminologie* 47 (2014): 203–229. doi:10.7202/1026734ar.

Musso, P. *Réseaux Et Sociétés. La Politique Éclatée. PUF Ed*. Paris, 2003.

Noiriel, G. *Etat, Nation Et Immigration, Vers Une Histoire Du Pouvoir*. Paris: Gallimard, 2005.

Pasha, M. *Colonial Political Economy*. Oxford University Press: Oxford, 1998.

Scott, J. C. *Seeing like a State: How Certain Schemes to Improve the Human Condition Have Failed. Yale Agrarian Studies*. New Haven: Yale University Press, 1998.

Serres, M. *Atlas*. Paris: Julliard, 1994.

Spivak, G. *Chakravorty. A Critique of Postcolonial Reason: Toward A History of the Vanishing Present*. Harvard Univeristy Press, 1999.

Strange, S. "The Limits of Politics." *Government and Opposition* 30, no. 3 (1995): 291–311. doi:10.1111/j.1477-7053.1995.tb00129.x.

Strange, S., R. Tooze, and C. May. *Authority and Markets: Susan Strange's Writings on International Political Economy*. Houndmills: Palgrave/Macmillan, 2002.

Susan, S. *States and Markets*. London: Pinter, 1988.

Tillt, C. "Political Identities in Changing Polities." *Social Research* 70, no. 2 summer, (2003): 605–620.

Tilly, C. *Identities, Boundaries, and Social Ties*. Boulder, CO: Paradigm Publishers, 2005.

Torpey, J. *The Invention of the Passport Surveillance, Citizenship and the State*. Cambridge: OUP, 2000.

Walker, R. B. J. *Inside/Outside: International Relations as Political Theory. Cambridge Studies in International Relations; 24. Cambridge [England]*. New York: Cambridge University Press, 1993.

Wallerstein, I. "The Rise and Future Demise of World-Systems Analysis." *Review (F. Braudel Center)* 21, no. 1 (1998): 103–112.

Index

Note: Page numbers in *italic* type refer to figures
Page numbers in **bold** type refer to tables
Page numbers followed 'n' refer to notes

actionable intelligence 73, 79
Actor-Network Theory (A-NT) 97, 99, 114
African Rhino Specialist Group (AfRSG) 34
Agnew, J. 150
Amicelle, A., *et al.* 1–11
Amoore, L. 96
Amsterdam treaty (1999) 95, 105
Appadurai, A. 154
area of freedom, security and justice (AFSI) 95
Aron, R. 144–145, 148
Australia *see* G20 Brisbane summit (2014);
Queensland Police Service (QPS)

Badie, B. 147
Balkans 102
bankers as unelected politicians 148, 152
Basic Law of Hong Kong 64, 70n41
Bauman, Z. 5, 123, 153
Bennett Moses, L., and Chan, J. 85
Bigo, D. 5, 139–157
bilateral treaties 66, 70n59
Block, L. 57
Boer, M. den 58
border security governance, EU 4, 5
borders, maritime 110, 112
Boston Marathon bombers 73
Bowling, B. 58
British police, as machine organisation 124
Brodeur, J. -P., and Dupont, B. 96–97
bureaucracies, rank-structured 124, 126

Canadian Centre for Justice Statistics (CCJS) 81
Canadian Police College 78
Canadian policing: crime analysts 77;
technological, organisational, and cultural
capabilities 81
Castells, M. 2, 37
central command centres 15, 16, 22
Centre for Information, Discussion and
Exchange on the Crossing of Frontiers

and Immigration (CIREFI) 99–104, *101*, *103*,
113
centres of calculation 94, 97, 98, 113, 114
CEPOL (European Police College) 63
Chan, J. 75; and Bennett Moses, L. 85
Chatterton, M. 124
China 65, 67, 68; and EU 64–66
Chinese criminal code 64, 70n43
citizens' rights 55
civil liberties 19
Civipol Conseil 110
command structure levels 23, 29n102
common information sharing environment
(CISE) 111, *112*, 113
Common Integrated Risk Analysis Model
(CIRAM) 104–109
common pre-frontier intelligence picture (CPIP)
92–93, *93*, 109–113, 115
communication technologies, hate speech 7
computerised information sharing mechanisms
95
Condon, C., and Sanders, C. B. 73–91
congestions 59
control, social 3, 14
Convention on International Trade in
Endangered Species (CITES) 36, 37, 38, 40–41,
48n18
Convention on Mutual Assistance in Criminal
Matters (EU) 61–62, 69n29
cooperation, informal 56–57, 61
Cope, N. 75
Corkhill, J., and Joseph, J. 76
Cox, R. 149, 150
crime: analysis 5; governance 1–3, 6; property 2
criminal codes 64, 67, 70nn43&44
criminological research 55
criminological scholarship 2
criminology 1–9; contemporary risks 4; filtering
flows 2; governance of crime 1–3, 6; human–
machine interactions 7–8; kinds of mobilities

7; mobility problem 6; policing of/through flows 5–8; research on flows 55; state-organised social control 3; University of Montreal workshop 3–4

cross-border law enforcement 54–71; bilateral treaties 66, 70n59; Common Centres 60; congestions 54, 59, 64, 68; criminal codes 64, 67, 70nn43&44; criminological research 55; dams 55; death penalty 64, 65, 67; drug precursors 57, 67, 69n11, 70n60; EU Council instruments 57; Germany and China 67; goals 63; Hong Kong and Mainland China 65, 68; human rights framework 56, 58, 66, 68; informal cooperation 56–57, 61; instrument creation 67; international legal assistance 55; liaison officers 61, 67; locks 55, 60, 61; Memoranda of Understanding (MoU) 56, 67; metaphors 55; narcotics 57, 67, 69n11, 70n60; national police agencies and human rights 58; personal contacts 60, 63–64, 68; policing flows between EU and China 66–68; regulating flows of policing in EU 59–64; regulating flows of policing in greater China 64–66; research (authors) 56–57; shared moral norms and values 59; sovereignty/protection of national laws 55; Taiwan and Mainland China 65; trust and congestions 59; trust and legitimacy 62; trust (personal and institutional) 68–69; weirs 55, 58

Cross-Channel Intelligence Conference (CCIC) 60

Cross-Strait Joint Crime-Fighting and Judicial Mutual Assistance Agreement (2009) 65, 70n53

cybercrime, professional organisations fighting 150

cybersecurity professionals 150

data: access 81, 82; fusion 92, *see also* policing through flows of data

database policing 75–76

de Lint, W., and Hall, A. 25

de Menezes, Jean Charles 54

death penalty 64, 65, 67

decolonisation, intellectual 152

Deleuze, G. 14, 154

democracy, survival of 140

Department of Environmental Affairs (DEA) 38, 42, 48n34

Department of the Prime Minister and Cabinet (DPM&C) 16

discretionary powers 19

disease management strategies (Foucault) 5–6

drug precursors (narcotics) 57, 67, 69n11, 70n60

Dupont, B., and Brodeur, J. -P. 96–97

early warning system (EWS) 100–102, 109

East Sea (freighter) 110

Ebola 6

Elias, N. 149

Ericson, R. V. 84; and Haggerty, K. D. 14, 129

eu-LISA 95, 96

Eurocentrism 143, 152

Eurodac 95

Eurojust 62, 70n34, 95

European Border Police Force 105

European border policing 92–117; ad hoc information exchange 102, *103*; centres of calculation 94, 97, 98, 113, 114; CIREFI ad hoc information exchange form 102, *103*; CIREFI data 99–104, 113; CIREFI standard form *101*; common information sharing environment (CISE) 111, *112*, 113; Common Integrated Risk Analysis Model (CIRAM) 104–109; common pre-frontier intelligence picture (CPIP) 92–93, *93*, 109–113, 115; computerised information sharing mechanisms 95; early warning system (EWS) 100–102, 109; FRONTEX 95, 99, 104, 105, 108–109; ICONet 104; illegal border crossings (Greece/Turkey) 108; illegal immigration indications and facilitator networks 101–102; immigration liaison officers (ILOs) 102–104; knowledge and calculation 94–99; knowledge work and centres of calculation 96–99; knowledge work/production of knowledge 93–94; National Coordination Centres (NCCs) 109, 111, *111*; Risk Analysis Centre (RAC) 105, 107–108; risk analysis formula (CIRAM) 106, *106*; risk assessment 105–106; risk indicators (CIRAM) 106–107, *107*; risk indicators (FRAN) 108, *108*; surveillance of maritime borders 110, 112; technology (roll of discussions) 114–115; undocumented persons (arrivals by boats) 110

European Convention on Human Rights (ECHR) 58

European liberal modernity 144

European Police College (CEPOL) 63

European Union (EU), border security governance 4, 5

European Union Judicial Cooperation Unit (Eurojust) 62, 70n34, 95

Europol 60, 61, 62, 63; Analytical Work Files 95

Europol Convention 61, 69n22

events and flow management 12–29; civil liberties 19; command structure levels 23, 24, 25–26, 29n102; control and regulation model 12–13; field intelligence officers 22; front-line police 24–25; intelligence operations 22, 29n96; lawful powers 19; legal architecture 19; managing external flows 18–21; managing internal flows 21–23; negotiated management 15–16; physical barriers 20, 25; reflexive systems of command and control 23–25; security operation staff 17; soft policing response 21; sovereignty practices 21; spatial control tactics 25, *see also* G20 Brisbane summit

exclusion notices 19

experiential knowledge 75

INDEX

fences, transparent 20, 25
field intelligence officers 22
financial markets, flow architecture 16
Finnish Frontier Guard 105
fire-brigade policing 124
flow-based architecture 16
fortification logic 2
Foucault, M. 4, 145–146; disease management strategies 5–6; *Security, Territory, Population* lectures 12–13, 14
Franko-Aas, K. 55
free choice, illusion of 146
freedom of movement 146, 153, 154
freedom of protest 19
FRONTEX 95, 99, 104, 105, 108–109
frontline police 24–25
functional differentiation 127
Fussey, P. 25

G20 Brisbane summit (2014) 4, 16–26; arrests 19; capability coordinators 23–24; command and control structure 21–22; command structure levels 23, 24, 25–26, 29n102; concentric theory metaphor 18–19; field intelligence officers 22; front-line police 24–25; intelligence operations 22, 29n96; interviews 17–18, 21, 22, 24, 28n56; legal architecture 19; lessons learned from Toronto-G20 24; managing external flows 18–21; managing internal flows 21–23; physical barriers 20, 25; Police Operations Centre (POC) 22–23, 25–26; Queensland Police Service (QPS) 14, 23–24; security operation staff 17; soft policing response 21; sovereignty practices 21
G20 protests 13
G20 Taskforce 16, 17
game ranchers 39
gated communities 2
geographic borders, intellectual challenge 142
geographic proximity, friendship/animosity 153–154
Germany 67
Giacomanionio, C. 127
Gill, S. 149, 150
Gillham, P., and Noakes, J. 15
Global Political Geography 150–152
globalisation: conditions for 141; governments role 147–148; social forces 149
governance: crime 1–3, 6; security 1, 4, 5, 14–15
governmental order, realist story of 140
Gramci, A. 149

Haggerty, K. D., and Ericson, R. V. 14, 129
Hall, A., and de Lint, W. 25
hate speech, communication technologies 7
Her Majesty's Inspectorate of Constabulary (HMIC) 15

Hermitte, M. -A. 6
Hluhluwe-Umfolozi Game Reserve (South Africa) 39
Holy Roman Empire 144
Hong Kong 64, 65, 68
Hübschle, A. 4, 34–53
Hufnagel, S. 4, 54–72
Hughes, V., and Jackson, P. 130
human–machine interactions 7–8
hunting markets, policing 47
hunting trophies 35, 37, 38–39, 41, 42, 43

ICONet 104
ideal types of flows management (Foucault) 6
illegal border crossings, Greece/Turkey 108
illegal immigration indications and facilitator networks 101–102
immigration flows, migratory controls 18
immigration liaison officers (ILOs) 102–104
incident management 125
individuals, attacks against 2
information, insufficient flow 54
Innes, M. 127; *et al.* 76
instant messaging, illegal trade 44
Integrated Border Management System 110
intellectual decolonisation 152
intelligence: actionable 73, 79; operations 22, 29n96; products 83
intelligence-led policing 122, 125, 130, 132
International Association of Crime Analysts (IACA) 78
International Association of Law Enforcement Intelligence Analysis (IALEIA) 78
International Convention on Civil and Political Rights (ICCPR) 58, 64, 65
international flows and political order 139–155; bankers as unelected politicians 148, 152; dualities 148; Eurocentrism 143, 152; European liberal modernity 144; fixist approach 146; flows and change 153–155; flows and globalisation 141–142; flows and state (order and change) 142–144; global political geography and post-colonial studies 150–152; globalisation (governments role) 147–148; intellectual decolonisation 152; international and global political economy 148–150; International Political Sociology 151, 153; liberal order 146; liberal transnationalist approach 140; logical conservatism 144; market deregulation by political authorities 146–148; policing flows (smarter mechanisms) 151; primacy of order 139–140, 152–155; prioritisation of order over change 144, 145; regional grouping collaboration 146–147; state border control 145, 150–151, 152; states management of flows 144–146, 147; technological advancement 141–142; Westerners view of flows 144; world history 141–142, 143

162 INDEX

international letters of request (ILOR) 62
international order, controlled by states 143
International Political Economy (IPE) 148–150
International Political Sociology 151, 153
international political summits 13, 19
Interpol 65
issue-motivated groups (IMGs): engagement with 20–21, 25; threat matrix 20

Jackson, P., and Hughes, V. 130
Jeandesboz, J. 5, 92–121
joint investigation teams (JITs) 61–62, 63
Joseph, J., and Corkhill, J. 76
Justice and Home Affairs Council (EU) 99

Keohane, R. O., and Nye, J. S. 146
key performance indicators (KPIs) 124, 125
Klauser, F. 15, 25
knowledge: of crime (who benefits) 150; experiential 75; networks 15; as social power 94; socially dirty and dangerous 126–127; management systems 130; sociology of 97, 99; work 97, 98, 129
Kruger National Park (South Africa) 39, 47, 49n72

labour, invisible and subjective 85
Laitinen, I. 105
Lapérouses expedition 97–98, 114
Lapid, Y. 142
Latour, B. 97, 98, 99, 114; and Woolgar, S. 114
law enforcement see cross-border law enforcement
Law, J. 114
lawful powers 19
laws, protection of national 55
legal assistance, international 55
Lemthongthai, C. 42
leprosy 5
liaison officers 61, 67, 102–104
liberal governance: Foucault on 146; freedom of movement 146; urban environments 14
liberal modernity, European 144
liquid modernity, Bauman's notion of 123
liquid modernity (police and information flows) 5, 122–134; cybernetic model 128–131; democratic influence 132; intelligence or evidence 127; intelligence-led policing 122, 125, 130, 132; local community policing 131; machine thinking 123–126, 132; Mobile Data Computers 129; operational/policy manuals 129; patrol officers 126–127; police accountability 128; rank-structured bureaucracies 124, 126; security governance 131; security partnerships 130–132; social justice 132; technological solutions/actual police work 130; traditional hierarchical model 128–129; training for new technology 129–130; workload distribution 124, 125

Lisbon Treaty (2010) 60
Lo, S. 56
Loader, I. 95
local community policing 131
locks 55, 60, 61
London Metropolitan Police 1, 123
London riots (2011), public order policing 15

Maastricht treaty (1992) 94–95
Macau 64, 65
machine politics 124
Maguire, E. R. 127
management, harm 2, 8n5
management of change logic 148
Manning, P. K. 74, 123, 124, 125
Marine Police Force 1
Marks, M., and Shearing, C. 122–123
Marx, G. 115
Mayne, R. 123
Mayo, E. 124
Memoranda of Understanding (MoU) 56, 67
migrants: imprisonment 2; majorities fear of minorities 154; undocumented arrivals by boat 110; undocumented (North African nations) 4
migration, association with infiltration 144
Mobile Data Computers 82, 129
mobility 6; restrictions on 146, 153, 154
modernity: European liberal 144, see also liquid modernity (police and information flows)
Molnar, A. 4; and Whelan, C. 12–32
moral norms 59
Morgenthau, H. 145
municipal police institutions, Peelian model 124
Mutual Case Assistance Scheme (MCAS) 64–65

narcotics, drug precursors 57, 67, 68, 69n11, 70n60
nation-state, territorialised activity 94
National Coordination Centres (NCCs) 109, 111, 111
Neal, A.W. 109
network society 37
Niche 81
North African uprisings 104
Nye, J. S., and Keohane, R. O. 146

Olivier, J. 42, 49n50
Olympic Games 13, 26n13
Ontario police services, crime analysts 77
Operation Rhino 39
Operational Coordination Group (OCG) 22–23
organised crime networks, wildlife products 35–36, 46

passage point urbanism 19
patrol car mobile computer terminals 82, 129
patrol officers, information flows 126–127
Peel, Robert 123

INDEX

163

Peelian model, municipal police institutions 124
physical barriers, transparent 20, 25
piracy, East African coastline 47, 50n74
police: accountability 128; British 124; frontline 24–25; management 83–84; statistics production 124, 125, *see also* liquid modernity
police agencies: dilemmas and challenges 5; displacement of responsibility 126; national 58; regulation of external flows 21; situational awareness 15; specialist police units 127; technologies and strategies (adaptation) 13; training for new technology 129–130
police cooperation: international regulations 56; police-to-police strategies 57
Police Operations Centre (POC): command structures 25–26; Operational Coordination Group (OCG) 22–23
police stations, dematerialisation 129
policing: border 93, 115; Canadian 77, 81; database 75–76; fire-brigade 124; intelligence-led 122, 125, 130, 132; pre-emptive 73; technology-led 115, 129–130, *see also* European border policing
policing practices: contemporary 2; internal dynamics 13; moral hazard 131
Policing the Risk Society (Ericson and Haggerty) 129
policing through flows of data 73–87; analysis (economic and organisational shaping) 79–80, 86n50; analysis unit 77, 78–79; cognitive effects and the reappropriation of analysis 82–84; crime analysis (defining and understanding) 77–80; crime and intelligence analysis (distinction) 79, 86n49; crime map 83; crime reporting 79, 80, 84; crime reports and bulletins 82–84; data access work 81, 82; incident focus of systems 81; intelligence technologies and database policing 74–76; intelligence-led and predictive policing 84–85; interviews 76, 77, 78, 79, 80–81, 83–84; IT adoption and enhancement decisions 81, 87n60; organisational training 78; study methodology 76–77
political order *see* international flows and political order
political summits, international 13, 19
politicians, unelected 148, 152
politics, machine 124
population flows, transgressive qualities 20
powers 19
pre-crime surveillance 13
pre-emptive policing 73
predictive policing science 154–155
Private Rhinos Owner Association (PROA) 39
property crimes 2
protest flows 13
protest movements: disruptive tactics 15; engagement with 20–21, 25; freedom of protest 19
pseudo-hunting phenomenon 40–42, 45

Queensland Police Service (QPS) 14, 18, 28n56; capability coordinators 23–24; Police Operations Centre (POC) 22–23; reflexive dramatisation 20, 25

rank-structured bureaucracies 124, 126
real-time analytics 16
records management systems (RMS) 75, 81
reflexive dramatisation 20, 25
reflexive systems of command and control 23–25
regulatory actors 7
Reiss, A. 124
relationship-building, protest movements/ police agencies 20–21, 25
Rescher, N. 142
rhino horn: authenticity 43–44, 45; market 4; price 35, 44
rhino horn flows and fluid interfaces 34–50; confiscated rhino horn 45; Convention on International Trade in Endangered Species (CITES) 37, 38, 40–41; dehorning 40, 45; Department of Environmental Affairs (DEA) 38, 42, 48n34; diplomats role in illegal markets 43, 45, 49n56; disrupting the illegal economy 46–47; distribution and trade 44–45, 49n65; flows out of South Africa 37–42; grey flows 39–40, 45–46; hunting trophies 35, 37, 38–39, 41, 42, 43; illegal market flow 35–37, *38*; illegal markets in Vietnam 42–43; militarisation of law enforcement 47; national moratorium on trade 37–38, 45, 46; poaching suspects deaths 47, 49n72; private rhino ownership 39–40; pseudo-hunting phenomenon 40–42, 45; regulatory loopholes 37, 40; research 35, 47n6; rhinos kills in South Africa 34, **35**; sex workers as trophy hunters 41–42; transportation to market 43–44, 49n63; Vietnamese crime groups 40–41
right of passage between states 143
rights, citizens 55
Risk Analysis Centre (RAC) 105, 107–108
risks 4; European border policing 106–107, *106, 107*, 108, *108*
Ronn, K. V. 131
Rosenau, J. 147
Rowan, Colonel C. 123
Roy, A. 123

Sakhalin 97–98
Sanders, C. B. 5; and Condon, C. 73–91; *et al.* 75
Sangatte Protocol 60
Sartre, J. -P. 144
Schengen Convention (1985) 60; framework 102
Schengen Information System (SIS) 95
Schmitt, C. 140
scholarship, criminological 2
science and technology studies (STS) 97, 99, 114

Seattle World Trade Organisation protests (1999) 15

Security, Territory, Population (Foucault lectures) 12–13, 14

Serres, M. 154

Shearing, C., and Marks, M. 122–123

Sheptycki, J. 5, 58, 96, 122–138

Sino-British Joint Liaison Group 65

Sistema Integrado de Vigilancia Exterior (SIVE) 110

situational awareness 15

smallpox 6

smart cities 16

social construction of technology 74, 75, 80

social control: practices 14; state-organised 3

social institutions, spatio-temporal fluxes 13

social justice 132

social media: hate speech 7; illegal trade 44; police access 81

sociotechnical work 74

soft hegemony 147

South Africa: Hluhluwe-Umfolozi Game Reserve 39; Kruger National Park 39, 47, 49n72; moratorium on rhino horn trade 37–38, 45, 46; rhino horn flows out of 37–42; rhino killings 34, **35**; wild animal ownership 39–40

sovereignty 55; territorial trap 150, 151

sovereignty practices: events and flow management 21; market deregulation 147

spaces of flow 37

spatial control tactics 25

splintering urbanism 14

state: legal terminologies and definitions 143–144; role of 147

state border control 145, 150–151, 152

state organisations, violence perpetrated by 140

state-organised social control 3

Statistics Canada 81

Strange, S. 148, 149, 150

street checks (crime report) 82–83, 84

supply chains, goods legal status 36

surveillance, pre-crime 13

surveillance practices, globalisation 12

Surveillant Assemblage 14

Tactical and Strategic Intelligence Analyst course 78

Taiwan 64, 65

Taylor, F. 124

Taylorism 124

techno-fallacies 115, 129

technology, social construction of 74, 75, 80

technology-led policing 115, 129–130

territorial political order 143

Threatened or Protected Species (TOPS) regulations 40

Tilly, C. 149

total security 13

Traditional Asian Medicine (TAM) 34

training by rote 124

trophy hunting 35, 37, 38–39, 41–43, 47

trust 59, 62, 68–69

undocumented persons 4, 110

Uniform Crime Reporting (UCR) 81

United States of America (USA): Department of Justice, intelligence-led policing 122; Peelian model of police institutions 124; specialist police units 127

University of Montreal workshop 3–4

urban environments: event regulation of 19; liberal governance 14; real-time functioning and management 16; security governance 2

urban surveillance system 16

urbanism, passage point 19

values 59

Via Rail bombers 73

video wall 22

Vietnam: Decision (11) 42–43; diplomats' role in illegal markets 43, 45, 49n56; illegal markets for rhino horn 42–43

Vietnamese crime groups 40–41

Visa Information System (VIS) 95

Walker, R. 150

Waltz, K. 145

Weatheritt, M. 125

Weber, M. 123

weirs 55, 58

Weisburd, D. 128; *et al.* 128–129

Western Balkans, European boarder policing 102

Western states, securitisation 94

Whelan, C. 4; and Molnar, A. 12–32

wild animal ownership, South Africa 39–40

Wildlife Justice Commission 44

wildlife products, organised crime networks 35–36

Wilson, J. Q. 126–127

Wilson, O. W. 124

Woolgar, S., and Latour, B. 114

Xaysavang Trading Export-Import 42

Young, M. 124

Zedner, L. 96

zero tolerance 128

Zika 6